D0712668

CHRISTOPHER ALEXANDER

The Search for a New Paradigm in Architecture

Frontispiece.
Jean-Michel Folon, "Le Funambule" Editions Gallerie Marquet, 1973

CHRISTOPHER ALEXANDER

THE SEARCH FOR A NEW PARADIGM IN

ARCHITECTURE

by

S*TEPHEN* G*RABOW*

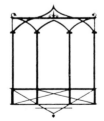

ORIEL PRESS

STOCKSFIELD

BOSTON   HENLEY   LONDON

1983

First published in 1983
by Oriel Press Ltd. (Routledge & Kegan Paul PLC)
Stocksfield, Northumberland NE43 7NA,
9 Park Street, Boston, Mass. 02108, USA,
296 Beaconsfield Parade, Middle Park,
Melbourne, 3206, Australia, and
Broadway House, Newtown Road,
Henley-on-Thames, Oxon RG9 1EN
Set in Bembo
and printed in Great Britain by
Knight & Forster,
Leeds
ISBN 0 85362 199 3

To

Eileen and Nicole

Form is both deeply material and highly spiritual. It cannot exist without a material support; it cannot be properly expressed without invoking some supra-material principle. Form poses a problem which apeals to the utmost resources of our intelligence, and it affords the means which charm our sensibility and even entice us to the verge of frenzy. Form is never trivial or indifferent; it is the magic of the world.

LANCELOT LAW WHYTE

Aspects of Form

CONTENTS

PART FOUR

PART FIVE

FOREWORD

by

CHRISTOPHER ALEXANDER

I am very happy to have the opportunity to introduce this book of Stephen Grabow's. It is, I suppose, a rare thing for a person to have a book written about him, under conditions where continuous consultation is going on between the author and his subject. However in this case, Steve spent six months in Berkeley, and we together spent hundreds of hours, discussing and arguing the many points which he makes in this book. These months were enormously stimulating for me. First, I had never had the opportunity to think over the whole of my work, in retrospect. Within myself I have always been aware of a single, unbroken whole in what I do . . . but I have never had a chance to write about it, and had, up until the discussions with Stephen, also never even been explicitly aware of the way it formed a whole. Steve's intuitive sense of the underlying unity behind the many ideas which I have expressed during the years, and his capacity to make this clear, were enormously exciting for me.

Even more important, his conviction that what was happening in my thought, represented a major break with tradition, and a "paradigm" shift, corresponded to deep feelings of unease which I was then becoming aware of. I had begun to experience opposition — almost violent opposition . . . of an almost irrational kind — far exceeding in emotional violence, what the subject itself, or reasonable discourse seemed to deserve . . . and I had begun to be aware that what I had discovered, the concepts which I had been formulating, were likely to stir, and reorganise our conception of the world or architecture in a shattering way. The apparently irrational disagreements which my discussions stimulated, were apparently caused by some fundamental, violent, almost devasting fissures in the intellectual whole which present day architects consider more or less intact. My works, by opening those fissures wider, and forcing people to confront the absurdity of their own beliefs, caused violent opposition, because it is indeed, a terrifying, anger-provoking thing, to find one's cherished picture of the world, threatened by its own internal contradictions. It is not surprising that

ix

works which shed this kind of light, as mine sometimes do, will be regarded by some people with joy (if they are already disentangled), and by others with dismay, hatred, or anger (if they are still entangled).

I am enormously grateful that Stephen has bought this issue into the open as clearly as he has, and with so much sympathy for my position. The time and patience he has given to this book, and his concern for what I have done, touches me very deeply.

In the years since we held the conversations, my own understanding of the magnitude of the shift which is necessary in order to perceive problems of architecture, building, and geometric order correctly has increased greatly . . . and now goes beyond even the point which Stephen himself has described in the closing chapters of this book.

I have come to believe that the problem of physical order — the kind of order which creates quality in architecture, which creates the "it" which I have spoken about in my tapes with Stephen — this problem is of so great a stature, that we shall have to modify our picture of the whole physical universe in order to see it clearly. That is, I believe it is not only architecture itself which requires change — (that is certain, and is clearly expressed in this book) — but that our picture of the nature of the physical world itself, will have to be modified altogether — so that what we know as physics, biology, chemistry . . . and other related fields, will all have to take on a different cast.

Our present cosmological picture is largely the one which was first sketched out by Descartes. This picture has been immensely influential — perhaps responsible — for the great success of science in the last three hundred years. It has been beautiful, awe-inspiring, wonderful, that this view has led so far, in teaching us, and helping us to discover, the nature of the physical world.

Nevertheless, I believe this view is so partial, so badly flawed, that one might have to say that in one respect at least, it is altogether wrong. The view which exists, does not have room within it, in any natural way, for the issue of value, for the character of order, for the "it", the quality without a name which I have written about.

I have now become convinced that it is possible to construct a modified view of nature, which does pay proper attention to the issue of order, and that in this new view, what we loosely call "meaning" and "significance" are not left out of the world picture, as they are left out of the present view created by recent science.

I am also convinced that a proper theory of architecture, a way of under standing the production of buildings as the production of deep order, can only be created, within this shifted world view. I have written a new book, The Nature of Order, which I suppose will not be finished for at least another five or ten years — in which this modified world view, and what I believe to be the proper view of order, are presented.

When I talked to Stephen about the fact that my earlier work, had now led me to these conclusions, and would not only make it necessary to modify our view of architecture, but also to modify our picture of the world . . . he felt it was difficult to include any discussion of this issue within his book . . . especially since my formulation of this view stemmed, in part, from just those conversations which are recorded here. However, he was kind enough to give me this opportunity, at least to record my own, most recent, shift of position, clearly.

I believe that the ideas which he has sought to make clear in this book, do lead, when one considers them carefully, to even vaster shifts in our picture of the world . . . and that when we are finished with these thoughts, we shall see architecture, and the problem of order . . . not as a subject which can be kept separate from physics or biology . . . but as the fulcrum of ideas which will cause revolutionary changes in the direction of all our thought.

In the past century, architecture has always been a minor science — if it has been a science at all. Present day architects who want to be scientific, try to incorporate the ideas of physics, psychology, anthropology . . . in their work . . . in the hope of keeping in tune with the "scientific" times.

I believe we are on the threshold of a new era, when this relation between architecture and the physical sciences may be reversed — when the proper understanding of the deep questions of space, as they are embodied in architecture . . . will play a revolutionary role in the way we see the world . . . and will perhaps play the role for the world view of the 21st and 22nd centuries, that physics has played in shaping the world view of the 19th and 20th.

Berkeley,
February 1983.

PREFACE

Architects and scientists are alike in that their vision of the world depends as much upon what they are looking *at* as upon what their previous experiences have taught them to look *for*. During revolutions, however, scientists actually see new and different things when looking in familiar places. The question is whether architects do the same.

Physicists, for example, looking at a swinging weight at the time of Aristotle saw constrained motion; but after Galileo they saw a pendulum. And astronomers looking at new celestial bodies at the time of Ptolemy saw stars and comets; but after Copernicus they saw new planets. At such moments, according to Thomas Kuhn, when the normal-scientific tradition changes, the scientist's perception of the world is reshaped.[1] He learns to see a new *gestalt;* and after he has done so the world of his research seems incompatible with the one he had inhabited before. In that sense, a pendulum was as inconceivable within the Aristotelian universe as a new planet was within the Ptolemaic. But for the transition to occur, a change in attitude was necessary in order to perceive the new phenomenon — or, to put it another way, to reinterpret the existing phenomena. Kuhn calls this change a *paradigm shift* — because it entails a reshuffling of the entire constellation of values, facts, beliefs, and methods which binds one to a shared view, or *paradigm,* of a particular field; and he likens it to a 'switch' in *gestalt* because it results in a revolutionary, although disciplined transformation of vision. At such tradition-shattering moments in the history of science, the foundations of the field itself seem to shake, although the ideas that precede these changes are themselves almost always rooted in tradition.

Copernicus for example was not the first to suggest the earth's motion, nor did he claim to have rediscovered the idea for himself.

In fact, as Kuhn points out, he cited most of the ancient authorities who had argued that the earth was acutally in motion around the sun.[2] But what made the idea stick after Copernicus — and cause a reshuffling — was the unprecedented mathematical system which he built around the phenomenon in order to explain the motion of the planets. That was what distinguished him from his predecessors and, according to Kuhn, "it was in part because of the mathematics that his work inaugurated a revolution as theirs had not." This is the crucial ingredient in paradigm shift — the ability to be precise about the consequences of a reality only believed to be exising independently of our knowing it.[3]

Although the chances for a comparable revolution in architecture will seem remote if not impossible to those rooted in current theory and practice, or to those who believe architecture to be neither paradigmatic nor comparable to science (mainly because "science" is, to them, dominated by positivism), this examination of the work of Christopher Alexander will suggest otherwise. It will try to show, for example, that what distinguishes his work from that of his architectural predecessors is the unprecedented linguistic and mathematical system which he has built around the ancient ideas of differentiating space in order to create a new type of building. It will also show that the notion that there exists, in space, a particular phenomenon which corresponds to those ideas, independently of any attempts to describe them, is as central to his work as the idea of the earth's motion was to Copernicus, and that his systematic description of its consequences will appear almost as tradition-shattering to modern architecture as the Copernican revolution did to medieval astronomy.

The idea of a centrally ordered conception of indeterminate space embracing aesthetic, functional, and technical elements — a unity of space — is not new. Its continuity however, seems to have been fractured with the so-called modern movement in architecture. According to Reyner Banham's history of the period, the chain is apparently broken with Walter Gropius and the general extension of the "International Style" as the dominant paradigm of the modern era:

> The human chain . . . that extends back from Gropius to William Morris, and beyond him to Ruskin, Pugin, and William Blake, does not extend forward from Gropius. The precious vessel of handicaft

aesthetics that had been passed from hand to hand, was dropped and broken, and no one has bothered to pick up the pieces.[4]

The idea that Banham is referring to is more than just "handicraft aesthetics"; it is the ancient, almost alchemical art of differentiating space — as mysterious and remote from both contemporary science and modern architectural practice as the closed world of the ancients was from the infinite universe of contemporary astronomy. And to assert its continuity today is not only incompatible with current practice but an historical admission of the absense of a systematic knowledge of its consequences. For without a systematically precise description of the consequences of any phenomenon — which is the basis of all paradigms — any assertions of fact are scientifically meaningless. The crux of the problem therefore, would seem to be whether or not it is possible to be systematically precise about such phenomena as the unity of space or, for that matter, any aspect of architecture.

The intellectual barriers which prevent one from entertaining such notions are considerable; after all, the problem is tantamount to resolving the conflict between the two worlds of art and science. And yet one is also struck by the increasing likelihood that, as William Thompson put it, "the key in which the nerves and the stars are strung is the same."[5]

The parallelism which seems to exist between Alexander's work and the paradigm model of change in the history of scientific revolutions goes beyond metaphor or even coincidence. Aside from the fact that Kuhn's model is itself borrowed from other fields, including art, the events and circumstances surrounding Alexander's work are so nearly congruent with the emergence of a new paradigm in the development of science that the parallel is too striking to ignore.[6] The story occurs however, when, independently of Kuhn's model, the current paradigm of architectural theory and practice has begun to break down during a period of profound professional crisis.

There are many reasons for the apparent failure of modern architecture, and a complete analysis of paradigm collapse has yet to be made; but it is clear that the constellation of shared values, facts, beliefs, and methods which have their origin in early 20th century architectural thought can no longer be relied upon solely to solve the variety of aesthetic, functional, or technical problems with which it is today confronted.

At such comparable moments in the history of science, different schools of thought compete for attention in an attempt to resolve the crisis and redirect the field. Whether the existing paradigm can survive the onslaught, whether the problem is postponed for another generation, or whether a new paradigm emerges to replace the old — these are questions which only future historians can answer with any degree of accuracy. My purpose here is to describe what I believe to be one of the most interesting candidates for the field.

As a theorist, Alexander belongs to the tradition of humanist thought that, in the 20th century, can be characterized by the application of scientific training in a painfully honest attempt to analyze the problems of personal existance against a backdrop of scepticism and doubt. Like H. G. Wells, Julian Huxley, Teilhard de Chardin, Abraham Maslow, Loren Eisley, or Gregory Bateson, he is convinced that the deep sense of human purpose and meaning previously provided by religion can be objectively rediscovered. As an architect however, he is more like the solitary figure of a man walking a tightrope in a poster by Folon.[7] He balances himself with a pole high above a flat expanse between the rectangular shapes of tall, anonymous buildings that could be taken from the drawing board of Le Corbusier. In front of him, in the middle of the wire, hangs a small heart-shaped pendant — almost invisible to the eye. Although the simplicity of the message is obvious, the vastness and color of the scene convey a deep sense of the complexity of the situation — and the importance of the outcome. The man's dilemma is our own and his success or failure is no isolated event.

Alexander is the man and the heart-shaped pendant is the beauty so painfully missing in the city below. The painting however, tells us nothing about the man or how he arrived at such a precipitous point — only that his steps are to be measured against the whole field. This book provides that explanation. It represents, in part, an account of several months spent with Alexander discussing his work in the context of these ideas. These discussions — which constitute a large portion of the text — provide more than a mere account or summary of the events and circumstances surrounding more than twenty years of extra-ordinary research and experimentation. Rather, they attempt to probe beneath the surface, to read between the lines of what is happening when someone is working just beyond the edge of "paradigm shift." The book therefore represents both a partial and highly selective view of Alexander's story. It emphasizes, for example, the intellectual and theoretical dimension of his work at the expense of fully describing the reality of his experiences in the making of buildings.

While it would be correct to say that the making of buildings is, in the end, what his story is about, my own purpose in writing this book was to present for the reader a portrait of what an architectural *paradigm* looks like and how it evolves. Since I am distinguishing here between a specific theory, or method, or style of building and the full constellation of elements which make up an architectural world view, the emphasis has been on the overall structure of thought rather than the details of building. As a result, the story is very different from the one Alexander would have told on his own, even although it is conveyed through dialogue with him. Throughout the book, there is a constant alternation between my own text, and Alexander's words, as he discussed these matters with me in our tape recorded sessions. His words are always set in italics.

This was an unusual project and I am grateful to various persons and institutions for their confidence and support in seeing it through to the end: to Joseph Toussaint, who unknowingly started it all; to Garrett Eckbo, John Friedmann, and Gabriele Gutkind for their initial encouragement, and to the National Endowment for the Humanities for providing the means with a research fellowship in 1976; to the University of Kansas for a leave of absence from the School of Architecture & Urban Design, and for the continuing support of the Faculty Senate Research Fund; to the University of California at Berkeley for the privilege of research facilities as a postdoctoral fellow in architecture during that same period; to Christopher Alexander, for his cooperation and patience during more than one hundred hours of taped interviews at the Centre for Environmental Structure in Berkeley; and to Bruce Allsopp, for his confidence in the value and importance of having this published.

Stephen Grabow

Lawrence, Kansas   December, 1981

xvii

REFERENCE NOTES

1. Thomas Kuhn, THE STRUCTURE OF SCIENTIFIC REVOLUTIONS, 2nd.ed. (Chicago: University of Chicago Press, 1970), p.112

2. Thomas Kuhn, THE COPERNICAN REVOLUTION (Cambridge: Harvard University Press, 1957), p.144; cf. Copernicus' Preface to DE REVOLUTIONIBUS ORBIUM CAELESTIUM (1543)

3. Cf. Michael Polanyi, PERSONAL KNOWLEDGE: TOWARDS A POST-CRITICAL PHILOSOPHY (New York: Harper and Row, 1964), p.311

4. Reyner Banham, THEORY AND DESIGN IN THE FIRST MACHINE AGE, 2nd.ed. (New York: Praeger, 1967), p.319

5. William Irwin Thompson, AT THE EDGE OF HISTORY (New York: Harper and Row, 1971), p.110

6. Kuhn even mentions that "historians of literature, of music, of the arts, of political development, and of many other human activities, have long described their subjects in the same way." (1970, p.208)

7. Jean-Michel Folon, "Editions Marquet," (1973); cf. POSTERS BY FOLON (New York: Harry N. Abrams, 1978). The title of the poster is 'Le Funambule'.

INTRODUCTION

Is there a current paradigm in architecture? And if so, what are its distinguishing features? If, by definition, one means the entire constellation of facts, values, theories, and methods which directs a community of practioners, then one way the question can be answered is by looking at the direction of the field since the *previous* paradigm.

The contrast between pre-industrial and modern architecture shows at once that in spite of any differences of style within each period, there is a completely different set of processes at work generating a completely different product — each recognizable as belonging to its own time. The transition period — say 1890 to 1920 — is blurred; but there can be no doubt that future historians will see modern architecture as a unified constellation of essentially similar buildings. One may choose to point out the differences between the buildings of Walter Gropius, Mies van der Rohe, and Le Corbusier, but compared with renaissance architecture, the similarities are more striking. For example, they are all united in their affinity for differentiating space into elemental compositions which are essentially cubistic in appearance and determined, in large measure, by the technological forces of the age translated — interpretatively — into built form by the architect. Within that paradigm there are of course endless variations which, to a lesser or greater degree, reflect these similarities; but in appearance and feeling they are all distinctly "modern."

In terms of the processes at work generating them, which is perhaps the invisible side of the paradigm, they also share the same facts, values, and methods. They are alike in their dependence upon industrial-economic space determinants, mass production and prefabrication of materials, standardization of construction practices, and the specialization and division of labor and activities.

1

And because the determination of these processes is, with the exception of the architect's individual interpretation of them, largely *external* when compared to the previous paradigm, there is an absence of any cumulative, internal body of knowledge which describes their consequences. Theory is derived from other disciplines — from painting, sculpture, mechanics, economics, sociology, philosophy, and history, translated through the personal experience of building — and replaces the ancient passing from hand to hand of handicraft aesthetics which is now regarded as incompatible with industrial and technological values.[1]

The paradigm itself is administered through a sequence of educational and professional processes which start in the schools of architecture. There, the student is given a problem, usually stated in the form of people and activities in search of an articulated and enclosed space. To solve it, he must first attempt to find out everything he can about these people and their activities — what they are like, how they behave, their values, their needs, how their activities need to be performed, what demands these needs make upon space, and so on. Then, based on analytical and heuristic skills in conceptualizing these facts, a scientific knowledge of structure, materials, and construction, and artistic abilities to arrange basic geometrical elements and compose space, he somehow designs a building that satisfies human needs, can reasonably be built and maintained, and is aesthetically pleasing. But these qualities of the solution — "commodity, firmness, and delight," as they were first called by Vitruvius — are themselves subject to the constraints imposed upon the design by the facts, values, and methods of the paradigm itself — which is why the solutions all look and feel distinctly "modern."

The breakdown of the paradigm occurs — just as it does in science — when external anomalies introduce contradictions within its order. In the case of science, phenomena may appear (or be invented) which cannot be accounted for or explained by the normal rules — just as the earth's motion contradicted Ptolemaic astronomy, or relativity contradicted Euclidean geometry. In the case of architecture, changes in the external environment may appear which prevent the normal rules from satisfying its own standards. This began to happen to modern architecture shortly after World War Two when increased industrialization, urbanization, and rapid social change revealed contradictions within the paradigm itself. The ensuing crisis — which strongly resembles the crisis of the previous paradigm at the end of the 19th century — consists in the recognition that modern architecture no longer produces buildings that satisfy people's needs, can reasonably be built and maintained, and are aesthetically pleasing. Research of the past decade (and conducted from within the paradigm itself) has conclusively shown that modern buildings are dysfunctional when evaluated according to *recent* standards of social and behavioral science; in addition, they are structurally and technologically inefficient when evaluated by *recent* standards of both structural engineering and environmental science; and finally, although their aesthetic appeal has always been essentially intellectual, they do not look and feel pleasing to an increasing number of architects themselves.[2]

Pre-industrial architecture experienced a similar crisis when new materials and methods of building, new functions connected with industrialization, and new values about the organization of people and space introduced similar anomalies. At first, the four-hundred year old tradition of classicism and historicism attempted to deal with these changes on its own terms by incorporating them within its own facts, values, and methods as well as by modifying those same facts, values, and methods. The railway stations that looked like palaces and the palaces that were stripped down like warehouses illustrate such a response. But finally, when the old paradigm no longer looked and felt good to architects themselves, a change was underway. At that moment, when competing schools of thought attempted to redirect the field, many architects were no longer trying to derive different styles from *within* the existing paradigm; they were then working in a new paradigm, one which we now call modern architecture.

These parallels with Thomas Kuhn's model of the structure of scientific revolutions are both striking and supportive of recent advances in the sociology of knowledge which demonstrate the essential similarities between the development of the arts and the development of the sciences.[3] Kuhn has also shown that, in science, acquisition of a "paradigm" and of the type of research it permits is a sign of maturity in the development of any given field. But the history of science is also the history of "revolutions," periods of transformation when one paradigm is rejected in favour of another. Such changes, together with the controversies that almost always accompany them, are "the tradition-shattering complements of the tradition-bound activity of normal science."[4] They bring with them not only a new basis for professional conduct and practice, but a new basis for seeing the world within which professional practice is conducted.

History suggests that the road to the acquisition of a new paradigm is both inevitable and extraordinarily arduous. There is first of all the period in which the existing or current paradigm starts to break down in the face of novel events that it cannot explain or deal with. Then, as these events become increasingly anomalous, the attention of the community is directed more and more toward resolving them within the famework of the current paradigm. A period of crisis then follows in which the paradigm's ability to resolve the anomaly is questioned. More and more adherents begin to search for alternatives in an attempt to solve the problem. This is the period of transition in which competing schools of thought attempt to gain attention in the search for a new paradigm. Because it demands large-scale paradigm destruction and major shifts in the problems and techniques of normal scientific activity, the emergence of these new thoughts is generally preceded by a period of pronounced professional insecurity. But finally, a new paradigm emerges which resolves the anomaly and begins to guide normal research, even before full consensus is achieved and the battle over its acceptance is won. "When the transition is complete," says Kuhn, "the profession will have changed its view of the field, its methods, and its goals."[5]

The importance of Kuhn's model lies not only in its ability to explain the periodic discontinuities which historically punctuate cumulative growth, but also in providing an inner light on those non-cumulative episodes in which an older paradigm is replaced in whole or in part by an incompatibly new one. Consequently, it permits one to dispassionately step outside one's own field, if only momentarily, and assess its historical possibilities through an understanding of the dynamics of change which characterize its development. In particular, it enables one to distinguish between modifications and extensions to an existing paradigm, and discontinuities which are genuinely incompatible with its

4

1

2

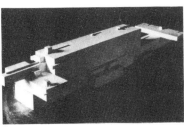

3

4

5   6

1. Filippo Brunelleschi, Pazzi Chapel, Florence.
   The pre-industrial paradigm.

2. Gerrit Rietveld, Schroeder House, Utrecht.
   The modern paradigm.

3. Kasimir Malevitch, Architectural Composition.
   An affinity for differentiating space into elemental compositions which are
   essentially cubistic in appearance . . .

4. Eliel Saarinen, Helsinki Railway Station.
   Railway stations that looked like palaces . . .

5. Peter Behrens, Electrical Factory, Berlin.
   Palaces that were stripped down like warehouses . . .

6. Otto Wagner, Design for an Exhibition Hall.
   The transition period is blurred . . .

PLATE I

7. Skidmore, Owings and Merrill, Alcoa Building, San Francisco.
Determined, in large measure, by the technological forces of the age.

8. Ludwig Miës van der Rohe, One Charles Center, Baltimore.
Industrial-economic space determinants, mass production and pre-fabrication of materials, standardization of construction practices, and the specialization and division of labor and activities.

PLATE II

structure. This latter type, which Kuhn calls "extraordinary science," is based on a reality believed to be existing independently of our knowing it, entail a reshuffling of the elements of a particular field, and result in a revolutionary transformation of vision.

This same type of *disjunction* however also occurs in art. "The constant unmasking of previous symbolisms," as Ernest Jones calls it, and the recognition that what was previously thought to be literally true is only an aspect or representation of truth of which our minds were at the time capable, is very similar to the process of paradigm shift in science.[6]

Diana Crane has even suggested that the violence of the emotions that accompany such shifts is probably related to the degree of comittment to the older conceptions and perhaps to the length of time during which a particular conception has gone unchallenged.[7] Kuhn however shows that in more scientific fields the reason is related to an important professional need to resist paradigm change. For even when confronted by severe and prolonged anomalies, even though they may begin to lose faith and then to consider alternatives, scientists do not renouce the current paradigm *until* an alternative candidate is available to take its place. In science at least, the decision to reject one paradigm is always simultaneously the decision to accept another. And the reason is obvious: to do otherwise would be to reject the field itself. This built-in conservativism is therefore essential to the survival and continuty of the field. The emergence of a new paradigm will therefore be subject to much greater professional scrutiny and resistance than mere paradigm extensions or modifications.

The proponent of a new paradigm will typically encounter otherwise inexplicably violent and hostile reactions to his ideas — ideas which by definition have little basis for reality within the existing paradigm. This is why his success depends so much upon a systematic and precise desription of the consequences of his findings, for although the existing paradigm may be in trouble, the burden of proof is on himself.

Often, however, such an effort starts out as only a modification or extension of the existing paradigm. In Kuhn's analysis, the proponent of a new paradigm is first seen to be pushing the normal rules of practice harder than ever to see, especially in the area of crisis, just where and how far they can be made to work. He will also seek ways for magnifying and making more striking the obstacles to success within the existing paradigm. He will often seem a man searching at random, trying experiments just to see what will happen, looking for an effect whose nature he cannot quite guess until, finally, the new route, or a sufficient hint to permit later articulation, may emerge all at once. "Almost always," says Kuhn, "the men who achieve these fundamental inventions of a new paradigm have been either very young or very new to the field whose paradigm they change."[8]

These characteristics are certainly descriptive of Alexander's situation. His first publication (written in 1958) was a re-examination of the perceptual qualities traditionally attributed to the Golden Mean — a highly regarded proportional ratio occuring in classical buildings.[9] It represented an attempt to push certain current beliefs up against what was then known in cognitive psychology. His second publication was a good example of paradigm extension — a call for agreement on the need to refine the developments of the previous "revolution."[10] It was an attack on the cult of individualism and on the lack of cumulative improvements in the standard of building since the 1930's. His first book (coauthored with Serge Chermayeff in 1962) was an analysis and critique of the capacity for current methods of design to satisfy the complex system of human needs in a building program from the standpoint of what was then known in information theory.[11] And in NOTES ON THE SYNTHESIS OF FORM (published the following year) he argued that the purely intuitive approach to architectural design was no longer capable of adequately responding to the complexities of industrialization, urbanization, and social change. This was felt to be true by architects in general, but it was never before very precisely spelled out. The *symptoms* of this incapacity were only vaguely perceived in the dehumanizing qualities of the concrete, steel, and glass boxes that were increasingly dominating the built environment after World War Two. Alexander's contention however was that the *causes* were to be found in the nature of the design act itself — in the lack of congruence between the statement of the problem and the solution. But in seeking to rationally understand the act of design, his first attempt was like opening an exit door on the current paradigm of architecture.

6

Alexander was a scientist (trained in physics and mathematics) *and* an architect, and he approached the question — What is design? — with a kind of scientific rationalism that was not normally associated with architecture. Modern architecture had been called "rational," for example, but it was the kind of rationality that Karl Mannheim called "functional": shaped exclusively by external realities and void of any final purpose.[12] On the other hand, Alexander's rationality was obviously *substantive,* the kind of pure rationality that distinguishes extraordinary from normal science and which seemed to flow naturally from his training as a mathematician.

Although architecture is, by definition, both the art *and* science of building, the "science" side of the equation is usually interpreted to mean *applied* science — the realm of structure, materials, construction, and the technological hardware of building operations. Occasionally a structural engineer or a technologist will conceive of the problem of design in terms of their particular disciplines; but this is quite different from the perspective of pure science or mathematics.[13] Nevertheless, the "art" side of the equation is usually reserved for the question of design — the realm of the synthesis and generation of architectural form. In terms of tradition then, the architect is fundamentally an artist, but one who *understands* science and can *apply* it to the problem of building. Although he may have great respect for science, even be fascinated or inspired by it, he is not a scientist. Even the few scientists who were also architects, like Leonardo da Vinci and Christopher Wren, treated the question of design as a purely artistic problem. Architectural history records few, if any instances of architects treating the question of design as a *scientific* problem.

The current role of theory in architecture illuminates this distinction. In the making of buildings and towns, the crucial test of the reality of a theory is the extent to which practical work depends on its existence. But in the case of modern architecture, most of what passes for "theory" is really just a manipulation of design concepts and ideas already derived from the experience of building. In other words, it exists in a peculiar relation to the final product. Such theory does not help create designs; it only explains them — a fact which always comes as a shock to most students of architecture. For this reason the *act* of design has remained a creative mystery, somehow transferable but not rationally communicable. As a science however, such theory is primitive. It cannot really be used by anyone else; each designer must re-invent the act himself; and as a result, there is practically no internal, cumulative body of architectural knowledge. In that sense, modern architectural design is very similar to pre-Newtonian optics where, says Kuhn, "being able to take no common body of belief for granted, each writer on physical optics felt forced to build his field anew from its foundations."[14]

On the other hand, treating the question of design as a scientifc problem presupposes a totally different kind of theory. Such theory would first of all have to *precede* the act of design. Secondly, it would have to lead directly to the act of building in much the same way that the purely intuitive process, regardless of its shortcomings, does generate an end product. In other words, it would have to *generate* designs rather than just explain them. And thirdly, it would have to be *general* enough to permit its applicability to an endless variety of individual circumstances. In other words, it would have to be compatible and congruent with the freedom and creativity necessary to produce a work of *art*.

Such presuppositions are enormous. No wonder Kuhn calls these kinds of theories "extraordinary" and the road to the acquisition of a paradigm "arduous." Yet the possibility of such a theory in architecture is both exciting and disturbing. No one really knows what buildings and towns generated by theory would be like. Most informed architects know that the popular image of the architecture of the future — the space-age fantasies of Hollywood, comic strips, and science fiction — is fundamentally incorrect, a misuse of science. A truly scientific (as opposed to technological) theory of architecture would be much more concerned with unlocking the creative processes that produce buildings than in the application of scientific technologies to buildings already produced. Yet the idea of discovering a set of steps or even "rules" which actually *creates* something is profoundly disturbing. Even the obvious benefits of the accumulation and expansion of knowledge that such discovery would permit are overshadowed by the belief that somehow such processes can never be known, only constrained or modified. But this is not only true for architects; it exists in other, more scientific fields as well.

8

For example, prior to the discovery of the structure of DNA molecules in the field of biology, the "laws" of nature were considered to be unknown except insofar as they were constrained or modified by natural selection. Natural selection could not account for genetic processes, but it could explain their characteristic behaviors.[15] Similarly, prior to the discovery of generative grammars in the field of linguistics, the origin of language was considered to be unknown except insofar as it was constrained or modified by the rules of grammar. You could not invent a sentence by following such rules, yet the rules seemed to explain their characteristic behaviors.[16] The same distinctions could be made in architecture. Prior to the discovery of a generative theory of building, the act of design would appear as an unknown creative process except insofar as it was constrained or modified by architectural "rules" like "commodity, firmness, and delight." Of course one cannot design a building by simply following such rules, although they do help to explain the final product. But the building itself is presumed to come from somewhere else — a presumption which ironically reinforces its dependence on *external* realities.

The idea that a set of known rules could actually generate a building is as disturbing as the idea that a human being is generated by a few genetic rules operating on chromosomes or that a poem is generated by a few grammatical rules operating on language. And yet that is precisely what Alexander is claiming. For him, the two examples just cited — genetics and linguistics — are not just analogies. In each case there is a principle of "generativity" involved, and Alexander is not just interested in a *theoretical* equivalent of this principle. He is actually interested in generativity itself and therefore serious about a set of rules which generates buildings — not as a mechanical technique (as might perhaps be naively understood in the automobile industry) but as a structural principle of natural creation as it is understood in modern science.

These ideas are of course disturbing because they challenge the long-standing separation of art and science into "two cultures," as C. P. Snow put it.[17] And yet it is precisely this "bifurcation of nature" that is so disturbing to Alexander.[18] In an allusion to Herman Hesse's great imaginary game in which all structures — musical, mathematical, social, political, physical, chemical, biological, and visual — could be represented in a single way, he posited what he called the "Bead Game Conjecture." "It is possible," he wrote "to invent a unifying concept of structure within which all the various concepts of structure now current in different fields of art and science can be seen from a single point of view."[19] This was a fascinating conjecture, if taken seriously, but it isn't until one sees Alexander's work over the ten-year period following the publication of NOTES ON THE SYNTHESIS OF FORM that these connections between theory, scientific paradigms, architectural paradigms, and the relationship between art and science can be made.

From NOTES on, Alexander's work has been characterized by a gradual but intensely persistent honing-in on the very heart of the creative process in what *appears* to be the search for a generative theory of architecture. For him, this search takes the form of several basic questions that need to be answered: What is an environment? How does it affect us? Is there any objective sense in which it can be good or bad? How is it generated? And under what conditions is the process which generates it capable of making the kind which is good?

This last question however, seems to suggest that it isn't just any generative theory of architecture that is important. It is a particular kind of generative theory — one that generates processes that produce "good" environments. And as it turns out, the search for a generative theory is incidental to this other search. In fact, the "theory" is simply a device which has to be created along the way because it is necessary in enabling Alexander to get where he wants to go — to make beautiful buildings. But in light of the effort which eventually went into the creation of such a theory, this is a bit like inventing the calculus simply in order to solve a particular equation, or creating the laws of motion simply in order to be able to ride in a car. Yet this is close to what Alexander has had to do in the case of architecture.

In THE TIMELESS WAY OF BUILDING, A PATTERN LANGUAGE, and THE OREGON EXPERIMENT, Alexander and his associates have published the first of several works which attempt to lay the foundation for an entirely new approach to architecture. At its core is a scientific attempt to account for the act of design — "an age-old process by which the people of a society have always pulled the order of their world from their own being."[20] For Alexander, this account takes the form of several basic facts: that the actual substance of which the environment is made consists of *patterns* rather than things; that the distinction between good and bad patterns is not arbitrary but can be arrived at *objectively;* that if you ask, "Where does the environment come from?", the fact is that it is generated by language-like systems called *pattern languages;* that its successful adaptation to a complex system requires an enormous amount of minute local adaptations which insists that *large numbers of people* have to be engaged in the process; and finally, that the environment properly constituted has an objectively definable morphology to it with *specific geometric properties* that must be present if it is to be beautiful.

The procedural consequences of these facts include practical changes in the relationship between the architect and society, in the relationship between the architect and the building contractor, in the processes of construction, in the flow of money through the environment, and finally, in the politics of land ownership and control. Taken as a whole, this work forms a new *paradigm* of architecture because it leads directly to a fundamentally different way of perceiving and making buildings and towns than current theory and practice requires.

Although paradigm claims have been made before in the history of architecture — namely in the 1920's — their appearance is all too rare to be dismissed lightly. These particular claims by Alexander certainly have a unique origin. They represent more than two decades of extraordinary research and experimentation into the nature of the built environment in the search for a way to make beautiful buildings. Regardless of the outcome, whether in the end one agrees or disagrees with the results, this particular evolution of a new paradigm is unique in the intellectual history of the profession. But because the proponents of competing paradigms will often disagree about the list of problems that any candidate must resolve, because their standards or their definitions of the discipline itself are not even the same, and because they see different things when they look from the same point in the same direction, the emergence of a new paradigm, even in science, is not the sort of battle that can be won by proofs. For these reasons, an account of the events and circumstances which led to its original formulation play an important role in the *sociological* processes by which such transformations occur.

Kuhn has shown that when a new candidate for paradigm is first proposed, it has seldom solved more than a few of the problems that confront it, and that most of the these solutions are still far from perfect. Ordinarily, it is only much later, after the new paradigm has been developed, accepted, and expanded that apparently decisive arguments can be formulated. But while the debate goes on, the opponents of a new paradigm can legitimately claim that even in the area of crisis it is hardly superior to its traditional rival. In addition, the defenders of traditional theory and practice can almost always point to problems that its new rival has not solved but that for their view are not problems at all. But in architecture, as opposed to pure science, the problem-solving abilities take on a special significance, even in the early stages of the debate. This is because the problems themselves are determined by societal urgency.

Only some of the problems which Alexander's work can claim to solve are generally shared by the architectural community as being the most important anomalies of the crisis. There is first of all the claim of providing a thorough-going connection to real functional problems within a comprehensive and rational procedure that clearly states what to do and in what order. In this view, the body of work represented by THE TIMELESS WAY OF BUILDING, A PATTERN LANGUAGE, and THE OREGON EXPERIMENT is seen as *information*. In other words, it solves the problem created by the absence of an internal and cumulative body of architectural knowledge. It satisfies not only those architects who simply cannot handle a large, complex body of facts, but also those who feel that there has just not even been any reasonable body of facts, particularly in terms of human social problems. And on its own, this "information" is sufficient to cause considerable changes in the current theory and practice of architecture. But they would be essentially modifications of extensions of the existing paradigm. They would not specifically account for the anomalous discrepancy between the obviously beautiful buildings of traditional societies and the lack of beauty which Alexander perceives in modern buildings and towns. This is the crucial distinction, and whether or not it is perceived as necessary by proponents of the old paradigm, further claims are made.

There is the claim of providing a direct link between design processes and social and political processes which directly involve both the architect and the user. Then there is the claim of providing a more profound connection between the engineering structure of a building and its social form and between the processes of construction and the quality of the finished product. And finally, there is the claim of providing an objective account of beauty which removes the distinction between aesthetics and function all the way down to the level of ornament and color and which provides an explicit solution to the problem of uniqueness and variety.

Yet paradigm debates are not really about problem-solving ability. Instead, the issue is which paradigm should *in the future* guide work on problems that neither competitor can yet claim to resolve completely. A decision between alternate ways of practising a discipline is called for, and that decision must be based less on past achievement than on future promise. What is called for in accepting a new paradigm at an early stage is faith that it will succeed with the many large problems that confront it, knowing only that the old paradigm has failed with a few. This is one of the reasons why, in Kuhn's analysis, prior crisis proves so important. But crisis alone is not enough. There must also be a basis for faith in the particular candidate chosen. Something must make at least a few practitioners feel that the new proposal is on the right track. Sometimes it is only personal and aesthetic considerations that can do that, as Einstein's general theory attracted scientists for many years principally on aesthetic grounds, an appeal that few people outside of mathematics have been able to feel.

To most people, science is valuable chiefly for its practical application. Yet most scientists will not even consider a theory if it doesn't have an aesthetic appeal, especially in mathematics and physics. "Beauty," "elegance," "simplicity" — these terms are not only used daily by scientists but they are imporant signposts in the search for scientific discoveries that lead to paradigms. This is not to suggest that new paradigms triumph ultimately through some mystical aesthetic. In the end it is of course the paradigm's ability to solve the problems and resolve the crisis that would eventually lead a profession to desert one tradition for another. But in the case of science, if there are two or more theories that equally seem to cover the facts, the choice will always be the one that has the greater aesthetic appeal because it gratifies our desire for comprehension. When we have forgotten the details of a particular theory or method, the degree to which it remains in our minds and continues to unify our acts is dependent upon the depth and comprehensiveness of its vision. As in art, this is the light that pervades the whole work and gives it a harmony that lies much deeper than anything the artist may achieve by the mere technical dovetailing of the elements of his work. The chief function of art is to communicate this vision.

In science, the search for universal laws and comprehensive theories is a manifestation of this same impulse. But the comprehension bestowed by a work of art is really the communication of the artist's personal vision. The comprehension bestowed by science is not so obviously personal. Yet the scientists who have branched away from the main road and have thereby given science a new direction are the ones who have put to themselves entirely new questions. It is here, of course, that the personal element in the creation of a scientific theory is most clearly revealed. The history of science is not the history of some sort of "automatic development," as J. W. N. Sullivan put it. "The actual course that science has pursued depends very largely on the types of mind which, as historical accidents, happen to have risen to the level of genius at favorable instants."[21]

For these reasons, biographical accounts of the events and circumstances which lead to the original formulation of a theory or a discovery can help to explain the personal and aesthetic considerations that are important in the initial attractions of a new paradigm, in spite of its problem-solving claims or abilities. In the case of Alexander's work, which exists equally in the world of art and in the world of science, this is especially true and constitutes, I believe, one of the most interesting chapters in the history of architecture.

REFERENCE NOTES

1. Reyner Banham, THEORY AND DESIGN IN THE FIRST MACHINE AGE, 2nd.ed. (New York: Praeger, 1967), p.319

2. In addition to Banham, OP. CIT., the same conclusion can be drawn from: Charles Jencks, MODERN MOVEMENTS IN ARCHITECTURE (New York: Anchor Press, 1971); Brent Brolin, THE FAILURE OF MODERN ARCHITECTURE (New York: Van Nostrand Reinhold, 1976); Peter Blake, FORM FOLLOWS FIASCO: WHY MODERN ARCHITECTURE HASNT WORKED (Boston: Little, Brown, 1977); and Tom Wolfe, "From Bauhaus to our House," HARPERS (June and July, 1981)

3. See Diana Crane, INVISIBLE COLLEGES: DEFINITIONS OF KNOWLEDGE IN SCIENTIFIC COMMUNITIES (Chicago: University of Chicago Press, 1972), pp.129–142

4. Thomas Kuhn, THE STRUCTURE OF SCIENTIFIC REVOLUTIONS, 2nd.ed. (Chicago: University of Chicago Press, 1970), p.6

5. IBID, pp. 84–85

6. E. H. Gombrich, NORM AND FORM (London: Phaidon Press, 1966), cited in Crane, OP. CIT., pp.132–133

7. Crane, OP. CIT., pp.135–136

8. Kuhn, OP. CIT., p.89

9. "Perception and Modular Coordination," ROYAL INSTITUTE OF BRITISH ARCHITECTS JOURNAL, 66:12 (October, 1959), pp.425–429

10. "The Revolution Finished Twenty Years Ago," ARCHITECTS YEARBOOK, 9 (1960), pp.181–185

11. COMMUNITY AND PRIVACY: TOWARDS A NEW ARCHITECTURE OF HUMANISM (New York: Doubleday, 1963)

12. Karl Mannheim, IDEOLOGY AND UTOPIA (1937)

13. I particularly have in mind Pier Luigi Nervi and James Marston Fitch. The former is representative of the "structuralist" movement in architecture; the latter the "environmentalist" movement. Cf. Nervi, AESTHETICS AND TECHNOLOGY IN BUILDING (The Charles Elliot Norton Lecutres, 1961–1962), trans. by Robert Einardi (Cambridge: Harvard University Press, 1965) and Fitch, AMERICAN BUILDING: THE ENVIRONMENTAL FORCES THAT SHAPE IT (New York: Schocken Books, 1975)

14. Kuhn, OP. CIT., p.13

15. For a simple, non-technical account, see Julian Huxley, NEW BOTTLES FOR NEW WINE (1959)

16. For a simple, non-technical introduction to modern linguistics, see John Lyons, NOAM CHOMSKY (1970)

17. Cited in Colin Wilson, BEYOND THE OUTSIDER (London: Pan Books, 1965), pp.77–84; cf. C. P. Snow, THE TWO CULTURES AND THE SCIENTIFIC REVOLUTION (1959)

18. IBID.; cf. Alfred North Whitehead, SYMBOLISM: ITS MEANING AND EFFECT (1959)

19. "The Bead Game Conjecture," LOTUS, 5 (Milan: 1968), pp.151–154

20. From the statement appearing beside the title page in each of the three books (New York: Oxford University Press, 1975, 1977, and 1979)

21. J. W. N. Sullivan, THE LIMITATIONS OF SCIENCE (New York: Viking Press, 1933), p.169

PART ONE

I

THE PROBLEM

From the start Alexander has been preoccupied with the question of what it is that makes things beautiful, especially buildings. The standard reference point for this question has always been the great buildings and towns of the historical past: Greek temples, gothic cathedrals, renaissance villas and the vast number of anonymous, indigenous buildings and towns of the Greek islands, the Italian hillsides, or the English countryside. Such examples of beautiful environments form the standard of reference of preindustrial architectural achievement. But the world has changed considerably since the advent of industrialization in the nineteenth century. Not only are buildings and towns made differently today, but the kinds of functional and technological demands which they are now required to meet did not even exist in preindustrial societies. In our own time, these demands have become so complex that the main problems confronting architects today center around the need just to have reliable information — information that can be translated directly into things like buildings and towns, regardless of their appearance.

Under these conditions the question of beauty has become even further obscured, surfacing variously as the attempt to express the aesthetics of machine technology, urban amenity, or cultural pluralism. And yet the anomaly remains that the buildings and towns of our time do not even approach the beauty of the great buildings and towns of the historical past. Consequently, no clever aesthetic theory can explain away the striking lack of beauty in such buildings as those which currently epitomize the state of the art, regardless of "style."

It is also true however, that in rare instances the work of some of the great architects of the twentieth century, such as Frank Lloyd Wright, have come close to recreating the quality that one feels in beautiful buildings and towns; yet these instances play a curious role in modern theory and practice. They are the exception rather than the rule. In fact, at such moments, it is as if the accepted rules of building were somehow cast aside and other, perhaps unknown "rules" were permitted to come into play. In architectural circles, such instances are considered to represent unique accidents of genius, when particular forces came together for an unrepeatable moment. But even if they were knowable and repeatable, the assumption is, finally, that they would be impractical and unfeasible under present conditions.

The current status of aesthetics in advance industrial societies reinforces this dilemma. The prevailing view is that beauty is just so much cream on the surface of things, the final icing of the cake. Actually, as Herbert Marcuse showed in his analysis of the philosophical history of the term, that view was fixed in the second half of the eighteenth century, about the time that scientific rationalism began "whittling down" the content and validity of the aesthetic imagination.[1] According to Marcuse, the sensuous realm of beauty — the realm of feeling — became relegated to the icefields of metaphysics, and what remained was the mere *appearance* of a thing — the way it looked. But perhaps even more devastating than this stripping away of the content of beauty was the implicit repression of its actual validity by the claims of subjectivism. The result is that, today, the average person assumes that not only does beauty have to do with just the appearance of things (and therefore an extravagance, to be added or subtracted as funds permit), but that it is also "subjective," a matter of personal taste or preference, and cannot be meaningfully discussed. And in this they have been supported by important philosophers, critics, and even artists who have come to the same conclusion. In summarizing this state of affairs, Guy Sircello points out how indeed it *is* almost impossible to discuss the subject objectively:

> We hear from one side that the very search for necessary and sufficient conditions [of beauty] is perverse; from another that it is reckless and irresponsible because it will take the mystery and splendor out of our experience of the beautiful; from another that in making such a search we lose integrity because we are merely aping "science"; and from another that in trying to put soft, aesthetic

notions on the same footing as hard, scientific concepts we are being presumptuous.[2]

This is the climate in which, today, the question of what makes a building or a town beautiful has to be asked. If such "rules" or "conditions" existed in the past, what were they, how had they become lost, under what circumstances might they be recreated, and how could such circumstances be made practical and feasible? Questions like these are the kind that Alexander has had to answer — and the starting point is his vision and definition of a beautiful building:

I am trying to make a building which is like a smile on a person's face, and which has that kind of rightness about it, and which is really like that and not just saying it is like that.

If you just take that very simple idea for a moment and try to imagine what it would mean to do that, you can see at once that it is very, very difficult. Admittedly it is somewhat nebulous put that way, but knowing the sort of incredible way you reverberate when a person smiles at you, and how you feel, and the opening and relaxation which takes place — in that person and in you — and you actually imagine simply trying to do that, then it is an accurate description. It is not simply a metaphor.

When someone smiles it is as though the fabric of the universe seems to melt. In other words, something happens in that the order of things actually relaxes in a peculiar way. And it can happen in a million different ways. But one would not ordinarily say that such things are beautiful, except in some incredibly rarefied sense of the word. And yet, the fact is that somehow, at such moments, things are completely orderly and at peace with themselves — not at all in the pretentious sense that we tend to call beautiful, but in an incredibly simple and straightforward and at the same time deep and mysterious sense.

If you contrast the beauty of a person's face (which roughly parallels the ordinary use of the word) with the beauty of a smile on a person's face (which is much closer to what I am talking about), then what I am trying to do bears the same relation to what one normally calls "beautiful" as the smile does to the face. Of course it is infinitely more wonderful and more precious, I think. It is also much more serious and closer to the hearts of everybody. Because if you think about the smile, the question of whether it is a beautiful face, in the ordinary sense of the word, is completely irrelevant. By the standards of the smile, the actual contents of a person's face are incredibly unimportant.

21

With this simple example Alexander achieves an almost figure-ground reversal between the prevailing view of beauty and his own. And yet, in the case of architecture, the question of whether a building "smiles" is certainly related to what is typically called beauty in the sense that places that have that kind of quality are places that one might easily call beautiful. It is just that, somehow, the word in its current 20th century usage is so unusual that the statement that Alexander, or anyone else, is trying to make a beautiful building has totally different connotations. It does not really convey the idea of trying to bring into existence those places in the world that are like the smile on a person's face. And yet it is clear that there are some places in the world that are like this:

Suppose that you imagine the most beautiful place that you know in the world. When I say "place," I am including exceptionally lovely buildings, like the buildings of Pisa, or the Alhambra, or the great buildings of Isphahan. And then you also include all of the ancillary, more modest buildings and streets and open spaces that were built in the heyday by the people in that same state of mind. For me, the whole thing is very, very simple. I want to reach the point of actually being able to do that. I want to be able to show a place, let us say for the sake of argument, ten blocks by twenty blocks, which has got that kind of order. It would have that kind of order on a very informal, rambling level; but it would also contain certain spots or buildings of almost excruciating beauty that would exist naturally within. And what I hope to do, if I live long enough, is to actually be able to set in motion what it takes to do that.

Now Alexander knows that this cannot be done by any of the normal procedures that architects have been working with for the past fifty or more years. So of course it becomes necessary to discover all of the processes which will actually permit this to happen:

First of all, there are the processes needed to do it; and secondly, there is the actual doing of it. It is a question of being in a position where people have enough confidence to permit me to regulate the processes in a sort of restricted area for a long enough period of time so that this could actually happen once. But it will take quite a long time to actually succeed in implementing one case because people will still be skeptical about whether it can actually be done at the level of intensity that I speak of.

The other part is that the processes are so explicitly clear and powerful that they ultimately do not depend on me at all. So at that stage, my doing of

*it once would be merely a demonstration. It would in fact replicate itself —
and of course in a million different versions. But the possibility of doing that
would then be something that belonged to everyone and would have nothing
special to do with me. And that is of course the reason for writing all of these
processes down in the form of books. The reason for writing them down is
not only to be able to share them with other people. It is essentially in order
to be able to do it the first time — because I know that it cannot be done
without getting these processes right. So if indeed we succeed in doing this
once, it also becomes public property and is actually capable of doing this
wonderful and miraculous thing to the environment all over the world. But
it hinges on understanding what that means.*

*If one has got some experience of the world and therefore knows what it is
like when a place really is breathtakingly beautiful and does not confuse it
with the Hyatt Regency House, for example, and provided that one has
been in enough places to know what that is really like — full-fledged, no
compromises, the real thing — and to understand what we are after here,
then I think you have a clear description of the goal.*

What is not clear, perhaps, is what that goal entails, because the
problems that need to be solved in order to accomplish it are
enormous. In Alexander's case a considerable amount of time has
gone into the development not only of the architectural processes
necessary to succeed but of the theory behind them — not for any
desire to be a theorist but simply because the problem demands it.
And this is where some confusion may lay — in understanding the
difficulty of the task:

*You can say that a lot of architects want to do this — or think they want to
do it; but there are actually very, very few that take it seriously because it
happens to be incredibly difficult. I am not interested in the ten percent,
twenty percent, or thirty percent versions because it is actually just not
worthwhile. The interesting thing is actually to be able to do the real thing
— which is incredibly hard.*

*Take someone who has struggled for years to do something that was
difficult to do and that a lot of people said could not be done — as in the case
of the Wright Brothers. Their tenacity came from recognizing how difficult
it was to fly but wanting very much to do it. That certainly is my situation.
I want to do this very much, but I am not willing to make do with second
best.*

Alexander refers to the early experiments in manned flight; but in
the case of the Wright Brothers, for example, no one had ever flown

before. Consequently, there was no precedent and no image of how long it would take to succeed — or what was actually involved in the task. But in the case of architecture, regardless of Alexander's feelings about how it is presently being conducted, it does exist, it is thousands of years old as an art form, and there are precedents. Someone can say that, of course it is not easy; but surely it is being done. But for Alexander, what he is trying to do has not been done for hundreds of years:

This is why I think it is difficult to communicate this goal. I do not think that people realize that it is not being done today and that it has not been done for hundreds of years. In fact, when I started out I had not even realized that myself. But the historical question is not really important. What is important is to be fantastically demanding and true to the facts about when it is really happening and when one is kidding oneself that it is happening.

I think there are many people who realize that there are obviously heights of attainment, or heights in the beauty of a thing, which are very rare. Literally hundreds of thousands of people appreciate that, for example, the Blue Mosque, or some small English Church is an incredibly beautiful place. There is nothing new in that. And I think it is also true that most of the architects who are working today fully recognize that there is an order of magnitude of difference between their own work and those works. I would say that even the so-called great architects of our own period have been conscious of the fact that some of these buildings I am speaking about were near miracles.

What I am trying to say is that the first half of this observation is quite common. Many people have a very clear perception of how beautiful some things are and that the things that are being made today are just not nearly that beautiful. But it is not simply that people are making fairly beautiful buildings today that are just not quite as beautiful as some that have been made. The fact is that they are not doing that at all. The real essence of the matter, which touches human life and human spirit and all of these things in a genuine way — that is not happening in kind. This is not a matter of degree. It is not happening, period! And what is peculiar — and this is the only respect in which I think I am somewhat unusual — is to take seriously the possibility that we could do that kind of thing, or even to make is a sort of moral imperative that it is not worth doing anything less — and to accept all of the consequences of that. I am actually serious about that.

Le Corbusier wrote a great deal about the cathedrals and the Parthenon.

24

9

10

11

9. Khwaju Bridge, Isphahan.
10. John Portman, Hyatt Regency Hotel, San Francisco.
11. Mosque of the Yeni Camii, Istanbul.

"If one has got some experience of the world and therefore knows what it is like when a place really is breathtakingly beautiful and does not confuse it with the Hyatt Regency House, for example . . ."

PLATE III

12

13

12. Courtyard of the Lions, Alhambra, Grenada
   "Spots or buildings of almost excruciating beauty . . ."

13. Cathedral of Strasbourg, Alsace
   "Even Le Corbusier wrote a great deal about the cathedrals and The Parthenon. He was very moved by many of these buildings."

PLATE IV

He was very moved by many of these buildings. But my experience of architects is that, even knowing these things, they have made do with some sort of incredibly mediocre second best. In fact, they are even playing tricks on themselves in order to permit this to happen. They have shut out all of this as being completely impossible, definitely belonging to the past, not being appropriate to the modern age, and a host of other slogans and interior mental attitudes which suggest that they feel comfortable with what they are making and have persuaded themselves that it is a reasonable height of attainment. Of course there are skills within the level. Low level as it is, you can do it well or badly. But my situation is simply that I am not willing to tolerate that. It is completely uninteresting and it does not mean enough.

Alexander's position is clear. He has set a standard for himself that he will not compromise. But the attempt to measure contemporary architecture up against such a standard is one thing; to make it a sort of "moral imperative" that nothing else is worth doing, and then setting about to do it is another. From the standpoint of traditional theory and practice, his assessment of the existing paradigm is outrageous. He has not only claimed that practically *all* of contemporary architecture is out of joint, he has also claimed that contemporary architects are either unaware of it or pretending that this is not the case. Are they wrong or mistaken? Or is Alexander simply mad?

According to Kuhn, such cognitive dissonance is typical of paradigm shift. For example, the men who called Copernicus mad because he asserted that the earth moved were not necessarily wrong or mistaken. Copernicus was only reopening an ancient debate about the motion of the earth. But part of what his opponents meant by "earth" was fixed position:

> Their earth, at least, could not be moved. Correspondingly, Copernicus' innovation was not simply to move the earth. Rather, it was a whole new way of regarding the problems of physics and astronomy, one that necessarily changed the meaning of both "earth" and "motion."[3]

Without the changes proposed by Copernicus, the concept of a moving earth actually was mad. On the other hand, once they had been made and understood, the question of the earth's motion no longer had any content for scientists. Kuhn's point is that the proponents of competing paradigms practice their trades in different ways and see different things when looking at the same world. Consequently, the transition between such incommensurables cannot be made without a change in the world view, or new *gestalt*.

That is what is being proposed here. Alexander is not just criticizing contemporary architecture and saying he can do better by its own standards. If that were the case his claims could easily be verified or rejected *prima facie*. Instead, what is being proposed is not only a different set of standards but a different definition of the field itself. Consequently, the assessment of Alexander's abilities to do what he has set out to do must be understood in the context of such a change in world view, or new *gestalt*.

REFERENCE NOTES

1. Herbert Marcuse, EROS AND CIVILIZATION (Boston: The Beacon Press, 1955), pp.157–179

2. Guy Sircello, A NEW THEORY OF BEAUTY (Princeton: Princeton University Press, 1975), p.5

3. Thomas Kuhn, THE STRUCTURE OF SCIENTIFIC REVOLUTIONS, 2nd.ed. (Chicago: University of Chicago Press, 1970), pp.149–150; cf. Kuhn, THE COPERNICAN REVOLUTION (Cambridge: Harvard University Press, 1957) and Max Jammer, CONCEPTS OF SPACE (Cambridge: Harvard University Press, 1954), pp.118–124

II

EARLY BEGINNINGS AND THE PERCEPTION OF ANOMALY

Alexander was born in Vienna in 1936. His parents were both classical archaeologists whose careers were becoming increasingly tenuous during the years immediately preceding the War. In 1938 German troops moved into Vienna and Austria became a part of the Third Reich. With the onset of war, Alexander and his parents left for England. Their contact in Oxford was Sir Gilbert Murray, a classical scholar. He took care of them, helped them get settled, and find work. Eventually, Alexander's parents both took modern language degrees as a basis for teaching German. As a result, he grew up in Oxford and started speaking English at the age of six. He attended the Dragon School where, except for mathematics and chemistry, he was not considered a very bright pupil. At the age of eight however, he made the decision to become a chemist.

In the spring of the last year in English preparatory schools there are examinations for going on to the public schools (which are comparable to the private academies and prep schools in the United States). A very small number of scholarships are given. In Alexander's case a scholarship was a matter of necessity since his parents could not possibly afford to send him to one of these schools. But when it was first proposed that he even take the scholarship exam his teacher was outraged because, first of all it was a year too soon and, secondly, he was considered to be no more than an average student. His father intervened and insisted he sit the exam for Oundle — then considered to be the best school for future scientists, having been the first public school to teach science in the 19th century. To his teacher's amazement, Alexander won the top

27

scholarship and eventually went to Oundle.

There he continued very much along the lines of mathematics and chemistry. Because in England one specializes quite early, he studied practically nothing but these subjects from the age of fourteen. He did quite well and this time it was his teachers who proposed he take the scholarship examinations for going on to University. And again he won the top scholarship, also a year ahead of time. The circumstances of the examination however were both unusual and prophetic:

I remember that in the physics practical exam we were asked to measure the earth's magnetic field — a sort of classical experiment one was expected to know how to perform. I got about half way through when the numbers started coming out unbelievably strange and did not really make sense. There was a temptation to want to correct them because the second part of the exam that was coming up was dependent upon the results of the first. Well, I never got to the second part. Instead, I sketched out a little theory about what possibly might be going on to explain these weird numbers. When I left the exam, I compared notes with the other students. They had all finished both parts of the exam, and I was convinced that I had failed.

However, as it turned out, luck was on my side. The physics practical had been held in the Cavendish laboratory, immediately over a room that contained a giant electromagnet. The magnetic field in our examination room was totally unlike the earth's magnetic field. So my idiot insistence to refuse to cook the results the way they were "supposed to be", and instead to write down the real numbers that I got, had been the right thing to do. In a sense, I was the only student who had faced the peculiarity of the situation, with complete honesty, even though it was uncomfortable and inconvenient. So that is probably why I won the scholarship.

Alexander's choice was Cambridge, but he was too young to go directly to University and so he decided to work with his chemistry teacher back at Oundle in order to see what it would be like to be a research chemist. It was the first time he had actually sat down and tried to see what the life of a chemist might be like and he very quickly became bored. It appeared he was not going to be a chemist after all. At the same time however, an exhibit of photographs of modern buildings was being shown at the school. It was to have an important and decisive effect on Alexander:

I was extremely excited by this exhibit and the first thought that passed through my head was that the people who were making these buildings were doing what I was doing when I painted — except that they were making a respectable living at it. My paintings were not particularly abstract; in fact, they were mainly pictorial. But I had the general sense that they were doing what I was doing — dealing with form. I did not particularly like their forms, but I went home the next weekend and told my father I was going to be an architect and that it was an unequivocal decision.

He was horrified. He thought architects were disreputable and idiotic. Here was his son that he was taking so much care of in the direction of science and it was as if I had announced to him that I was going to be a clerk. So we had a long talk about it. It was 1953 and I was seventeen and we worked out a bargain. He said I could do what I wanted but strongly advised me to get another kind of degree first and then do architecture. And on that basis, rather than doing chemistry, I chose mathematics because that seemed to be the most fundamental mental preparation for any other activity.

After he left Oundle, Alexander went into the Army; but it was only after he had been in for several months that it was discovered his eyesight was not good enough. Although he did not actually get discharged until after the fall term at the university was well under way, Cambridge agreed to accept him late. He actually entered the second year of a three-year program having missed all the introductory lectures. Nevertheless, he managed to catch up and finish the first year on schedule.

Almost every single lecture he went to for two years had to do with mathematics. It was even more specialized than at Oundle. One was assumed to already have a general education and that if there was anything else to be learned it was acquired on one's own. There was always a tremendous intellectual fervor going on quite informally at Cambridge and so Alexander was able to maintain his interest in architecture during this period:

I read a great deal about architecture and began to write about aesthetics. From the very beginning I was quite concerned about what made things beautiful. I went to art galleries, read a lot, and wrote a great deal about these kinds of things. It was strange, because there was nothing at Cambridge in any department that dealt with that question. So I actually went to the lengths of hiring, at my own expense, a philosophy tutor in aesthetics. This was unusual to do because theoretically I could get anything I wanted from the University. It took me some time to realize what an incredibly dry and bloodless subject aesthetics can be. I read Kant,

Schopenauer, and the early British philosophers — anything I could lay my hands on that had to do with this. I was fascinated by it but also found it quite dry. I even went into it to the extent of giving papers at the Cambridge Philosophical Society. There were a lot of intellectual games going on there but I was only a boy and felt both inadequate and frustrated because no one was willing to deal with the question of how to make something beautiful. But I did read a great deal, including psychology. My concerns were not just with buildings. In fact, it was mainly painting and music. But I was looking for properties rather than skills. I was astonished that in what I was reading there was no attempt to deal with this. My main feeling, however, was one of being overawed by everyone around me and so was unable to articulate these misgivings.

The two years rushed by at an incredible pace, and after finishing up with an honors degree in mathematics, Alexander entered architecture school at Cambridge. To him it was as though he had come to an insane asylum:

I was simply shocked. Here I was, still young, swimming up to my neck in mathematics, quite challenged, but able to hold my own. Then I get into this program and it was quite clear to me that it did not make sense on any level. I was asked to do incredible and absurd things which did not relate to each other or even make sense individually. I was lost and became quite angry — but also quite panicked.

The basic instruction consisted in teaching about modern art — a peculiarity of this program. There was an intense focus on painters like Mondrian and vanDoesburg, with occasional references to Mies van der Rohe and Le Corbusier. But mainly it was focused on painting. It was unclear to me what these painters were trying to do, although that was not even discussed very much anyway. Somehow, the implication was that what they were trying to do was what we were trying to do — and that we had to get a sense of what that was and then do it in buildings. There were all the typically crazy exercises, like making a formal garden in which you place one large cone, one large pyramid, and one large sphere. But the crux of all this came in my second term.

We were asked to design a house. Of course we were told nothing about what a house was, architecturally. I remember sitting in the studio just doodling and I made this drawing that sort of looked like a vanDoesburg — just black and white. And I thought, "That must be what they were talking about." So I said to myself that each one of those black lines is a brick wall and then I enclosed all of it in a rectangular glass cage with some of the walls jutting out and separating the inside and outside. We were taught to draw quite well and I did it up on very beautiful paper.

After I turned it in I got a call that the Director of the School wanted to see me. I just panicked. I thought, "Oh God. I know what I'm doing doesn't make any sense and they have discovered this and he is going to tell me I have to leave the School." The Director's office was at the end of an incredibly long corridor which went through four houses. I knocked timidly at the door and was quaking. He asked me to come in and said he wanted to discuss my work. I thought for sure that now my worst fears were coming true. As he pulled the drawings out I felt sure that he would tell me that I had to leave the school. But instead he came over to me, put his arm around my shoulder, and said: "Chris my boy, this is exactly what we want!" And I thought that now I really was in a lunatic asylum. Here I am putting this doodle on a piece of paper and here is this guy saying that it is exactly what they want. But I was too timid to say anything. I simply decided to get out of there as soon as possible because I realized then that there was nothing more to learn. I made the request to be able to take the second and third years concurrently and, although there was some resistance, I rushed through as fast as I could!

This of course did not deter me from trying to make a nice building; but as long as I was there I could not figure it out. I was completely frustrated and deeply dispirited. Yet at no time did I doubt that modern architecture was correct. I admired Mies and Corbu but could not understand what they were doing. In retrospect I think I had simply convinced myself that it was good. I just did not realize until after I had left England that I was afraid to be honest with my true feelings about it. There was a tremendous amount of pressure to accept it. The experience in the Director's office however, led me to believe that there was something strange going on. I was lucky. By accident I had got a glimpse of the sheer absurdity of it all. And this was very fortunate. Since I was supposed to be at one of the tap roots of contemporary modern architecture at that time, recognizing that absurdity was much more fundamental than if I had been in some architectural backwater.

Nevertheless, during this period Alexander made friends with painters, pursued his independent investigations with aesthetics, and became further interested in psychology. Except for his experience with architecture school, it was a very rich time for him. He lived a classic Bohemian life, full of fantastic parties, mischievous adventures, and unpredictable social and personal situations. As a result, he loved Cambridge very much, but as the third year of architectural studies was coming to an end he was in a shaky state and quite depressed. His teachers were never quite aware of the fact that the was interested in beauty. They considered him to be a mediocre student — but one who had to be contended with intellectually. He knew he did not want to go on to the fourth and fifth years of architecture school — the so-called diploma years. He rejected that completely. Eventually it came down to three options. One was to go to London University for a Ph.D. in aesthetics; the second was to work at the Building Research Station, also in London; and the third was to go to Harvard:

I thought perhaps I should just continue my own work in aesthetics, but under formal tutelage. So I went to London and spoke to A. J. Ayer because he was chairman of the philosophy department there. I discussed this with him and I remember I got a very uneasy feeling that he would not welcome a serious investigation of what made things beautiful and that somehow it was going to be treated as a verbal problem — although I had actually been impressed by his book LANGUAGE, TRUTH, AND LOGIC and that was why I went to see him. So I did not like that option very much.

The Building Research Station was a place where I could clearly get a job because of my background. There were a lot of people there doing empirical research on various aspects of building. I had already written a paper on modular coordination which was being published at the time and which fit in nicely as part of my credentials.

The third option came about quite unexpectedly. I lived in Trinity College at Cambridge for three years, and during the last year an American from Harvard had the rooms underneath mine and we became very good friends. We did crazy things together, ate peanuts with chopsticks, and generally had a good time. And it was just as a result of knowing this person that, for the first time, it occurred to me that I would like to visit the United States. Since he was from Harvard — studying literature at Cambridge as a Marshall Fellow — I wrote there to find out if I could take a Ph.D. in the architecture school. They had just announced a new program and I was accepted. I was too poor to go without money, but eventually they offered me a scholarship.

My original thesis proposal was to continue my work on modular coordination. One of the things I became involved with at Cambridge in my attempt to find out what made things beautiful was the whole theory of proportion — the Golden Mean and so forth. There is quite a bibliography on the subject. The Golden Mean interested me very much, but I was also

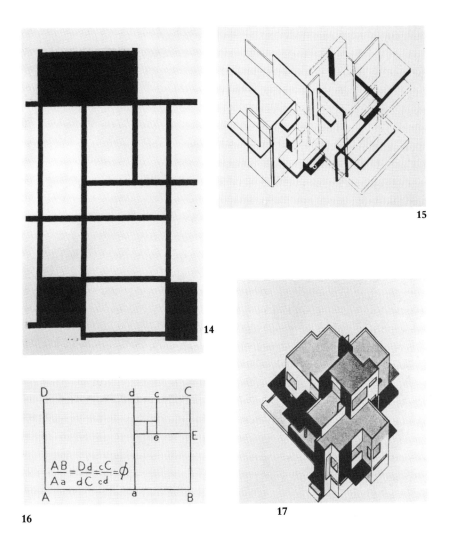

14. Piet Mondriaan, Composition, 1921.

15. Theo van Doesburg, Architectural Compositon, 1925.

17. Theo van Doesburg and Cor van Esteren, Project for a Private House.

   "Somehow, the implication was that what they were trying to do was what we were trying to do — and that we had to get a sense of what that was and then do it in buildings."

16. Geometrical Construction of the Golden Mean.

   "I thought it very strange that an irrational number like 1.618 . . . could have so many wonderful things claimed for it."

PLATE V

18

18. Ludwig Miës van der Rohe, German Pavilion, Barcelona, 1929.

"I began to realize that everybody in the world knows that modern architecture is strange . . . but dare not admit it."

PLATE VI

extremely skeptical about it. I was only nineteen or so, but I thought it very strange that an irrational number like 1.618 . . . could have so many wonderful things claimed for it. Obviously perception does not work like that. One cannot perceive the proportions of a rectangle to that degree of finesse — certainly not more than to the first decimal place. So I was suspicious. And that is what I wrote the paper about. But I was aware, nonetheless, that there was something there. I ended up by claiming, in this paper, that there were certain combinatory schemes that created harmony, but that they did not have to do with these irrational numbers. They had to do with the nature of their combinatorics and that had something to do with modular coordination because it was the simplest kind of combinatory scheme — although the least interesting.

The original impetus to go to Harvard however, was meeting this American. He was very refreshing and had an almost 180° opposite point of view on everything that was current on the Cambridge intellectual scene and that was just fascinating to me because he always had good arguments to explain his point of view. In retrospect I must have felt a bit stifled in this world of vanDoesburgs.

Alexander also wanted to go to Martinique. He was very much in love with a girl from Martinique and he wanted to spend the summer there before going on to Harvard — which he did. That was in 1958 and he wrote two things while he was there — a book that was never published called "What is Beauty?" and an essay entitled "The Revolution Finished Twenty Years Ago":

The book was hopeless. I took it with me to Harvard and quite correctly got some unfavourable opinions. The central point of it was that beauty was not the presence of something but the absence of something. Whenever something was not beautiful, there was something wrong with it, which was irritating. But in the absence of all presence you were still left with some ground. It was all quite childish but did give me the experience of writing a long work.

"The Revolution Finished Twenty Years Ago" was published in THE ARCHITECT'S YEARBOOK in 1960. Although critical of the cult of individualism in modern architecture and of the lack of a cumulative body of architectural knowledge since the previous "revolution," it never challenged the existing pardigm:

I really did not dare. I did not have an alternative, so what could I say? I do not think that I realized then that my dissatisfaction was more than a personal experience. I thought the faddism of modern architecture was

33

idiotic; but what was not clear to me was that everybody else knew that also.

Throughout it all I have felt the archetypal fairytale experience, right up to this moment, of "The Emperor's New Clothes." I feel like the little child who shouts out that the Emperor has no clothes. At the time — 1958 — I began to realize that everybody in the world knows that modern architecture is strange. The unpeeling of this fact is one of the most incredible things. First I had to realize that that is what I thought, which I did not realize at the time that I wrote the article. I still thought Gropius and the others had figured it all out. Then I had to realize that everybody else thought so, too. And finally, I had to realize that even architects thought so — but dare not admit it. It was not until that crystallized in my mind that I could criticize the architecture school at Cambridge; but by then I no longer cared.

I constantly feel myself to be in this fairy tale position. I really find myself to be saying the obvious all the time and, indeed, everyone knows the obvious but dare not admit it. They are too deeply locked into this lie. I remember once that I was talking to a woman at a fashionable cocktail party and she said, "Oh, you're an architect" and she opened some magazine lying on the cocktail table and said, "Oh look at this fabulous house!" It was some sort of slick, chromium-plated vanDoesburg and I said, "You don't really like this, do you? You don't have to pretend to like it because I'm an architect. Honestly, do you really like it and do you want to be there?" She was completely taken aback by this and she said, "No, actually I think it's terrible."

It was literally like the "Emperor's New Clothes." And I have frequently felt how devastatingly this game has worked, so that almost the whole western world, up until about 1970, has been conned into believing that this was very beautiful and was foolish in not being able to see it. This is what the tailors in "The Emperor's New Clothes" do. They tell the Emperor that only he can see and that foolish people cannot, and since he must be clever he sees it, etc. So it's the threat of being called a fool if you do not see it, if you do not have confidence in your own eyes. For example, take the column with or without the capital. Everyone knows that it looks more comfortable with the capital. But of course ever since the Bauhaus there are no more capitals. And it is incredibly hard to get architects to admit that it does look better the other way. Its like you have to keep punching that person's stomach and finally they let out an incredible gasp and they can admit they really like the column with the capital.

Such resistance to the perception of anomaly is characteristic of a paradigm in crisis. According to Kuhn, even in science the awareness of anomaly "emerges only with difficulty, manifested by resistance, against a background provided by expectation."[1] The recognition that something has gone wrong only occurs for the person who knows with precision what he should expect. Of course Alexander did not know fully what he should expect either — certainly not in 1958. He was still operating within the existing paradigm when he arrived at Harvard. And in fact, it would be another ten years before he would discover that there was something else to architecture than what the prevailing constellation of facts, values and methods would allow. But the exit door had already been opened. In the meantime, he would be pushing the existing rules to their limit, just to see how far they could be made to work.

REFERENCE NOTES

1. Thomas Kuhn, THE STRUCTURE OF SCIENTIFIC REVOLUTIONS, 2nd ed. (Chicago: University of Chicago Press, 1970), p.64
2. "The Revolution finished twenty years ago." ARCHITECTS YEAR BOOK 9, 1960 pp.181-185.
3. cf THE LINZ CAFÉ (New York, Oxford University Press, 1981) Chapter 12.

III

PUSHING THE RULES

The point of departure is Alexander's doctoral dissertation at Harvard — NOTES ON THE SYNTHESIS OF FORM. To a certain extent, the book was a theory and method for tackling the staggering complexity of trying to satisfy human needs in the design of an urban house. This was the problem posed by Alexander's work with Serge Chermayeff in COMMUNITY AND PRIVACY. Aside from helping Chermayeff to analyze the problem, Alexander's contribution was primarily in exploring ways to make the solution of a design problem congruent with the statement of the problem:

I explored a tremendous variety of possible approaches to the "decision problem" in architecture — which is a very broad and generic way of asking "What is design?" That question was being asked in a number of fields at the time. There were psychological as well as mathematical theories of decision-making which I studied. For example, the whole question of what are the units in perception — which is important in perception itself, gestalt psychology, and linguistics — is related to the question in my thesis which is "What are the units of the problem?"

NOTES represent Alexander's attempt to find out "What's actually going on" in a good design. His thesis was that the ultimate object of design is form. The *problem* of design is to fit the form to its context. Form is that part of the environment over which we have control; context is that part of the environment which puts demands on this form. As in nature, a good design is a good fit, one in which form and context are in frictionless coexistence. Such a design is further distinguished by the clarity of its articulation. "A well-designed house not only fits its context well but also illuminates the problem of just what the context is."

So far there is nothing unusual about these ideas, except perhaps what Alexander means by "good design." Rather than choosing the

36

so-called master works of modern architecture to illustrate his thesis, he used indigenous buildings made in pre-industrial, traditional societies:

One of the first things that really presented itself to me as absolutely true was simply the fact that buildings made in traditional societies were so beautiful. Since I grew up in Europe, they were accessible to me. But obviously as a student at Cambridge I never permitted it to become clear in my mind that traditional architecture was more beautiful than what was being built as so-called modern architecture. Indeed I thought the reverse. And even in 1958, although still skeptical, I was still in that state. But since the first part of my thesis dwelt with what was happening in traditional societies, I obviously gave it some respect. So I must have gradually been growing toward the realization. Although working with Chermayeff, who was part of the modern movement, we never really touched on this fact. He was critical of the functional organization of modern buildings, not their basic conception. But to me, this core fact about buildings in traditional societies being beautiful nonetheless had to be accounted for, and the idea that buildings of our time, by comparison, were so oppressive and ugly, even the best of them, gradually emerged in my mind. That it was uncompromisingly true only came later. But it was that kind of thinking with which I tried to come to grips.

I was trying to look and ask what is the most fundamental thing that is actually happening in architecture — really and truly what is it — and then concoct a way of looking at it that fit what was actually going on. And the reference point was traditional buildings and the success of their adaptation. So I gradually began to look for ways of describing how one talks about the phenomenon of something being adapted or well adapted — and under what circumstances — which is what the book is really about.

In NOTES Alexander asked whether this kind of adaptation has an underlying structure or pattern to it and, if so, can it be represented logically? The obvious reason for attempting this feat is that if you could represent the structure of a problem logically, it would be much easier to achieve a congruence with its solution than by guesswork or intuition. It would not only permit one to solve simple problems more successfully, but to solve complex problems more simply.

In the context of the existing paradigm, the attempt to make an explicit map of the structure of a design problem may have appeared too mathematical, too abstract to be useful to architects; but for Alexander, the difference between mathematics and architecture was inessential:

> The shapes of mathematics are abstract, of course, and the shapes of architecture concrete end human. But . . . the crucial quality of shape, no matter of what kind, lies in its organization, and when we think of it this way we call it form. Man's feeling for mathematical form was able to develop only from his feeling for the processes of proof. I believe that our feeling for architectural form can never reach a comparable order of development, until we too have first learned a comparable feeling for the process of design.[1]

But the fundamental reason for his approach had very little to do with any great desire to develop a mathematical feeling for architectural form. The real reason stems from Alexander's belief that the correspondence between the structure of the problem and its solution is a source of goodness (or beauty) in traditional buildings. As he wrote at the end of NOTES:

> My main task has been to show that there is a deep and important underlying structural correspondence between the pattern of a problem and the process of designing a physical form which answers that problem. I believe that the great architect has in the past always been aware of the patterned similarity of problem and process, and that it is only the sense of this similarity of structure that ever led him to the design of great forms.[2]

Yi-Fu Tuan, in his review of NOTES, correctly observed the meaning of this intent: "The explicit mapping of the problem's structure, which Alexander advocates, is not just an isolated exercise in design; the structure, if successful, will *clarify* the life it accomodates."[3] This is an important point, because it eventually appears as an essential characteristic of what Alexander means by the unity of space. Yet the emphasis in NOTES was on "method," not ultimate intent. Since the attempt to make an explicit map of the problem's structure was unique in design thinking, the need to invent a conceptual framework for such maps necessarily became a central concern of the book. The so-called method which resulted from this concern consisted of writing the requirements of a program, analyzing their interactions on the basis of potential conflicts or "misfits," decomposing them into a hierarchy of manageable parts with the aid of a computer, making small diagrams which match each part, and putting them together into

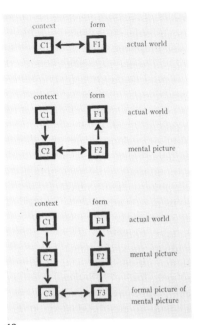

context form

C1 ⟷ F1   actual world

context form

C1   F1   actual world

C2 ⟷ F2   mental picture

context form

C1   F1   actual world

C2   F2   mental picture

C3 ⟷ F3   formal picture of mental picture

19

20

19. Mapping the Structure of a Design Problem.

20. Bjølstad Farm, Heidal, Norway.

"I was trying to look and ask what is the most fundamental thing that is actually happening in architecture — and then concoct a way of looking at it that fit what was actually going on. And the reference point was traditional buildings and the success of their adaptation."

PLATE VII

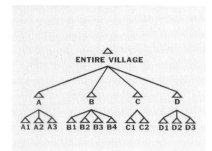

21

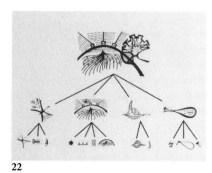

22

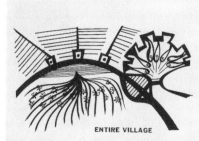

23

21. Hierarchical Decomposition of the Program.
22. Hierarchical Composition of the Diagrams.
23. Synthesis of the Diagrams.

These kinds of diagrams were unlike anything anyone had seen before. Their visual impact was unprecedented for something so abstract. But aside from their unique appearance, one acutally had the feeling that they originated directly from the theory; there seemed to be no other source from which they could have come.

PLATE VIII

more and more complex diagrams:

> The hierarchical composition of these diagrams will then lead to a physical object whose structural hierarchy is the exact counterpart of the functional hierarchy established during the analysis of the problem; as the program clarifies the component *sources* of the form's structure, so its realization, in parallel, will actually begin to define the form's *physical* components and their hierarchical organization.[4]

The kinds of diagrams which Alexander generated from this method were unlike anything anyone had ever done before. Their visual impact was unprecedented for something so abstract. But aside from their unique appearance, one actually had the feeling that they originated directly from the theory; there seemed to be no other source from which they could have come. As Charles Jencks put it, "The result was fantastic. Not only did the final form reflect all the criteria but ... the form was pure, forceful, honest, and strictly relevant. It had all the passionate intensity of ... a pure response to specifiable parameters."[5] Although it was not at all clear how these diagrams might turn into buildings, the implication was that it was actually possible to have a *productive* theory of architecture. As a result, Alexander quickly became identified with a whole new field called "design methods," an identification from which he would eventually have to disassociate himself. For the time being however, it was assumed that by following the method outlined in NOTES one could eventually design buildings that were more successfully adapted to functional requirements than was otherwise possible. Although still remote from the ultimate intent, NOTES was an important base from which Alexander could pursue a variety of unanswered questions during the next five years. The first of these had to do with where the problem's "requirements" were actually coming from; the second, with the overly simplified hierarchical structure of defining the problem itself; and the third, with the way in which the solutions could actually generate real buildings.

In NOTES, and even in COMMUNITY AND PRIVACY, the listing of requirements — the so-called program — was not very precisely spelled out. As in the existing paradigm, one was presumed to develop a "feel" for the problem through research, interviews, and consultation with real or simulated clients. In practice it is exhaustive, time-consuming, and essentially arbitrary.

Even in NOTES, where the focus of concern was for potential conflicts or "misfits" that might occur in the final design, there was no way of knowing that the system itself would even behave as described. This became apparent in 1964 when, after moving to California, Alexander was hired to apply NOTES to the analysis of the then proposed San Francisco Bay Area Rapid Transit System (BART):

I spent quite a bit of time discussing the question of when a [diagram] was a good one or not and I realized for the first time that it was not based on requirements. I remember that one of the diagrams we did for the BART study concerned the system of forces surrounding the ticket booth. Even though there was an elaborate terminology about misfits, essentially, on the everyday working level, one was really writing down requirements of things that ought to be happening. We had 390 of those. In the ones that surrounded the ticket booth there were things like people being able to get their change, people not having to wait too long in line, people with tickets being able to pass those waiting to buy tickets, and so on.

But as we studied that system it became clear that in a certain peculiar sense there were forces there beyond our control which were not accounted for by requirements. For example, if congestion was to develop around the ticket booth and actually disrupt the flow of people coming into the station, that was an internal problem in the system, not based on any requirements — just that the forces that were developing were coming from within the system. Suppose there was a phenomenon such that a person standing in place in line would attract another person next to him in such a way that very quickly you would have a knot of people grow rather quickly and paralyze the whole entrance — like an Italian traffic jam. But the forces creating this thing were not part of our requirments. Of course we had a requirement not to have congestion, but we did not have a requirement saying that people could not stop and stand next to someone else. But it was also true that if one did not deal with that phenomenon the system was going to ball itself up.

So it became clear that the free functioning of the system did not purely depend on meeting a set of requirements. It had to do, rather, with the system coming to terms with itself and being in balance with the forces that were generated internal to the system, not in accordance with some arbitrary set of requirements we stated. I was very puzzled by this because the general prevailing idea at the time was that essentially, everything was based on goals. My whole analysis of requirements was certainly quite

40

congruent with the operations research point of view that goals had to be stated and so on. What bothered me was that the correct analysis of the ticket booth could not be based purely on one's goals, that there were realities emerging from the center of the system itself and that whether you succeeded or not had to do with whether you created a configuration that was stable or unstable with respect to those realities.

A sceptic could have said that you still have some goals and that there are just some extra constraints, but I was not happy with that. It seemed to me that there was something radically peculiar here and that there was an essential arbitrariness about goals and a non-arbitrariness about this system telling you more about itself and putting more into your lap, so to speak, than the theory of goals was admitting. All I knew was that there was something fundamentally screwed up in my analysis, that the program of requirements was just not the correct picture, that there was some sense in which one was now confronting the reality of the system itself and that it almost determined its own correctness or not. It was not possible for an arbitrary act by a designer or by some group of people stating requirements. The system was somehow stating its own requirements.

This was just one of several new lines of thought. Yet regardless of the answer to where the problem's requirements were coming from, there was still the question of the analytical structure of their interactions. In NOTES, that structure was described as a hierarchical tree of interacting sets. It was assumed that the decomposition of this "tree" into dependent subsets would permit the designer to work on small clusters at a time, gradually building them up into larger and larger patterns. But in reality, the subsets are rarely independent, discrete entities. In fact, their interconnections are far richer than was implied by the tree-like structure described in NOTES. To account for this, Alexander did a comparative analysis of a large number of modern city planning schemes that resulted from a tree-like structure in their programs. In an attempt to be precise about what was wrong with them he became aware of the fact that in traditional, unplanned cities the richness of their patterns was the result of an *overlapping* structure. To him, the deathly simplicity and blockishness of the newer schemes was a result of their overly simplified "tree-like" structure. As he formulated these observations, they took on wider implications:

> For the human mind, the tree is the easiest vehicle for complex

41

thoughts. But the city is not, cannot, and must not be a tree. The city is a receptacle for life. If the receptacle severs the overlap of the strands of life within it, because it is a tree, it will be like a bowl full of razor blades on edge, ready to cut up whatever is entrusted to it. In such a receptacle life will be cut to pieces. If we make cities which are trees, they will cut our life within to pieces.[6]

A mathematically more accurate representation of this overlapping structure would be a "semi-lattice," in which millions of subsets could result from a few elements. These ideas were published in 1965 as "The City is Not a Tree" and, as Jencks observed, it was picked up by many magazines and republished around the world, gaining particular influence in Italy, France, England, and Japan. Along with the work of Ada Louise Huxtable and Lewis Mumford, it was given the Kaufman International Design Award for being one of the most effective statements in the field of design during the previous five years. But it was still a diagram. Although the so-called semi-lattice was actually a precursor of the eventual pattern language, the question of its relationship to real buildings was, in 1965, far from answered. Several events however, opened up the possibility that the structure of the diagram itself might have a *generative* capacity. The most important of these events occurred in connection with the BART study.[7]

Alexander and his colleagues were working for the firm of architects hired to program all the transit stations. In all, about thirty stations were to be built. The work of the firm was not to design any one station, but to provide material for the design of *all* the stations. Each individual station would then be designed by a different architect.

The study was very extensive. With three hundred and ninety requirements the number of subsystems was immense and the computer program for decomposing the structure was gigantic. It became intuitively clear that it was quite impossible to imagine conducting such an effort to design a single building, although there was some relief in the knowledge of doing something that would have value thirty times over — namely, for the thirty different architects of the individual stations:

The idea that these diagrams would represent generic entities from which a specific design could be composed began to emerge partly in response to that situation. In NOTES it essentially said to break the system down into subsystems, construct the diagrams, and build the solution out of the

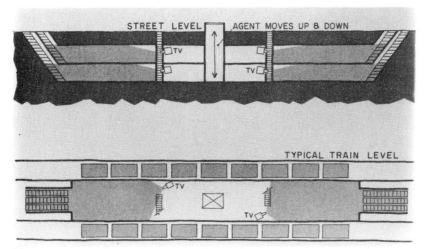

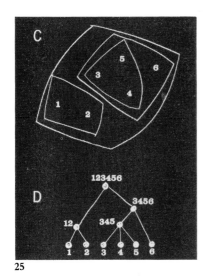

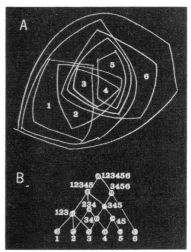

24. Diagram of the Transit System Ticket Booth.
    "The system was somehow stating its own requirements."

25. Diagram of a Tree-like Structure.

26. Diagram of a Semi-Lattice Structure.

    "The City is not, cannot, and must not be a tree."

PLATE IX

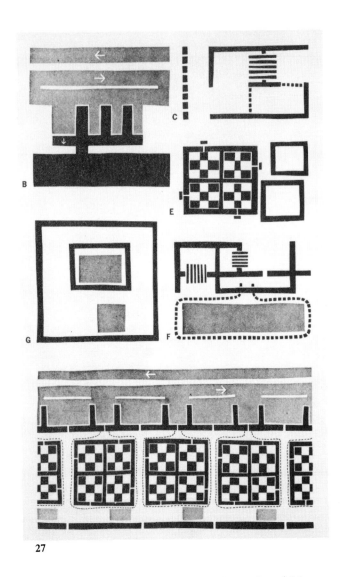

27

27. Synthesis of Housing Diagrams from *Community and Privacy*.

PLATE X

diagrams. But that was all in response to one *design problem. Now here we were experiencing the situation where the design problem is incredibly complex, very expensive, very time consuming, and it was obvious that this huge activity we were engaged in was not going to happen everytime someone was going to build a building. But it did become plausible that perhaps this material could become valuable if it could be used over and over again. So the idea that the diagrams were generic entities playing a combinatorial role — such as the patterns do in the current theory — began to emerge as a necessity forced by the reality of that huge situation.*

Of the three ideas developed since NOTES — that every system somehow has its own requirements, that these requirements have a complex, interacting structure like overlapping sets (i.e., the semi-lattice"), and the mappings of those sets represent generic entities — this last one was the most difficult to formulate. First, it opened up a whole new line of research. Basic questions — like what is an environment, what are its components, and how does it get its structure? — had to be asked. But more importantly, the basic line of inquiry itself was fundamentally incompatible with the existing paradigm.

By "generativity," Alexander means the processes which actually produce the structure of the environment. The current view is that architects, operating within a set of constraints or "requirements," *create* the structure out of their imagination. Even Louis Kahn's statement about what the building "wants to be" means what the architect *imagines* it wants to be. In other words, the transition from the problem to the solution is mediated by a conceptual process unique to the architect or builder. Aside from being unique — and therefore closed to systematic analysis — it is also presumed to originate outside the problem, as in Le Corbusier's machine metaphors for example. Although, as in Kahn's case, the problem may stimulate the development of such imagery, the environment is presumed to get its structure from the superimposition of this conceptual process over the context of specific problems. Even although the agreed objective of good design is a "fit" between the form and its context (i.e. "program"), the actual generation of form is presumed discontinuous with its context. Consequently, the architect is seen as creating order out of chaos.

Up to this point, Alexander's work has not differed

43

fundamentally from this view. The attempt to make the requirements of a problem explicit by mapping the structure of their interactions, the development of diagrams to match the solutions within that structure, and even the observation that the requirements are originating from within the context itself (as Louis Kahn also observed) can all be viewed as attempts to bridge the gap between the final form and its context. But the question of where that form actually comes from is not raised, except implicitly by the unspecified role of the diagrams. For the diagrams to actually become generative — to finally bridge the gap — the conceptual process of the architect's creative imagination would have to be replaced. But by what? The diagrams, by themselves, were incapable of fulfilling that role because on the one hand they were based, in part, upon an arbitrary set of requirements and, on the other hand, because they were two-dimensional abstractions.

To tackle this problem it was necessary to break out of the bind of having to view the question of the structure of the environment from within the prevailing constellation of architectural facts, values, and methods and see architecture as a special case within the environment — itself a generating system.

REFERENCE NOTES

1. NOTES ON THE SYNTHESIS OF FORM, p.134
2. IBID., p.132
3. Yi-Fu Tuan, "Notes on Computer Architecture," LANDSCAPE (Winter, 1964-1965), p.14
4. NOTES ON THE SYNTHESIS OF FORM, p.131
5. Charles Jencks, MODERN MOVEMENTS IN ARCHITECTURE (New York: Anchor Books, 1971), p.354
6. "The City is not a Tree," ARCHITECTURAL FORUM (May, 1965), pp.58-62
7. "Relational Complexes in Architecture," ARCHITECTURAL RECORD, 140 (September, 1966), pp.185-190

IV

THE SEARCH FOR A GENERATIVE STRUCTURE

For Alexander, a generating system is like a kit of parts or components, together with the rules for combining them to make wholes — "a way of focusing attention on some particular holistic behaviour in a thing, which can only be understood as a product of interaction among the parts."[1] By pursuing this line of inquiry he was able to make two paradigm-shattering observations. First, that the actual substance out of which the environment is made consists of relations, or patterns, rather than *things;* and secondly, that it is actually generated by the implicit, language-like system of rules which determines their structure. The first observation took years to develop:

During the early years of the formulation of the pattern language we had a very peculiar problem. We had both "things" and "patterns" which were connecting those things. This seemed like a very inelegant formulation. In discussing this with mathematicians it was intuitively clear to them it would be better if there were "patterns of patterns" rather than "patterns of things." In 1967 this seemed like a beautiful idea but it did not seem to have any reality. It seemed too abstract. It finally became clear that it was much more lucid to say that there were just patterns.

Its one thing to say in a kitchen, for example, you have a certain relationship between a counter, a refrigerator, a sink, and a stove. Everyone can see that. But in that view of the thing, you still consider the kitchen to be made of the counter, refrigerator, sink, and stove and their relationship is kind of playing a secondary role in trying to organize it. But when you look more closely you realize that the stove is a relationship between an oven, some heaters, and some switches and furthermore, that the switch is a relationship between something you can turn with your hand and some electrical contacts, and so on. Finally you realize that the whole substance of all this is in fact made of these patterns and that the "things" are just convenient labels which we give to bundles of patterns, or patterns themselves.

Although this is a pretty difficult thing to realize, it is consistent with modern mathematics and physics. In that sense it's not a surprising development. But from the standpoint of common sense it is not completely natural. To some extent its counterintuitive. Its startling. It seems to contradict common sense. Language is involved here. We give names to things but we don't give many names to relationships. Our language is full of nouns. The idea that the noun is merely a label for a bundle of relationships that is real is not supported in verbal experience, although Whorff suggests that there are some traditional languages where the opposite is the case. Most Western languages tend to perpetuate the illusion that it's the object which is real. This is a problem in modern physics — the incompatability of the language with some of the concepts that are currently used. The idea that an atom, for example, is a "thing" is a popular view, when actually it is not. So there are quite a few problems involved in seeing patterns rather than things as fundamental, and not merely adjuncts to reality.

The second observation — that the patterns in the environment are generated by a language-like system of rules, or "pattern language" — actually goes against architectural dogma:

The idea that the structure comes from these languages rather than from the creative brilliance of designers is initially repulsive. Architects imagine they are creating buildings and, by extension, towns or parts of towns and that these entities are the products of the fertility of the imagination. To have a theory which claims that there are these systems of rules and that we, by embodying these rules, produce particular versions of the structure implicit in the rules — but no more than versions — and that it is really the implicit structure which governs, is pretty much of a shock to the ego. Even lay people tend to think that architects control the environment. The basic attitude is that architects bring order into an otherwise chaotic situation — instead of recognizing that the order comes through this system of rules which, in some version or other, exists anyway. Its the same difficulty one has in understanding that a bird can be made from a set of rules. People just won't believe it.

The first observation says that relations are fundamental; the second one says that these relations are generated by rules. In nature, a particular robin is ultimately a product of the rules inherent in the gene system and that those rules interacting create an egg, and then a chick, and then a robin. But such a process is not real for most people. Its not even that real for biologists. Its intellectually real, but not emotionally real.

It is now known that even humans are produced by the interactions of certain genetic systems and that the generative rules are relatively simple in comparison to the complexity of the end product. This is now accepted as a part of biology, but for most people it is not emotionally real. Its just too incredible. And I think the reason is that we have not yet succeeded in simulating the process. So the idea that there can be a set of rules which ultimately generates the environment is difficult to take. But the simple fact is that the structure of the environment comes from the languages that the people who made it are using. And the difficulty with accepting that is similar to the difficulty we have in accepting that a robin is made by a set of rules. But that is what is going on. Yet one feels that somehow the miracle of creation is not fully accounted for by these interactive rules.

In architecture, everyone knows that there are rules, but the current view is that they are "constraints" — which is very different. In the literature you will find no mention of anyone believing these rules are generative. In genetics itself the idea is only ten to fifteen years old. In linguistics it's only ten years old. As far as I know the topic has not yet been discussed in architecture. Consequently, the idea of systems of rules actually generating structure is not widely shared. It is different from the idea, normally accepted, that rules merely restrict the field of possibilities until there is just one structure, essentially created by a process of elimination. In the generative sense however, the rules actually create the thing. The question is whether or not anyone seriously believes you can generate a whole building or town by such rules.

It is a touchy subject in architecture because it fundamentally touches the ego of the creator. So long as you view the rules as constraints, its as though the creative core was still lying independent and the constraints are merely impinging on them and shaping it. But once you admit that the rules are generative then you have sort of got right into the heart of the creative core and one starts to wonder what exactly is the role of the creator in all this. A generative system is one in which the interaction of the rules, and nothing else, will create the thing. There is no intermediate force of any kind.

It was not until Chomsky's work that anybody succeeded in formulating the rules which actually generated sentences — which is quite a different thing from saying that a sentence has to obey certain rules of grammar. That is why Chomsky's systems are so different from "grammars" evolved over the past two hundred years. Earlier grammatical rules did not generate

47

sentences. They merely put constraints upon what a sentence has to be. But the crux of the issue is generativity.

Suppose we agree that there are these rules, by all means. The conventional architectural attitude to all that is, indeed, there are all those rules and, working within those rules, I create something as an architect. But I'm making the statement that I can actually set up those rules so that if you follow a sequence of them in the order prescribed you will have a building. Furthermore, you will have created a building which has never been seen before and which is also capable of being as beautiful as any other building. Now that is the sort of extreme of what I mean by "generative." But if you say that was how the cathedral at Chartres was made, people will freak out. They will say, "My god! Are you trying to mechanize great works of art?" But the crucial thing is that in an embryo, for example, that is precisely what happens of course. You have these systems, and they come into play in an absolutely established order during the course of embryonic development and eventually you get a robin. And the fact that I'm claiming to put out here is that environments are also generated by systems of rules. They do not have systems of rules which sort of "constrain" their creators. They are actually generated by them.

As an empirical fact about my own work and experiences of the last few years, this is definitely the hardest thing for an architect to swallow. Lay people find it amazing and feel they just won't be able to do it; but they have no prejudices against the idea. Architects, on the other hand, do not want it to be true, don't want to try it, don't want to believe that other people can do it, and have a vested interest in this not being true because conceptually it threatens to replace them — although the practical question of what an architect should be doing and what makes architecture a great creative art is actually another question.

With the onset of computers, for the first time it has actually been possible to study the effect of certain interacting rules. Suppose you take the shape of a wave breaking, for example. You can ask, "Do I understand what is happening?" So you write a set of rules — an algorithm — which is supposed to depict the history of a wave. Then you can run these rules through the computer and generate a pattern of dots on a cathode ray tube. It might be no more than a dozen rules, but if you keep going through those rules, over and over again, in different combinations of sequences, and you are successful, you will actually see this pattern of dots forming a breaking wave. But to write a set of rules which actually generates a life-like wave is incredibly difficult. It might take two years of mathematical research

48

playing around with those rules until you generate a breaking wave, complete with a curl. Yet it is a very simple case of interacting hydrodynamic rules. It does not involve the sort of complexities going on in a linguistic system or an embryonic system. But it is nonetheless tremendously exciting because you feel that you have sort of entered into the heart of nature. So far from mechanizing the environment, or belittling the architect, it does nothing of the sort. It is a miracle that all of these interacting rules can produce a complex fabric rather than chaos.

A few years ago, mathematicians became aware, purely on a childish level, that even if you were to take three or four rules, you could already generate orders of complexity much greater than any mathematically describable geometry. Now when we talk about things like the breaking of a wave, which is a bit more complicated, we might be up to a dozen rules. In the case of an organism, there are about fifty thousand genes responsible for an incredible number of interactive rules. In the case of environments, there are hundreds. This kind of complexity cannot be accounted for by the kind of mathematics which D'Arcy Thompson is speaking about.[2] And indeed, it is only by studying the process which consists of the interaction of the set of rules that you can begin to generate that kind of complexity. So the fact that the environment is created like this — generated like this — is a very remarkable thing. It is miraculous and beautiful.

Now, once we get into linguistic systems, and pattern languages specifically, you not only have these very complex rules that generate things but you also have the power of choice — so that you are free to make something that has not been made before by allowing the system of rules in your mind to do it. This is another step which goes further than saying that, indeed, nature is produced by interacting rules. In a linguistic system or in a pattern language you not only have very complex sets of interacting rules but you have choice. You can say any sentence you want to say at a particular moment in order to make a response to something and, similarly, you can create something that is appropriate to a particular environmental situation which was never made before. But it is the structure of your rule system or language that is enabling you to do this. And that same structure ultimately resides in the finished product, although you have still made it and have created a thing never before created in that specific framework. But to realize that there is no opposition between the immense creative power and the power of the rules — that is difficult to grasp.

In the two examples — the wave and the sentence — there is an important distinction. Being able to write generative grammars was not a trick, as in the case of the wave. With the wave it is just a trick — a simulation of the processes that are going on in the real world. In the case of the grammars there is an important difference. And that is, that it is fairly widely considered to be true that these generative rules are actually the ones that we have in our heads. In other words, it is not a sort of cute description of something. The assumption is that this system of rules is real and actually exists in the brain in that form. In the wave, however, it is merely presumed that the natural processes have a structure which is similar to the rules which are used to simulate the wave — it's a model, although a generative one. But in the case of linguistics and genetics, we are saying that the rules actually exist. They are not just a conceptual model to explain what is going on — they are in the real thing, although you have to discover them by inference. This is very important in the case of the environment because what I am claiming to have discovered is that there are rules operating in this same way in the environment. I am not saying that this is a handy simulation. I am saying that these rules are actually there, in people's heads, and are responsible for the way the environment gets its structure.

Chomsky's work on generative grammar will soon be considered very limited. It happened to be brilliant in the sense that it was the first part of linguistics to receive this attention. But in fact, it does not deal with the interesting structure of language because the real structure of language lies in the relationships between words — the semantic connections. The semantic network — which connects the word "fire" with "burn," "red," and "passion" — is the real stuff of language. Chomsky makes no attempt to deal with that and therefore, in a few years, his work will be considered primitive. In that sense, pattern languages are not like generative grammars. What they are like is the semantic structure, the really interesting part of language and which only a few people have begun to study. The structure which connects words together — such as "fire" being connected to "burn," "red," and "passion" — is much more like the structure which connects patterns together in a pattern language. So pattern languages are not so much analogous to generative grammars as they are to the real heart structure of language which has hardly been described yet.

The question of what Alexander means by the "real heart structure" of a system — analogous to the semantic connections in language — goes back to his work in cognitive psychology at Harvard and his little-known association with Jerome Bruner at the Center for Cognitive Studies in the late 50's and early 60's. The connection is important for two reasons. First, it broadens

Alexander's credibility in terms of these obvious cross-disciplinary references, especially to linguistics.[3] Harvard and MIT were real hotbeds of this kind of thinking and Alexander (as a member of the Joint Center for Urban Studies as well as The Center for Cognitive Studies) was in touch with these ideas around the time they were being formulated.

The second reason the connection is important is that it brings the inquiry back to the ultimate intent of NOTES — the attempt to discover and describe the structural correspondence between a good form and its context. The good form, it was observed, not only fits its context well but also clarifies the life it accommodates. We perceive this clarity by the richness and wholeness of its structure. But what about the bad forms — the so-called misfits that confuse the life they accommodate and which we perceive as static and fragmented?

At the time of NOTES, Alexander suspected that the source of the difference had something to do with how forms were perceived and represented in the brain and what the difference was between the ones that seemed whole and the ones that were not whole.

The results of his work at the Center for Cognitive Studies, published in four journal articles between 1959 and 1968, connect up to the question posed by the need for the diagrams to become generative and prefigure his later work on the geometry of unified space.[4] The connection comes from the observation that the spatial structure of certain forms is congruent with the basic cognitive structure in the brain out of which other structures are built — that there is a correspondence between the holistic behaviour of a thing and its perception. The observation is paradigm-shattering because it ultimately leads to the conclusion that the distinction between good and bad forms is a matter of fact, not value. The idea, however, is more widely shared than one might think possible within the prevailing nominalism of the current paradigm; although most of the research has been at the level of urban rather than architectural form.[5] In architecture, Christian Norberg-Schultz's concept of spatial structure as a concretization of environmental schemata or images that form a necessary part of man's general orientation in the world is an important step in the same direction, but it is primarily speculative.[6] Alexander is unique in actually attempting to carry the idea to its inevitable empirical conclusions.

After 1965, the main ingredients for a full-scale investigation had been assembled. The idea that the real structure of the environment comes from overlapping sets of interacting rules — rules representing relations between patterns in the environment and which correspond to the holistic perception of structure — provided Alexander and his colleagues with the basis for thrashing out a general theory of the "pattern language" over the next few years. The immediate questions that had to be answered dealt with the need to identify such rules operating at all levels of the environment, the overall structure which binds them together and makes them whole, and the problem of generativity — the actual production of objects which embody those rules with infinite variety.

In one essay, "From a Set of Forces to a Form," he compared the process of generativity in design to the formation of sand ripples in nature. Drawing upon the physics of blown sand, he showed how the wave-like rippled form is generated by the interaction of five rule-like forces working upon any level surface. "With the wind blowing, the level sand surface is an unstable form because it gives rise to forces which ultimately destroy it. The rippled form is stable because the forces which it gives rise to maintain the form."[7] The key process here is the interaction of forces to maintain the stability of the system.

In the realm of design, the comparable question is: "Given a set of needs, how can we generate a form which meets those needs?" If one could replace the concept of "need" by the concept of an active "force," it might be possible to study the interaction of human needs in space as a generative process comparable to and with the same precision as the form-generating processes in nature.

These questions were first pursued formally during a year-long seminar in Berkeley between 1966 and 1967 and discussed in various journal articles during the same period.[8] The idea to continue the work in the context of an ongoing research institute emerged in 1967 with financial support from the Edgar J. Kaufmann Foundation and from the National Bureau of Standards (and later from the National Institute for Mental Health). "The Center for Environmental Structure" was created in Berkeley with Alexander as Director. Its statement of goals listed three main activities. First, to undertake contracts to develop specific patterns and systems of patterns within a pattern language, and to design buildings and parts of cities according to the language; second, to undertake basic research concerning the pattern language itself; and third, to publish and distribute the coordinated pattern language as it would evolve.[9]

For Alexander, the feeling of committment to see this work through to the end had now solidified. With the formation of the Center an intense period of experimentation and testing began. In three projects — a multi-service community center in New York City (for the Human Resource Administration), an educational research facility in Southern California (with the architectural firm of Skidmore, Owings, and Merrill), and a low-income residential district in Lima, Peru (for a United Nations Competition) — the strengths and weaknesses of the ideas which had developed since NOTES would emerge.[10] Reviewing the work of this period, Roger Montgomery said that"already, in the three years or so that it had been in development, the pattern language has proven effective in practice. At the same time, its conceptual basis has been strengthened and enriched by further analysis."[11]

Progress had been made on the format for writing patterns and on the language of rules for their combination into complete environments. Each pattern consisted of an "if-then" statement representing a context-form ensemble. The "if" statement defined precisely the situation in which the pattern applied; the "then" statement contained the spatial configuration which was necessary to the life of that situation; and both were accompanied by a problem statement giving the background for the pattern and any specific data on which it was based. This format seemed to make each pattern open to criticism, modification, and continual reassessment. In Montgomery's opinion, "the importance of these three fundamental aspects of patterns, which give them a certain formal rigor, stands out sharply in the experience which has been built up in using them, as well as in the intensive theoretical effort carried out over the last few years at the Center."[12] But the structure of their interactions was still unaccounted for. Particularly in the multi-service center project, the way in which the patterns were combined took the form of a "cascade" representing sequential combinations of progressively smaller configurations. But it was not yet a language:

It was completely clear that there was really no language — that the word "language" was in some sense a hope, a promise, rather than a fulfillment. In other words, if one actually presented another person with this, that person would have to be an architect in order to be able to do it. That was the crux of the matter.

This weakness became clear because in each of the projects a final design was required and so it became necessary to "bridge the gap" intuitively — by the traditional methods:

Of course, our own designs and sketches were themselves made without any real knowledge of building. They certainly were not diagrams; but they were not ordinary plans of buildings either. They had some of the whacky character of modern architecture; on the other hand they were sort of faintly just beginning to move into some new realm. But they were actually quite thin. We did not yet have the muscle within ourselves. We did not have the substance to actually present a coherent and solid and definite thing that had to be done.

During the next two years these problems would be hammered out, but the investigation splits at this point. The need to continue to expand the collection of patterns and the question of a generative structure which binds them together into complete environments became both a purely technical as well as an intuitive concern. It was clear from the BART study, for example, that the key to the structure was somehow contained in the free functioning of a system and its ability to come to terms with itself internally. In the case of the multi-service center project and in the Peruvian housing scheme, an intuitive grasp of this ability had permitted the design to be completed in the absence of a clear analysis of the structure. The problem, therefore, was not exclusively structural. Something was going on that appealed to the intuition more than to formal logic. But what was it?

One source of discovery was an intense desire on Alexander's part for basic improvements in the institutions of society and his belief that the work he was doing had the power to help put things right socially. There was a general feeling in the 1960's that both society and the environment mirror each other and that if one starts to take the structure of the environment seriously enough one inevitably becomes involved in the reconstruction of society. This is not a particular social philosophy, just a recognition that by

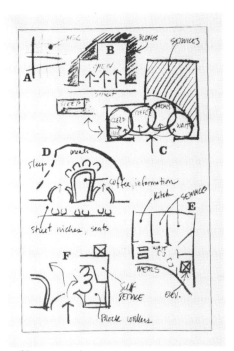

28

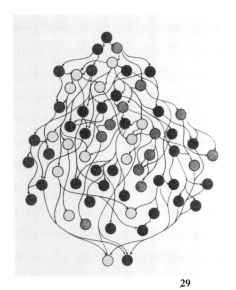

29

28.　Pattern Diagrams for a Multi-Service Community Center.

29.　A Cascade of Patterns.

　　In the multi-service centre project, the way in which the patterns were combined took the form of a "cascade" representing sequential combinations of progressively smaller configurations. But it was not yet a language.

PLATE XI:

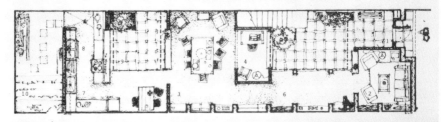

First floor

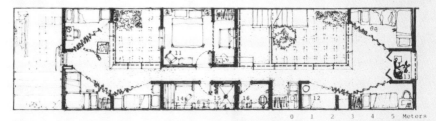

Second floor

0 1 2 3 4 5 Meters

30

31

30. Peruvian Housing Project, plans.
31. Peruvian Housing Project, sections.

PLATE XII

"patterns" one means patterns of behaviour as well as patterns of space and that if an institution is basically dysfunctional, nothing that is done solely to the physical environment will bring it to life. The free functioning of a system therefore was not only the key to its structure but the source of any holistic properties that it might have.

In NOTES, Alexander said that a good design was one in which form and context were in frictionless coexistence. This now goes a step further. In this view, a building is basically a living organism in which certain things are happening — as opposed to being a shell made of glass, bricks, and mortar. And the things that are happening are patterns of behavior as well as patterns of space. Consequently, by searching for what is the correct structure of the environment, one is led to uncover what is the proper form of social institutions.[13] At the same time it was also clear that social institutions are themselves only large-scale patterns of millions of very minute events. In the work on the pattern language, therefore, there was an attempt to build up a fabric of such events — like opening a window and taking a deep breath, walking down a garden path and picking a flower and putting it in a buttonhole, having a cup of coffee and a piece of toast and talking to someone at the same time, all the way through everything that is going on in the city and all through its various institutions, but always built up out of very minute events — much as a novelist, like Tolstoy for example, would describe a human life. And it was an intuitive sense of the structure of such a fabric that, in a very limited way, enabled the early projects to be completed and, to a greater extent, guided the work on the structure of the pattern language itself.

The idea that a building is as much, if not more, the life that goes on inside as it is the "shell" which encloses that life is of course congruent with the observation that the environment is made of patterns, not "things". But it is equally paradigm-shattering because it leads logically to the conclusion that the correct adaptation of the environment requires an enormous amount of minute local adaptations between the buildings and the users. It completely rules out, for example, pre-fabricated, standardized, and modular construction — the hallmarks of modern architecture. Although this incompatibility would not become completely clear to Alexander until he actually started to build, it was a source of friction between the Center and other professional architects engaged in the work of the early projects. But the idea is paradigm-shattering in another way.

The modern, so-called objectivist view of aesthetics insists that the source of beauty of an object is contained primarily within its formal properties. In the case of a building, this means *how it looks,* independently of the life that goes on inside. The exclusive appeal of this view is evident in the tendency for modern buildings to be photographed for publication *without* people in them. The so-called subjectivist view however is equally unsatisfactory. It holds that what makes something aesthetically valuable is not in its own properties but its relation to the personal preferences of its perceivers.

This antimony has no place in Alexander's view. For him, the beauty of a thing does not rest entirely in its appearance but rather in its *existence:*

For me, the beauty of a thing is not purely in how it looks. It has to do with how it is. Now how it "is" essentially involves a relationship between the various events that are going on there. It happens to be true that when a thing is transparently true to itself we then somewhat naively think of it as beautiful. The naive part actually consists in attempting to analyse that intuition and mistaking it for being a comment on how it looks. But when it is correctly understood it happens to be only a comment on how it looks in passing. Appearances can be deceptive. If you are looking at a racehorse naively, for example, you might mistake the saccharine quality of the beauty of the horse for the actual appearance of things like the flaring of the nostrils or other characteristics which are present in a horse that is going to run like hell. Such a horse is certainly not going to be ugly; but it is not going to be that saccharine look for which somebody might naively paint a picture of a racehorse either. In the human realm we are clearly aware of this. We distinguish between the saccharine exterior and the appearance of a person who is actually resolved. So it is ultimately the inner life which is the thing that matters. And when I say that basically I am concerned with making things beautiful, that is what I am speaking about.

Here again the inquiry comes to rest on some holistic property of structure. In this case it is the internal resolution that occurs when something is "transparently true to itself." As in the "goodness of fit" between form and context, or in the correspondence between the structure of a problem and the design program, or in the free functioning of a system, or in the overlapping structure of interactions, or in the "real heart structure of a language," or in the congruence between the holistic perception of a thing and its behaviour, all of Alexander's investigations during this ten-year period come down to this property of wholeness or richness or vitality that is present in beautiful buildings. To anyone trained in scientific method this would seem to suggest two possibilities. Either the investigations have been incorrectly biased from the start, in which case the pattern of coincidence is nothing more than an interesting tautology *or* there is some objective phenomenon at work which shows up no matter how one approaches the problem.

In science, the discovery of such phenomena is rarely sudden. Usually the investigator is inelectably driven to conclude its existence only after repeated efforts to explain something else come to rest on its probability. For Alexander, the idea that there might be some sort of phenomenological event occurring when something was "beautiful" was not even an attractive option. First, it places one in the extremely awkward situation of claiming something to exist when that existence seems highly problematic. Secondly, the burden of proof is enormously time consuming and often impossible within the lifetime of the person making the discovery. And yet, by the end of the late 60's there seemed no other alternative. It was clear that although progress on the pattern language was evident, each attempt to explain what was meant by the holistic property of structure opened up new questions. The results seemed to suggest some sort of hermetic circle of inquiry that led inexorably to the existence of some objective feature of reality that was logically accessible only by inference. If indeed there was such a phenomenon, by what means could one be precise enough to systematically predict its consequences?

Although the remainder of this book will attempt to convey as fully as possible Alexander's answer to that question, there are precedents in architectural theory and practice for the discovery or even the claim that there is such a phenomenon. A careful examination of Wright's discussion of "organic" architecture or of Le Corbusier's remarks about "ineffable space" suggests that both believed that what they were referring to were objective features of reality.[14] Eliel Saarinen believed that the search for form would result in objective conclusions — which he described in terms of a spatial "aura" — and that its fundamentals were "always the same, all the time, unchangeable and firm."[15] There is, however, no precedent for a systematic description of the consequences of such phenomena. Although such descriptions constitute the basis and prerequisite of scientific paradigms, their existence in architecture would radically alter the current conception of the field and shatter the prevailing constellation of facts, values, and methods upon which it is based. Because such an event seems so improbable, and because of Alexander's specific answer to the question, his inquiry itself constitutes an examination of the entire field.

REFERENCE NOTES

1. "Systems Generating Systems," ARCHITECTURE CANADA (November, 1968), p.40

2. Cf. D'Arcy Wentworth Thompson, ON GROWTH AND FORM (Cambridge: The University Press, 1966)

3. In fact it was Bruner who first nominated Alexander to Harvard's Society of Fellows of which he became a Junior Fellow in 1962.

4. "A Result in Visual Aesthetics," BRITISH JOURNAL OF PSYCHOLOGY (October, 1960), pp.357-371; "The Origin of Creative Power in Children", BRITISH JOURNAL OF AESTHETICS, 2:3 (July, 1962), pp.207-226;"On Changing the Way People See,"PERCEPTUAL AND MOTOR SKILLS, Vol. 19 (July, 1964), pp.235-253; and "Subsymmetries," PERCEPTION AND PSYCHOPHYSICS, 4:2 (February, 1968), pp.73-77. These are discussed at length in Chapter XVIII.

5. See Kevin Lynch, THE IMAGE OF THE CITY (Cambridge: MIT Press, 1960); Francois Vigier, "An Experimental Approach to Urban Design," JOURNAL OF THE AMERICAN INSTITUTE OF PLANNERS, 31:1 (February, 1965); Stephen Carr, "The City of the Mind," in William Ewald (ed), ENVIRONMENT FOR MAN (Bloomington: Indiana University Press, 1971); Carl Steinitz, "Meaning and the Congruence of Urban Form and Activity," JOURNAL OF THE AMERICAN INSTITUTE OF PLANNERS, 34:4 (July, 1968); Donald Appleyard, "Styles and Methods of Structuring a City," ENVIRONMENT AND BEHAVIOR, 21:1 (June, 1970); and Gyorgy Kepes, "Notes on Expression and Communication in the Cityscape," in Rodwin (ed.), THE FUTURE METROPOLIS (New York: George Braziller, 1961)

6. Christian Norberg-Schultz, EXISTENCE, SPACE, AND ARCHITECTURE (New York: Praeger, 1971)

7. In Gyorgy Kepes (ed.), THE MAN-MADE OBJECT (New York: George Braziller, 1966), p.97; cf. R. A. Bangold, THE PHYSICS OF BLOWN SAND AND DESERT (1941), pp.144-153

8. "Atoms of Environmental Structure," Ministry of Public Buildings and Works (London: 1966); "The Coordination of the Urban Rule System," REGIO BASILIENSIS PROCEEDINGS (Basle: December, 1965), pp.1-9; "Twenty-Six Entrance Relations for a Suburban House," Ministry of Public Buildings and Works (London: 1966); "Design Innovation: An Exchange of Ideas," PROGRESSIVE ARCHITECTURE (November, 1967), pp.126-131; and "The Pattern of Streets," JOURNAL OF THE AMERICAN INSTITUTE OF PLANNERS, 32:5 (September, 1966)

9. "Center for Environmental Structure: Theory, Organization, Activities" (Berkeley: 1967)

10. .Two of the projects were described in A PATTERN LANGUAGE WHICH GENERATES MULTI-SERVICE COMMUNITY CENTERS (Berkeley: 1968) and HOUSES GENERATED BY PATTERNS (Berkeley: 1969)

11. Roger Montgomery, "Pattern Language: The Contribution of Christopher Alexander's Center for Environmental Structure to the Science of Design," ARCHITECTURAL FORUM (January/February, 1970), p.53

12. IBID., p.54

13. These ideas were explored in several articles published in the late 1960's: "The City as a Mechanism for Sustaining Human Contact," in William Ewald (ed.), ENVIRONMENT FOR MAN (Bloomington: Indiana University Press, 1967), pp.60-109;"Cells of Subcultures," an occasional paper of the Center for Environmental Structure (Berkely: 1968); and "Major Changes in Environmental Form Required by Social and Phychological Demands," EKISTICS (August, 1969)

14. Cf. Frank Lloyd Wright, AN AUTOBIOGRAPHY (New York: Duell, Sloan, and Pearce, 1943) and Le Corbusier, NEW WORLD OF SPACE (New York: Reynal & Hitchcock, 1948), pp.7-9

15. Eliel Saarinen, SEARCH FOR FORM (New York: Reinhold, 1948), pp.vii,3

PART TWO

V

BREAKTHROUGH

Kuhn's description of the proponent of a new paradigm is worth recalling here. He is first seen pushing the normal rules of practice harder than ever to see just where and how far they can be made to work. He will also seek ways to magnify and make more striking the obstacles to success within the existing paradigm. And, he will seem a man searching at random, trying experiments just to see what will happen, looking for an effect whose nature he cannot quite guess until, finally, the new route, or a sufficient hint to permit later articulation, may emerge all at once. This kind of breakthrough occurred for Alexander between 1967 and 1969 when, after almost ten years of attempting to analyze the structure of a well adapted environment, he finally realized that there was something more to space than his investigations had thus far been able to reveal.

Up to this point, the ideas developed since NOTES can all be viewed as attempts to identify the structure of a well adapted environment as if its emergent properties — like goodness of fit, richness of fabric, or wholeness of form — were somehow dependent upon their correct description. In terms of aesthetic philosophy, this is what Monroe Beardsley calls "aesthetics from below" — to state problems of beauty in such a way that the empirical results of formal inquiry can be brought to bear upon them.[1] By contrast, "aesthetics from above" is congruent with a belief in the autonomy of a work of art — the idea that it has objective qualities in itself, independent of both its creator and perceivers. It is easy to see how, for Alexander, with an essentially scientific background coupled with an interest in both the adaptations and perceptions of the users of buildings, the idea that the beauty of a thing could have an existence all of its own might have little appeal. Yet he had already once pursued a not dissimilar line of inquiry.

In an unpublished and accidentally burnt manuscript called THE UNIVERSE OF FORMS he struggled for several years to find a general mathematical representation of all geometrical forms, a mathematical space in which all of these forms were located with respect to each other and, finally, the types of purely mathematical spaces that were occupied by the most beautiful ones. Yet the real change in the direction of a purely objective account came, ironically, when Alexander — like Rousseau — permitted himself to be guided by instinct and emotion more than by formal logic. As a result, he gradually became aware of a *particular quality* embodied in certain environments that was more fundamental than any of the properties he had so far been studying:

I began to see that there was something entirely different in space and which you might think of as the living heart of it. There was a particular quality in space that one could actually see in certain places that was very, very hard to create. It was as though you were almost calling on your soul to actually be able to produce it. It was obviously incredibly hard to do. It was very soft but at the same time very disciplined — very soft in feeling but not all in the sense that it had funny curves. It might be incredibly simple in its outward geometry but fantastically soft in the way that it actually was.

For example: if you imagine a brick wall that has been standing for one hundred and fifty years, and that some of the paving stones around its base have shifted slightly with the shifting of the earth's surface, and that there are mosses and grasses growing in between the stones, that the wall itself is essentially a disciplined wall and probably has a rather carefully made capping to it, and the bricks are almost perfectly regular, although not perfectly regular, and you imagine the tree that has grown against the wall, and that there has been a kind of progressive interaction between this tree (which might have grown over a period of fifty years) and the sun warming the wall and bringing the tree to fruit — I think it is quite clear that all of that has a particular feeling to it, if you forget what geometry it might have for a moment and just pay attention to the feeling.

It's fundamentally different from the feeling which is projected from the so-called master works of modern architecture. Their so-called very goodness lies in something that is much more like cardboard than what I have just described. It has something to do only with the geometry. The whole thing is very conscious and very hard. It may not actually be any more rectilinear than the wall I have just described — that is not critical. What is critical is that as an entity it is entirely different in feeling. [In contrast to the ordinary wall with the peach tree growing beside it,] it seems almost narcissistic. It is essentially made to be looked at. It is not made to be a living breathing thing. It is made to be photographed, to be walked past, and to be looked at.

The two things are physically quite different, so that immediately you know what kind of thing it is by looking at it, long before you know what is actually going on there. And of course, in part, you would see this quality physically because it would be the aggregation of all the things that had happened there, actually helping it to be what it is. But it's incredible softness has nothing to do with looseness of line, or being curved, or any of that. It happens to be accompanied by a fairly strong discipline of simple, orderly shapes at the same time that it has a tenderness to it.

Some of the sources of Alexander's awareness of this were distinctly architectural. For example, one was a drawing of a house made by Frank Lloyd Wright; another was a small road in Denmark; and a third was a temple in Japan — Tofuku-ji. This particular temple was simultaneously so disciplined and yet so continuous with the natural environment that it was to Alexander "as if someone had rolled up his shirt-sleeve and put his arm down into the heart of nature and had actually plucked up something and brought it to the surface." And yet the quality itself is not essentially architectural. For Alexander, it is a fundamental feature of reality — of which architecture is only one form of expression. It has other than architectural sources: it has to do with the process of achieving this quality in one's own life. This is an important point because it helps to explain both this quality and any claims made about its status.

For Alexander it is both objective and at the same time dependent upon personal experience — a philosophical distinction shared by several existential writers, particularly Sartre who spoke of the "being-in-itself" of a thing as well as the "being-for-itself" of its perception. When these two aspects were present in some thing or event, according to Sartre, it contained "measureless depths which speak to ourselves as persons."[2] The appeal is to a non-mystical realm of existence in which, very simply, reality appears unshakeably *authentic*. Philosophers and poets since Plato and Homer have attempted to describe it, some more successfully than others, but always in opposition to "normal" or everyday reality — as in the cave scene of the REPUBLIC — which is considered inauthentic, if not boring and unsatisfying.

Imagine that one is continually playing a movie to oneself and that what we think of as our waking life is actually being dominated by a little movie of continually changing images that have got nothing to do with our actual life as we are living it. If you could ever turn the movie off and be in touch with the actual life that you are living at the moment, you would enter into an incredible realm of freedom and oneness, a point at which you are doing just what you are doing and nothing else — like breathing very deeply.

For Alexander, this state is so fundamental that it is imperative to ask under what circumstances it occurs. It is a reasonable question for an architect to ask. Recall NOTES: "A well-designed house not only fits its context well but also *illuminates* the problem of just what the context is." Or Yi-Fu Tuan's review: "The structure, if successful, will *clarify* the life it accommodates." This is a level of "functionality" in architecture that is far and above what is normally understood by the term within the existing paradigm. Alexander is now talking about life itself, not just a system of activities that needs to be parcelled out into space with a minimum of conflicts. And somehow, the whole problem of beauty is deeply rooted in the question of what it means to be alive. Recall his comparison of beauty to the smile on a person's face: "By the standards of the smile, the actual contents of a person's face are incredibly unimportant." It is the phenomenon of the sense of being alive that is important and that determines the authenticity of the situation, not some frozen ideal. Alexander's concept of beauty is *visceral*. It cuts right through the standard aesthetic categories. It is the "inner paste" of things, the "measureless depths" of feeling. But how can one *see* it?

This is the breakthrough — the discovery that the sense of being completely alive has a clear phenomenological counterpart in space:

32

33

32. A Brick Garden Wall.

33. Ludwig Miës van der Rohe, German Pavilion, Barcelona, 1929.

PLATE XIII

D

34

34. Colonnade, Toshodaiji Temple, Nara.

PLATE XIV

a particular quality in space that one can actually see as well as feel. Eventually, Alexander would precisely identify the geometrical properties of this "quality", but the emphasis here is simply on the discovery itself and the important change in direction which it had on his work:

From that moment on it became quite clear to me that that was what this was all about — that actually everything that I had been doing essentially led in that direction but that I had not yet made the culminating step. And the whole question became how to actually have all the processes that I had been discovering and inventing, how to actually get them to lead to that point — that quality.

The specific context in which this discovery took place centered around the questions posed by the Rapid Transit Study: the observation that somehow the "system" was stating its own requirements and that something was going on which could not be accounted for by the analysis of the so-called program. Even before the breakthrough, work had progressed on analysing the structure of that program — regardless of where the system's requirements were actually coming from. But still, Alexander began to study that one question in the form of a separate book. This book — THE TIMELESS WAY OF BUILDING — eventually took fourteen years to complete.

In its initial form it was simply an attempt to connect up the many articles he had already written about design in the hope that by precisely identifying a single thread running through all of the investigations he would have the answer. Then there was a fairly immediate transition to a book called "The Environment". This was to be a completely scientific treatment of the central property of a system which accounted for its "wholeness." That phase lasted about five years — until the discovery that there was something else to space than his investigations had thus far revealed:

The third phase was recognizing fully that the quality I became aware of was fundamental and that you could not fool around with it. But it was much more difficult to explain than I had thought. I recognized, for example, that normal scientific discourse would not do it. All of that began to develop after the book already had its preliminary shape. In other words, a rough but complete draft of the book — in its scientific form — was actually finished when it was still called "The Environment." But I realized that I had not really hit the nail on the head. And I was then forced by various problems that arose to deal completely and honestly with this central issue.

One of the problems was that the wholeness concept was breaking down at the same time that the unresolved question of the reality of patterns since the Rapid Transit Study was looming larger and larger. The difficulty of giving an accurate account of when a pattern was a good one — which plays a fairly central role in the book — was becoming more and more critical. The gradual realization that, actually, a personal transformation was needed in order to do all of this and to liberate it, quite apart from whether you understood the thing intellectually, entered into the book in its last phase.

One of the key events was a conversation Alexander had with Murray Silverstein — then a colleague at the Center — about this central concept:

I used words like "wholeness" to try and explain the essential property, and after talking for several hours I went home frustrated by the fact that we could not really put a name on it. So I decided to write a chapter about that and, in so doing, called it "The Quality Without A Name." And it was at that time that the book changed its character and became THE TIMELESS WAY OF BUILDING.

In Kuhn's analysis of scientific revolutions, this is the relatively sudden and unstructured event like the gestalt switch of which scientists often speak as the "scales falling from the eyes" or the "lightning flash" that "innundates" a previously obscure puzzle, enabling its components to be seen in a new way that for the first time permits its solution:

> No ordinary sense of the term "interpretation" fits these flashes of intuition, through which a new paradigm is born. Though such intuitions depend upon the experience, both anomalous and congruent, gained with the old paradigm, they are not logically or piecemeal linked to particular items of that experience as an interpretation would be. Instead, they gather up large portions of that experience and transform them to the rather different bundle of experience that will thereafter be linked piecemeal to the new paradigm but not to the old.[3]

As a result of this development, the already formulated idea that the real structure of the environment comes from overlapping sets of interacting rules — rules representing relations between patterns in the environment and which, when properly adapted, correspond to the holistic perception of structure — could now be taken a step further. The holistic perception of structure was isomorphic with the perception of this particular quality in space — the "quality without a name" — and the fact that it was the exact same quality every time it occured provided a sort of "litmus test" for guiding the work on the completion of the pattern language; in particular, the expansion of the collection of patterns and the description of a generative structure which binds them together:

I was no longer willing to start looking at any pattern unless it presented itself to me as having the capacity to connect up with some part of this quality. Unless a particular pattern actually was capable of generating the kind of life and spirit that we are now discussing, and that it had this quality itself, my tendency was to dismiss it, even although we explored many, many patterns.

By claiming to have identified an objectively attainable quality, Alexander has set up a level, a goal, which is much higher than that to which contemporary architecture normally aspires. In that sense he has uncovered a genuine anomaly which places the existing paradigm in doubt because it cannot be dealt with. Yet this contrast obscures the fact that we are actually dealing with a continuum; and once the claim is made that this continuum is longer than had previously been assumed to be the case, that there are experiences which are quite removed on the scale from what constitutes "normal" or everyday realities, then sharp contrasts are automatically set up in trying to distinguish between the two ends:

I am certain that an architect functioning in today's terms cannot produce buildings that are alive. You can call that a black and white distinction. But what I am really saying is that there is a continuum and that there are certain processes which automatically place you very low down on that continuum because it is structurally impossible for them to reach the other end. And I think that what I have done is to attempt to identify, very sharply, kinds of properties, patterns, set-ups, conditions, or processes that tend to put you on the higher end of the continuum and to identify those that tend to put you on the lower end and make the distinction between them. And I think that what makes people so upset is that I am insisting that there is such a continuum.

The insistence is indeed upsetting. If this quality in space really does exist, and if it cannot be accounted for by the prevailing constellation of values, facts, and methods of the field, then a genuine paradigm crisis is under way. And as Kuhn has shown in the case of science, such crisis will be resisted by the proponents of the existing paradigm — if only to insure the continuity of their field. But in the meantime, the pressure will be on the new candidate to move on to new discoveries. In Alexander's case, it means taking this "quality" and providing a systematically precise description of its actual consequences — which is the province of science, not philosophy.

REFERENCE NOTES

1. Monroe Beardsley, AESTHETICS: PROBLEMS IN THE PHILOSOPHY OF CRITICISM (New York: 1958)
2. Cf. Jean-Paul Sartre, BEING AND NOTHINGNESS (1943)
3. Thomas Kuhn, THE STRUCTURE OF SCIENTIFIC REVOLUTIONS, 2nd ed. (Chicago: University of Chicago Press, 1970), p.122

VI

THE CONFLICT BETWEEN FACT AND VALUE

THE SIMILARITIES between Alexander's work and the emergence of a new paradigm in Kuhn's analysis of the structure of scientific revolutions have so far been mainly *procedural* — that is, similarities between Alexander's line of of inquiry and the patterns of investigation which occur during a period of paradigm crisis. The uncovering of anomalies within the field, the attempt to push existing rules beyond their normal limits, the isolation and magnification of their defects, the search for alternative solutions, the cognitive and intellectual shifts necessary to reinterpret existing phenomena, and the emergence of new explanations for the basic elements of the field itself — all these appear in Alexander's work during the ten-year period since 1958. But what about *content*? If the crucial ingredient in the evolution of a new paradigm — in science — is the ability to provide a systematic and precise description of the consequences of a reality only believed to be existing independently of our perception, what does this say about the *kinds* of phenomena which can be so described?:

Basically, science is concerned with those events that become visible or reproducable at will. You have to be able to tap somebody on the shoulder and say, "Look at this." But what we have here is somewhat different. It is not just any old event that anyone can look for, although it is as objective as these seemingly neutral events. It does take a certain amount of maturity to see it in order to tell whether it is present — or to what extent it is present. I definitely do not consider it subjective. On the other hand, it is a little bit more subtle than these events where you can tap somebody on the shoulder.

It is true that, in medicine for example, with microscopes, it does take a certain amount of training just to see an event that someone will say has to be explained. At the time Harvey was working on the circulation of blood, for example, even the most banal observations of bleeding required a trained eye to see what was happening. And in particle physics it takes a great deal of maturity as a physicist to interpret the tracks in a bubble chamber.

So we have the similarity that even in science, where things appear to be very straightforward, you still need to have a trained eye to even identify the events, congruent or incongruent with certain models. In that sense it is not totally unusual to say that this quality requires a certain maturity in order to see it. I do not think it is a unique vision. One can gradually be trained to see it for oneself. However, what is completely different is that this quality has to do with value.

In science, what one is doing is constructing various definitions and models in the hope that they will account for phenomena. Any phenomena which appear inconsistent with these definitions are grounds for challenging the definitions and reshaping them to fit the phenomena observed. In every case the phenomenon is an event; and it is always some sort of event which is not predicted by these models which challenges them and forces one to rearrange them or look for new ones. But the events are neutral. There is no question of whether they are good, bad, or indifferent. There is just the question of whether they occur or not.

But, if I think about all of this work, almost going back to the beginning and including the mature part, I suppose that the central issue is that there is something of value *in a building, or a town, or in a moment in a person's life. And all of what I am doing is trying to form models which may consist of rules, or principles, or processes, or definitions, not just which will account for this quality, but which will produce it. And I will keep knocking my models against whether they actually produce this quality. And to the extent that they do I will leave them alone; and to the extent that they do not I will junk them. Now on that level it is incredibly similar to science. In formal terms the parallelism is almost exact. But — and this is where there is a certain discontinuity — this event, this quality, has to do with what is* valuable.

This is the distinction — and a crucial one: that some events have more value than others. Yet compared to the kinds of phenomena science tends to describe, how could events of value be a matter of objective fact? Does not the passing of "value judgments" place one automatically in the *subjective* realm of personal preference and taste? Or — in the case of design — style?

These and similar questions arise from Alexander's claim that there is a certain state — *a unity of space,* in which a thing is "true to itself," or "completely resolved," or any other of his attempts to give it a name — that is preferable to other states. It is one thing to say that sand ripples, for example, can be explained in terms of the resolution of forces acting on the individual grains of sand (and that, indeed, the rippled state is the most stable since any configuration of wind and sand will tend *towards* it); but it is quite another thing to say that this is the best or preferred state. Even the deeper explanation, which would have the sand ripples as merely one state along a dynamic continuum, cannot account for why the ripples are more interesting to the human eye than any of the intermediate "ascending" or "descending" states.

Certainly the sense of "being and becoming" of sand ripples — that is, the process of formation up to and including the actual ripples themselves — is due in part to the dynamic character of *all* natural processes. They are in formation at every moment, including the forms that have special properties — like ripples; for these only break down and become part of a continuing process of formal adjustment and adaptation. But even although nature can be understood this way — as a formative process — certain *instances* of form indeed seem to have special properties in the sense that they attract the human eye (or other sense organ). Whether or not this is because of a corresponding pattern in the cognitive structure of the brain, these are like moments of local resolve — when the forces at work in the thing achieve maximum kinetic energy, as in the breaking of a wave or the full bloom of a flower. At these moments the form *appears* most perfect, and Nature *seems* to be revealing itself most fully. These moments interest the physicist as well as the poet because they *seem* to provide clues to the inner workings and otherwise hidden structure of the world.

When the ancients looked at Nature they were attracted to certain states more than others — in the rising and setting of the sun, in the eclipse of the moon, in the diurnal rotations of the seasons, in the blooming of the flower, or in the spiral of a Nautilus shell — and these states represented, for them, the perfection of the universe, worthy of reverence and respect and of study and abstraction into fundamental properties like harmony, rhythm, proportion, and balance. The expression of these same properties — in music, in dance, in athletic contest, or even in politics — was seen as a striving toward perfection and constituted the highest value of life (e.g., as expressed in the Greek word arêté).

This was more than just an example of "organic analogy" or "copying nature" — unless one can presume to *step outside* the universe and then look back and "copy it," as Descartes was supposed to have done. One either *recognizes* that one is a part of nature or not; and the mere existence of the phrase "organic analogy," for example, only presupposes an alienation — the source of which is often attributed to Descartes in the context of a hotly contested debate spanning almost two centuries of philosophic and scientific thought.

A central notion in Descartes' philosophy was the separation of mind and matter: the internal world "in here" and the external world "out there." The external world was knowable, but only through its impression on the mind. Descartes thought of his consciousness as a kind of dispassionate and uninvolved observer recording what it saw — like a reflective mirror, although his contemporary Spinoza, attracted to Descartes' attempt at finding an explanation, disagreed. To Spinoza, mind and matter were not separate but rather two different versions of the same thing. He agreed with Giordano Bruno that all reality was a single, homogenous substance and that every particle of reality was composed inseparably of both physical *and* psychical phenomena. There is only one entity, seen inwardly as "mind" and outwardly as "matter," but actually an inextricable mixture and unity of both. The mind is so passionately involved in the external world that, according to Spinoza, "the order and connection of ideas is the same as the order and connection of things."[1]

To Kant as well, the mind was not passive wax upon which the experience and sensation of the external world was etched; rather, it was an active organ which coordinated our perception according to an inherent structure. We might never know for certain the external world, but we might at least know how the mind perceives it, how it filters and organizes infinite stimuli through "categories" of space and time and shapes them into an ordered whole. Furthermore, this "transcendental unity of apperception," as Kant called it, was innate, *a priori,* like the laws of mathematics — so rooted in the nature of mind that it must be absolute and necessary to the scheme of things (i.e., matter as well): not only thoughts, but things themselves must follow the same laws, since it and they were one. In Hegel's formulation, logic and metaphysics were thus inseparable.

To these philosophers, the congruence of mind and matter was no mere coincidence; it was a fundamental feature of the structure of existence, underlying all events and things, and constituted the essence of the world. Consequently, moral and religious feelings of perception — like those held by the ancients — could not be dismissed as personal delusions simply because they were in the mind. It seems true — as rationalists after Descartes pointed out — that if it is a question of certainty, religion obviously falls a long way behind science. However, by showing that science was as much mind as matter, Kant reversed the argument. If *everything* was, to some extent, in the mind, then science is just as doubtful as religion — which is to say, as Colin Wilson points out, that religion is as certain as science.[2] "In one sweep," says Wilson, Kant had managed to reinstate religion — not as an institution of belief, but as a mode of perception. The *feeling* of unity between the "in here" and the "out there" (Kant's transcendental unity of apperception) was *the same as* the ancient awareness of God — "that great sum of being in which matter and mind, subject and object, good and evil, are one."[3] But "the same as" was not quite God. God was conceivable, but still not knowable (after all, Kant's great discovery was that we can never know for certain the external world, only our perception of it). Kant proved that it was possible to accept certain modes of awareness as corresponding to an object "out there" — and thus proving the existence of that object — but that such "transcendental" knowledge was the province of neither science nor religion because the understanding could never go beyond the limits of sensibility. God may thus have been saved from the growing scepticism of 18th century empiricism, but it also became separated from scientific inquiry. As Alexander Koyré put it, "Kant was unable to connect space with God and had to put it into ourselves."[4]

The distinction may seem subtle, but its consequences were part of a momentous series of intellectual developments in the history of science that lead to the eventual separation of fact and value. In Koyré's analysis, what we understand to be the "scientific revolution" of the 17th and 18th centuries is bound up not only with the development of theories concerning the nature of the universe (i.e., Copernicus to Newton) but with the development of theories concerning the relationship between mind and matter as well (i.e., Descartes to Kant):

> This scientific and philosophic revolution ... can be described roughly as bringing forth the destruction of the Cosmos, that is, the disappearance, from philosophically and scientifically valid concepts, of the conception of the world as a finite, closed, and hierarchically ordered whole ... and its replacement by an indefinite and even infinite universe which is bound together by the identity of its fundamental components and laws, and in which all these components are placed on the same level of being. This, in turn, implies the discarding by scientific thought of all considerations based on value concepts, such as perfection, harmony, meaning and aim, and finally the utter devalorization of being, the divorce of the world of value and the world of facts.[5]

And his conclusion is even more revealing:

> The infinite universe of the new Cosmology, infinite in Duration as well as in Extension, in which eternal matter in accordance with eternal and necessary laws moves endlessly and aimlessly in eternal space, inherited all the ontological attributes of Divinity. Yet only those — all the others the departed God took away with him.[6]

In the great debate over the relationship between mind and matter, duality had defeated unity and matter had edged out mind. Science justifiably aligned itself with the realm of matter which, in turn, became progressively stripped of the "value-concepts" imposed upon it by the mind. The universe was still "one," "simple," "eternal," "necessary" — all the ontological attributes previously associated with God — but it was no longer a whole in which the hierarchy of value determined the hierarchy and structure of being. Furthermore, this "utter devalorization of being," as Koyré calls it, meant that questions of value (and religion) could no longer appeal to the "facts" of the universe. Science, religion, and philosophy would go their separate ways and, in so doing, lose their single, unified, and powerful focus (like infinite extension, i.e., absolute homogeneity). As a result of this "bifurcation of Nature" (Whitehead's phrase), science would become progressively dehumanized (in spite of its incredible productivity after the 18th century), religion would remain hopelessly tied to institutional dogma (in spite of its great professed humanity), and philosophy (to use Schopenauer's phrase) would lapse into endless biographies of philosophers" — the central theme of which is an existential despair, a sense of "contingency" in a world without values.

Human values, which stemmed from man's ancient experience of congruency with the universe — no longer having a single point of reference "out there" — were cast adrift into a sea of subjectivity. Thus the 17th century poet John Donne wrote:

> ... new Philosophy calls in doubt.
> The element of fire is quite put out;
> The sun is lost, and th'earth, and no man's wit
> can well direct him where to look for it.

Beauty, for example, was no longer *in* the object of contemplation as one of its constituent properties; it became, for science, a quality the mind supplies before or after the act of cognition — arbitrary and purely subjective rather than a real property of the objective world. "And since," as Theodore Roszak so painfully puts it, "one person's taste is as good as another's, who is to say — as a matter of *fact* — that the hard cash of a strip mine counts for less than the grandeur of an untouched mountain?"[7] For Roszak, such "barbarism" cannot be blamed on science; but it is deeply rooted in the scientific principle of reality that treats value as a matter of subjective preference. In the case of architecture, this is what Ruskin meant by the "pathetic fallacy." Robert Herbert provides the explanation:

> Ruskin's great lament is that by his day man had cast out spirituality and substituted a purely mechanical, materialistic universe, so that his contemporaries were driven to nature as a *substitute for,* rather than a revelation of, the divine unity of purpose, the divine sense of order .... It pointed to a terrible loss for mankind, because nature was not seen as a manifestation of God.[8]

For Alexander, the same situation leads to an inherent paradox in the attempt to fuse art and science — namely, the practice of architecture:

> ....during the period from 1600 to 1800, roughly from Descartes to Leibniz, God was taken out of the world, and replaced by an endless, isotropic, homogenous universe, represented by a geometric structure, in which value had no natural place: indeed, it was value-free, and value could not be related to it, in any sensible, graspable way.
>
> We have grown up with this scientific heritage. Trying to be good

scientists — or at least believing in science — we have accepted the idea of a world picture without value in it. And yet we face a paradox, as architects, planners, faced with human decisions, decisions about the structure of our world every day, we patently face the issue of value constantly. Trying to keep faith with "Science," and therefore accepting the idea that there is no one Value essentially connected to the structure of things, we replace it with the idea of many values (little v), and try to let these little v values take the place of a world in which fact and value are united.

But this cannot be done. If the conception of value which we have, is purely personal, treats each person's values as interesting, deeply important, but arbitrary things, not essentially connected to the structure of things, we still flounder about in the value-free structure of science, trying artificially to graft on the little v values, which individuals have: and then we dignify this patchwork, and call it a theory.

Myself, as some of you know, originally a mathematician, I spent several years, in the early sixties, trying to define a view of design, allied with science, in which values also were let in by the back door. I too played with operations research, linear programming, all the fascinating toys, which mathematics and science have to offer us, and tried to see how these things can give us a view of design, what to design, and how to design.

Finally, however, I recognized that this view is essentially not productive, and that for mathematical and scientific reasons, if you like, it was essential to find a theory in which value and fact are one, in which we recognize that there is a central value, approachable through feeling, and approachable by loss of self, which is deeply connected to facts, and forms a single indivisible world picture, *within which productive results can be obtained.*[9]

Alexander is claiming that the moments of local resolve which we experience as beauty actually correspond to a state "out there" — a *unity of space* — which has investigable properties but which cannot be properly understood except in the context of value. Thus productive necessity demands the creation of a theory in which fact and value form "a single indivisible world picture." The problem is that normal scientific procedure, since the 18th century, does not lend itself to this kind of investigation:

Suppose that we are interested in a certain type of event perceivable at a gross level of observation in a bubble chamber. Let us say that a particular spiral occurs which is then going to be interpreted as the decay of a pi-meson, for example. But overtly, we are only interested in whether or not the spiral is there because when it is there the particle is apparently decaying into nothing. Now if we look at the two cases where the spiral does exist and where the spiral does not exist, no statement of any sort is being made that one of them is more valuable than the other. It is just an event — namely, that this spiral sometimes happens and sometimes it does not. No statement of the sort is being made along the lines that the essence of the universe is revealing itself more when the spiral occurs and less when it does not. In fact, such a statement would be so bizarre that it could not even be fitted into physics at all. And yet that is the sort of statement one is making when one says that this quality is there or not.

Talking about the quality is saying that, in some fashion, the essence of things is more present in one case than in another. The thing is more true to itself — or all the ways one can talk about this, such as my own efforts for example. But regardless of all of the verbal difficulties, we are ultimately talking about cases where a thing has got more of this quality or less of it. In the case of a rug, for example, it just happens to be a very beautiful and spiritual rug compared to a carpet for walking on which has no special qualities. It is like saying that at such a point man allowed nature to reveal itself more in one case than in another where it was perhaps obstructed or prevented. And this is not a fact which science deals with. So at the same time that you can call it an event, and in that sense is a part of science, it is a highly unusual event — almost a meta-event — and is not a part of what science wants to look at. If it did, it would be an extension of science.

An "extension" of science — but what kind? What if science could literally turn itself toward the beauty of a smile in a person's face, or the rustling of leaves in a field of wheat, the ease and gracefulness of a sunlit courtyard, or the warmth and coziness of a kitchen you can sit down in and talk about the most intimate things in your life? All these things — which are as valued as life itself — have been, by virtue of the historical separation of fact and value, denied the incredible understanding and productivity which the scientific imagination can provide. But in turning toward these matters, science itself would have to change; for it could not look at these things from a neutral standpoint. It could not even hope to understand these things without according them the same reverence for nature that once inspired the painstaking discovery of its very laws and processes. For Alexander, these things are indeed what matter most to human life and therefore, to all of existence — the physical world notwithstanding.

REFERENCE NOTES

1. Cited in Will Durant, THE STORY OF PHILOSOPHY (New York: Simon and Schuster, 1961), p.135

2. Colin Wilson, BEYOND THE OUTSIDER (London: Pan Books, 1965), p.58

3. Cited in Durant, OP. CIT., p.218

4. Alexander Koyre, FROM THE CLOSED WORLD TO THE INFINITE UNIVERSE (Baltimore: Johns Hopkins University Press, 1957), p.150

5. IBID., p.4

6. IBID., p.276

7. Theodore Roszak, "Science, Knowledge, Gnosis," DAEDALUS (Summer, 1974), p.26

8. Robert L. Herbert (ed.), THE ART CRITICISM OF JOHN RUSKIN (Garden City: Anchor Books, 1964), p.xxi

9. "On .Value," CONCRETE, 1:6 (November, 1977), p.6

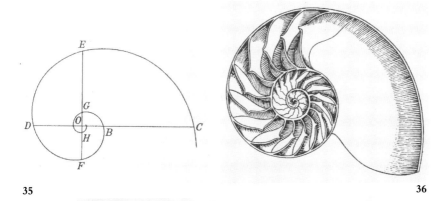

35

36

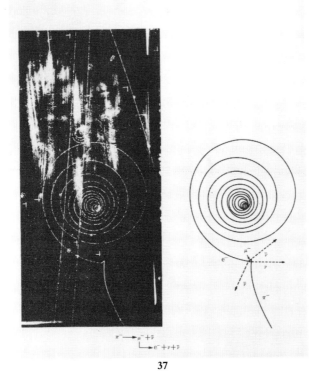

37

35. – 36.   The Equiangular Spiral of the Nautilus Shell

37.   Decay Sequence of a Pi-Meson.

"No statement of the sort is being made along the lines that the essence of the universe is revealing itself more when the spiral occurs and less when it does not . . ."

PLATE XV

38

38. Turkish Rug, Gilan.

"... and yet that is the sort of statement one is making when one says that this quality is there or not."

PLATE XVI

VII

THE MEETING OF THE PERSONAL AND THE IMPERSONAL

There are moments of local resolve in which both space and our perception of it are arranged holistically — a unity of space — which accounts for the existence of beauty in a thing. Since our own perception of what is valuable is involved, it seems reasonable to ask whether this is a matter of personal preference or objective fact. Does it exist in the mind, "in here?" or in the realm of matter, "out there?" The question implies a necessary split or *European* division, yet the break is really "historical" and corresponds to the Cartesian debate over the relationship between mind and matter.

Prior to the 17th century, God served as a reference point at which mind and matter followed the same laws; indeed, their congruence provided the only rational explanation for the existence of an absolute standard of values. But the removal of divinity from the analysis of the laws of the universe in the 17th and 18th centuries resulted in the separation of the world of facts from the world of values, leaving values stranded in a sea of "contingency." By the 19th century "positivism" had dominated scientific thought. But the victory against superstition and blind faith was hollow. A universe without values only leads to a contingency of perception, a subjectivity against which both "productive necessity" and ordinary consciousness rebels, demanding the restoration of an objective, absolute standard of values. (cf. Huxley's "Religion without revelation.") By the 20th century, phenomenology reveals that positivism incorrectly obscures the "real" relationship between mind and matter, "bifurcating" nature into an artificial duality.

81

Positivism tacitly assumes that scientific knowledge is sharply distinguished from other forms of knowing by its methods and concepts of impersonal and uncommitted modes of relation between the observer and the phenomena observed. But by demonstrating that into every act of knowing there enters a passionate contribution of the person knowing what is being known, Michael Polanyi argues that all knowledge is, to a certain extent, "personal."[1] By stressing the *active* components in scientific knowing — appraisal and commitment — Polanyi shows that such knowledge is less "objective" and more complex — more intentional — than is tacitly supposed. Knowing implies a foundation in skills, a confidence in one's ability to judge beyond the range of well formulated rules, and a belief in the existence of an answer to one's questions before the answer is actually in sight — all of which demonstrates that the knower personally participates in all acts of understanding. Finally, science involves, to use Polanyi's phrase, a "personal knowledge" of the bridge between subjectivity and objectivity and the committment to transcend one's own personal obligations to universal standards.

The way in which this knowledge comes together in extraordinary research depends upon the personality of the individual, the context in which he is working, and the historical forces which shape the problem that he has chosen to solve. In Alexander's case we have the situation in which the problem itself cuts across both the abstract and the concrete — that is, the realm of space and the realm of feeling — or what Polanyi would call the disjunction between objectivity and subjectivity. For Alexander they are inseparable:

Imagine doing physics from the standpoint of what it means to be a person. Suppose that you are asking yourself what it is like to be a person, just for the purposes of living, because it is your life and you have to be honest about it yourself; but somehow, the investigation — which has to do with the "out there" (as in the case of physics) — is tied to the answers.

Consider the architecture profession. There is the story that Mies van der Rohe, at the same time that he was doing what he did in architecture, lived in an apartment in Chicago with old Victorian stuffed chairs —the exact opposite of the kind of environments he was designing. Even if the story is not true, the archetype is. A lot of people are perfectly willing to project something onto the world "out there" and actually live something else — *and not be bothered by the discrepancy. I have never been able to do that. I ask myself questions about my own life all the time —ordinary, everyday things — and I reject anything in terms of what I am going to put "out there" that is not consistent with the answers to those questions.*

I do not necessarily mean incredibly deep, philosophical questions. For example, I know that it is very pleasant and relaxing to walk down the street in a village in England. It just makes me feel good. Now suppose I take that with extreme seriousness. If I do, then I cannot build something like Wurster Hall — the School of Architecture Building at Berkeley. I know my experience is not just idiosyncratic. It is deeply rooted in my daily life; and I kid myself if I say that something is enjoyable but that I am going to do something else.

This argument breaks down if I assume that it is all personal and that other people do not have the same experiences. But I make the assumption that I am like most people and that most people are like me. I assume that my innermost feelings are the surest guide to what is really going on. By making this assumption I come into a much more authentic contact with what people are all about and therefore permit myself to do for them what I would do for myself. I think my own life is very much on the fulcrum of the meeting between the personal and the impersonal.

Alexander's assumption about his "innermost feelings" may be correct; but only if they are congruent with the fundamental state of inner freedom and sense of being completely alive discussed in the two previous chapters and which is accompanied by the perception of a particular quality in space as a kind of phenomenological correlate. For Alexander it is a matter of being "fantastically demanding and true to the facts about when it is *really* happening and when one is kidding oneself that it is happening:"

I think we have not discussed my own characteristics very much, but that is one respect — one of the only respects — in which I truly differ from quite a few other people. I consider myself to be quite typical and ordinary in most other ways. But I think that having this standard and actually refusing anything but this standard is perhaps a slightly unusual combination.

This is obviously what Polanyi means by "the committment to transcend one's own personal obligations to universal standards." For Alexander, this committment was evident in NOTES (and which accounts for part of that book's unique appeal) and in most of his subsequent writings. It seems characteristic of almost his entire career that his own education as an architect has been conducted publicly. In literature, the German word *Bildungsroman* means "novel of education" — a form of writing in which the author sets out to describe the evolution of the protagonist's soul; it is a sort of laboratory in which the writer conducts an experiment in living at the same time that he is observing and evaluating what he is doing. NOTES is a kind of architectural *Bildungsroman* in which Alexander asks what is going on in architecture. Like Herman Hesse, he writes in the grip of a need to solve his own problems by seeing them on paper; but at the time, he had yet to undergo experiences that would make his analysis real to him. In 1964 the *Bildungsroman* was far from finished. And by the time he has awakened to the existence of a special quality in space, an even greater commitment is required — the process of achieving this quality in his own life. Only here the barriers are more formidable than they were while the problem was treated strictly "out there." For Alexander they entail an understanding of the colossal role that *fear* and the overcoming of fear play in the "education" of an architect:

There are two different versions of this fear and I think everyone encounters them, although it is not that common for people to deal with it. They live under the pressure of this fear but they do not know that it is happening. The first version is simply the fear of designing anything. The other is, given the willingness to design something, the fear of actually doing what you know to be sweet. *Obviously quite a few people overcome the first and, in fact, some people never even experience the first. But I think almost everybody experiences the second and I consider that to be of colossal importance. In a nutshell, the second of these fears is almost single-handedly responsible for everything that is wrong with the environment.*

I think that the fear is universal in the sense that it has existed at all times in history and is similar to the sort of fundamental fear which man has to struggle with over and over again in every generation and in every person. But there is an extremely acute version of it which is widespread today and which has got people so locked-in that is almost impossible, single-handedly to climb out. This is unusual. In traditional societies you could say that overcoming this fear was part of a known stage of growing up, whereas in our own society we have the unique situation where the majority of people do not pass through it.

To bring the point back to architecture, recall Alexander's comparison between the ordinary garden wall with the peach tree growing beside it and the modern, architecturally streamlined wall

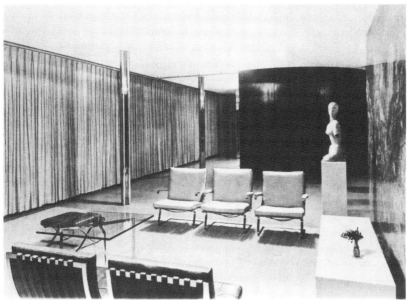

39

40

39. Ludwig Miës van der Rohe, Tugendhat House, Brno, 1930.
40. A 'Comfortable Living Room', New York, 1978.

— for a Japanese?

PLATE XVII

41

42

41. A street in Oxford, England.

42. DeMars, Esherick and Olsen, Wurster Hall, Berkeley.

"... I know that it is very pleasant and relaxing to walk down the street in a village in England. It just makes me feel good. Now suppose I take that with extreme seriousness. If I do, then I cannot build something like Wurster Hall — the School of Architecture Building at Berkeley."

PLATE XVIII

which, for him, "constitutes a very implausible creation to bolster up a terrified and dwindling ego:"

What I am saying is that the fundamental reason that someone would make such a cardboard-like thing is out of fear. It is out of fear of being laughed at, out of fear of not being famous — a whole series of wordly fears like that and which have essentially to do with what other people are going to do and say. And finally, there are the sort of more intimate fears which have to do with actually permitting the feelings that are necessary to produce the kind of wall that has the peach tree next to it to surface. There is an amazing amount of fear connected with permitting those kinds of emotions to see the light of day.

In traditional societies it takes a sort of journey to look this thing in the face. It is not so deeply buried that you cannot reach it. But in our own time, for the vast numbers of people, this thing is actually unavailable. And yet, there is no question in my mind that every single living person knows what this quality is. Very, very few people however, have the courage to live with it.

There is no question that I felt this fear myself. I became very strongly aware of it. I began to realize that I was afraid. As I say, in my case, I also experienced the first fear which was of designing anything at all. It was actually of the same type because, generally speaking, the form of the fear was whether I could make something for which I was not laughed at. But of course if one is living in a world where one is perpetually afraid of whether one is doing the right thing or not, you end up by not being able to do anything. And I think the current situation in architecture is very similar to that. In other words, everyone has in them the capacity to draw. That is obvious in the same sense that all children have the capacity to draw and make things. But most of the time, because there is what one might call a conspiracy of sneering to make you feel small, you become very, very nervous about whether you can do a thing in a fashion that will not cause somebody to sneer at you for it. And then of course people can manipulate you to an incredible extent into doing things in a certain manner — Frank Lloyd Wright's manner, or Le Corbusier's manner, or Mies van der Rohe's manner, or any sort of manner that happens to be fashionable and that creates the illusion of competence.

Overcoming that fear, breaking through it to the point where you just say, "The hell with it. I'm just going to make something!" is very similar to breaking through the other fear of actually making something in touch with this feeling I have been describing, instead of making something that is

85

an empty shell of images that has been learned from all these fear-makers. That is why I connected the two fears. As I say, even although I do not think everybody experiences the first, everybody does experience the second. There is in all of us a fear of doing things that are in touch with this realm.

At the end of ZEN IN THE ART OF ARCHERY there is a description of a man who comes to a swordsmaster to learn and the swordsmaster says, "You already seem to be a master." But the man says that the only thing he has mastered is the fear of death. And the swordsmaster says, "Then you are already a master!"[2] All of the Japanese arts recognize the fact that, finally, you have to meet the fear of death in order to do anything — landscape painting, flower arrangements, and so on. Of course you have to master the fear of death to be a swordsman; thats obvious. But what is less obvious is that to do anything freely, including the kinds of matters that we are speaking about, you have to reach the same point. And the reason for it is that if you take the fear of humiliation — of which we have been speaking — or the fear of exposing yourself, and you ask what is frightening about that and try to trace it, you realize that you have a whole series of linkages in your mind which ultimately go back to the fear of death. For example, if you are mocked you may lose your job, and if you lose your job perhaps you will end up in the gutter, and then you would be vulnerable to getting mugged, and of course there are a million different versions of this fantasy that can take place in your mind. But far from being an idle fantasy, that is actually the stuff that is controlling you, and if you were not connected up to all that you would not be afraid to do anything.

So it is actually the fear of death taking many, many different disguises. That is why I say it has to be faced over and over again by every society and for every individual. In other words, it is not only something peculiar to our time, although I think there is a particularly nasty and strange form of this fear in the recent past. In the architectural profession, the work of several decades of architects have contributed very strongly to the growth of that kind of fear. For example, I remember seeing a photograph of the teaching staff of the Bauhaus taken not long after its formation. I was intersested in the picture because in a sense they were one group of organized perpetrators of this fear, much like the tailors in "The Emperor'sNew Clothes." There were others, of course, but they were certainly influential. I looked at this photograph and it really looked like it was taken in a lunatic asylum. There is that insane look in their eyes!

I have no idea why that should happen, why people should try to

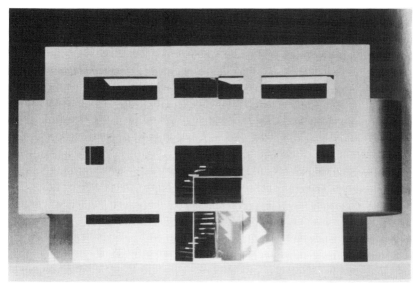

43

44

43. Richard Meier, House in Pound Ridge, New York.

   ". . . the fundamental reason that someone would make such a cardboard-like thing is out of fear."

44. Bauhaus Staff Photo.

   "There is that insane look in their eyes!"

PLATE XIX

45

45. A Zen Swordsman.

PLATE XX

perpetrate these fears. I am not sure it is because of a particularly widespread fear of death. If you go behind the immediate social exaggeration of it which exists in our time, even if you manage to get into a more normal state where one does not have to make apologies for putting up shutters on one's house, for example, you are then in a situation where there is still a fear of the same sort to be encountered, although much deeper, and that has to do with death. And it does not depend on the social context. It is just something a person has to face in order to become free in the creation of anything.

All of this is based on my own experience and on my experience of taking people through these layers of fears. It certainly is true that in my current work, no matter what theoretical subject we are working on, this is the number one event that is occurring — overcoming these fears and permitting oneself to do what is in one to do, both in myself and in my students. But if you make the statement that to teach somebody how to make buildings you have to help him strip away his own fear, this appears to be infuriatingly esoteric. But it isn't esoteric at all. It happens to be the kernel of the matter.

But the overcoming of fear is one thing; the actual meeting of the abstract and the concrete is another. As in swordsmanship, for example, without a mastery of the technical skills in handling a blade, it bears little resemblance to the task at hand.

REFERENCE NOTES

1. Cf. Michael Polanyi, PERSONAL KNOWLEDGE: TOWARDS A POST-CRITICAL PHILOSOPHY (New York: Harper and Row, 1964)
2. Eugen Herrigel, ZEN IN THE ART OF ARCHERY (New York: Vintage Books, 1971)

VIII

MAKING THINGS

What is not readily apparent from Alexander's writings is the concern for purely physical skills traditionally associated with architecture: clarity, proportion, attention to detail, craftsmanship, and a general sense of care which goes into the making of things. Although he would eventually have to draw upon all these resources in the actual construction of his own buildings, he is no stranger to this side of architecture.

As a child, the building of model railroads — including the detailed construction of the actual trains out of small pieces of brass and wood — was fascinating to him because it was "like creating a piece of the world." He also spent a great deal of time visiting medieval churches in order to make paintings of their heraldic devices — which he collected. And in later years he would build furniture and paint ceramic tiles on a continuing basis. This activity would serve several purposes in the context of mastering the physical skills necessary to succeed in the projects ahead.

First, it is an obvious and necessary counterpart to any theory of architecture in the sense that if you want to seriously consider the problem of how to make something you actually have to know how to make it:

Quite apart from my desire to work as a builder, quite apart from my desire to see buildings with this quality built, and quite apart from my belief that architects should be builders, there is just the simple, plain, ordinary fact of the necessity for having a first-hand acquaintance with building and making things. And it seems ridiculous to have to mention it except for the fact that most architects today do not understand this.

Secondly, the activity of making things over a long period of time provides an insight into the important role which "process" plays in acquiring skills as a builder:

In a woodworking shop, for example, one of the distinctions between somebody who understands working with tools and somebody who does not is to realize that the process of sharpening or sweeping up are absolutely fundamental to the activity of making something. Most people who do not really understand tools consider sharpening to be sort of an occasional event that happens only when the tools become blunt; whereas if you actually understand the tools properly, you realize that sharpening the tool is an integral part of its use. In other words, you sharpen the tool, you use it, you complete the work, and then you clean up the shop. Every craftsman knows that this is completely basic and that by getting command of these processes and taking all of them incredibly seriously, you finally get control of the medium. But for some reason this is just not clear on the level of architecture and planning.

Thirdly, there is the connection between making things and the realm of feeling. This has to do with Alexander's belief that those things which appeal most to our deepest feelings are those that have a strong sense of constructedness to them — as opposed to the minimally crafted, cardboard-like quality of modern buildings:

Something can have an immense amount of feeling and be made of an almost simple-minded precision of repeating blue and white tiles with an odd green one thrown in once in a while and placed diagonally on the facade of the building — and thats all. Its very much in the realm of craft; but the idea that you could create feeling that way is alien to the tradition of modern architecture.

On the one hand we have these very brutal cubistic buildings which are just not in the realm of feeling at all; and on the other hand we have the world of redwood burls and soft-cornered sculptures which has a soft, vaguely lovable quality but is not actually dealing with feeling either. Rather, it is a shriek of protest and outrage against the brutality of the cardboard-like world of cubism. Whereas this thing about blue and white tile might easily appeal to deep feelings — as a result of its very constructedness. Its comparable to the distinction between the music of Bach and some late 19th century sugary music. The Bach, which is much more precisely constructed, ultimately appeals to much deeper feelings.

And finally, there is just the fact that Alexander simply enjoys making things for the sheer pleasure of it.

Ever since I was a small boy, I have loved making things. At one time, when I was about fifteen, I spent almost a whole year, making one tiny locomotive. I went, first, to the Brighton locomotive works, to get a

89

blueprint of the engine . . . it was a type originally built in about 1880 . . . but they still had a blueprint of it. I took it home, and built a tiny model —— at 4mm to one foot —— of this engine. I made every single thing, the boiler, the wheels, the cab, the handrails on the cab, tiny faucets where the boiler can be emptied, on and on, day after day. I used to sit for hours, simply soldering two pieces of wire together. For instance, when you make a faucet, (in the model, the faucet is about ¹/₈th of an inch high), you have a tiny brass knob, you have to drill a hole through it; then you take a very fine brass wire, pass it through the hole; then you heat the whole thing up, and let the solder melt throughout the thing. Since it is so tiny, you cannot hold any part of it. You just have to heat it, the solder melts, and after trying perhaps thirty or forty times, the wire is in just the right place, when the solder melts, it doesn't move, and when it cools down you have a complete faucet. It might take me a day to make two faucets like that, perhaps two days. For month after month, I sat, cutting, shaping every tiny piece of brass, until I made the complete locomotive.

I have exactly the same love, today, in building buildings, or building furniture.

For example, during the years 1976–79, I used to spend day after day, out on the site in Martinez, trying our gunnite experiments. This is a way of building which I have developed, in which one shoots high strength stiff concrete, into flimsy wood, cardboard, and styrofoam guides, to build up a beautiful building.

The technique is very sophisticated technically. It took months, simply to adjust the equipment, get it running right. We would go day after day, shovelling concrete, running the compressor, trying different hoses, different nozzles, different additives, different ways of holding the hose, different pressures, different kinds of guidework.

Often at the end of a day of shooting concrete, I would be covered in sand, and concrete, from head to foot — especially your hair gets caked with it . . . and nothing in the world could make me happier.

I have a small workshop which opens directly from my living room, where I make furniture. I am never happier than when I am making something in this workshop — a tray or a small table . . . and I do many experiments there, too. I fire my own tiles, in a small kiln, make stamps for stamping and forming concrete, try the shapes of new elements of some building or another.

I mention all this, for two reasons. First, because I am quite convinced in my own mind, that the endless stream of theories which I have been making up, and all my efforts to find theories which do give us accurate pictures of what is going on when a building "smiles" . . . that all of these would have been quite impossible, if they had been developed from some purely theoretical point of view.

It is the love of making, and the instinct for making, which has led me in the right direction. Even though I have rarely written about this instinct, or this love of mine, in the books which have been published . . . still it is this instinct, and this love, which have really given the theories the shape and power they have.

I do not believe that someone more remote from the act of making, could identify what is going on in a made thing, with sufficient accuracy, to get anywhere near the truth.

So this is the first reason. The second reason has to do with the things which you were discussing in the last chapter: the subject of fear. And this I believe is a more universal, and wider reason for touching on this subject.

The fear which people experience, in the process of design . . . especially the fear of being vulnerable, the fear of making something which truly does have "it", because it communicates with a deeper level of the human person . . . I do not believe that this fear can ever be overcome, except within the context of a workshop, or the context of physically making things.

After all, there is something inherently false, about pretending to make buildings, while sitting at a drawing board. Part of the fear which people feel, when they are engaged in this activity . . . comes from the very natural sense of falseness which they must experience. Inevitably, when someone sits at a drawing board, and pretends to make a building, he must be full of a hundred fears, about the things which he pretends to know, but somehow studiously avoids. After all, a building is a huge thing . . . quite a rough thing . . . and the physical reality of backhoes, drilling rigs, the physical weight of a 30 foot 8 × 12, the enormous weight of 70 yards of concrete when it is poured, and the fearsome way in which that huge volume of material can get out of hand . . . the subtle difference between a piece of wood which is sanded, and one which is planed, the right way to drive a nail, the effect of putting a piece of glass into a window in one way or another, the enormous variety of color, and the almost amazing mess which can be created by a few gallons of paint, which are not perfectly right . . . all these things are remote from the drawing board, cannot be gauged or felt, by someone who has not experienced them.

Is it not natural, and right, even, for someone to feel afraid, if he pretends, claims, to have the authority to put up a building when he has no first-hand touching experience with these things, and yet somehow wants to pretend to lord it over them.

Of course, this person knows himself secretly to be something of a cheat — even a charlatan . . . and probably, is fearing, that one day someone is going to expose his deception . . . so like anyone, with a big secret hidden away, who goes in daily fear of being discovered . . . the person who pretends to be an architect, but knows nothing of these things, has his natural fear, increased enormously, by his deception, and by his own remoteness from the physical act of making.

And, really, the same even goes for the people who write about building, or who try to coin philosophy, or style, or design "aesthetic". It is impossible that any of this can be accurate . . . unless it is rooted in the everyday experience of making things . . . and unless, also, it is rooted in the love of making things.

Whether it is painting color tiles, or sawing pine planks, or handling wet concrete, Alexander feels more complete and alive as a person when he is engaged in that kind of activity than he does sitting in an office all day. And the reason is that when all the theory is said and done, it is the actual act of making things that puts one directly in touch with space, not the theory. And when all the fears of doing that have been stripped away, then one is free to create anything which has the quality of timelessness in it.

For Alexander, the ongoing activity of making things is a constant reminder of that basic fact and serves to ground him in the reality of his work. In the absence of the complete formulation of a new paradigm, this would prove to be a necessity. For as Kuhn points out, during the period when new theories are proliferated, the rules of normal practice become increasingly blurred and the foundations of the field seem to disappear. In the absence of a solid footing, one can easily lose one's way.

REFERENCE NOTE

The Collage which follows page 237 is particularly relevant to this chapter.

IX

EXPANSION AND
EXPERIMENTATION

In Kuhn's analysis, the work that is undertaken to articulate a paradigm theory consists primarily of resolving the ambiguities in its formulation and attempting the solutions of problems to which the theory had only previously drawn attention. For Alexander, this effort focused on the completion of the pattern language; namely, the expansion of the collection of patterns and the description of the generative structure which binds them together.

Patterns could now be seen as structural descriptions of situations in the environment that tend to embody the quality of timelessness — like window seats, alcoves, arcades, sunny courtyards, entry transitions, building clusters, street cafes, or promenades — and the generative structure binding them together is somehow the same as the cognitive structure in the brain which permits one to perceive this quality and out of which other structures are built (since they are the result of the pattern languages which the people who built them had in their heads). At the time, Alexander's understanding of this congruence was fairly strong. He had already conducted several related experiments in cognition at Harvard; and his own ability to perceive this quality was quite developed. But still, the actual structural properties of this quality in space were far from understood (and would not be for about another six years).

The only way to crack the problem was by trial and error. So, an intense period of experimentation set in at the Center for several years immediately following the completion of the Multiservice Center Project and the Peru Housing Competition. This

93

experimental work was supported, in large measure, by the National Institute for Mental Health:

They were very interested from a mental health point of view because this was one of the few pieces of work they had come across that represented the possibility of a serious connection between the problems of human emotion and the psyche on one hand and the built environment on the other. So it was very important to them. They saw us through about five years which gave us the opportunity to complete the pattern language. There is no question that without that help we would never have been able to do it because the sustained energy that it took to do that work was ferocious.

At the time that the Multiservice Center and Housing projects were over (as described in chapter four), the way in which the patterns were then combined took the form of a "cascade" representing sequential combinations of progressively smaller configurations. It may be recalled that such a structure was not yet generative; and that this weakness became apparent to Alexander because in each of the projects the gap had been bridged intuitively — by the traditional methods of design:

In spite of the fact that we were already working our way down the cascade of patterns in a sequential order — which is not that different from the way the final language actually works — there was the sense that we were groping our way toward something that we intuitively knew how to do but was not a transferable activity. You needed to be an architect in order to make use of that material.

What I mean by that is that you had to bring a whole lot of other stuff in to make it work, to make it into a building. And of course that meant that the structure was in no sense generative. It was just information that was basically helping some other process. And furthermore, that other stuff that was being brought in was rather ugly — monstrous and ridiculous assemblages, full of ego and fantastic images of giant concrete walls flying off in all directions. "Images" and "concepts" are words architects use quite often. But the fact is that most of the really ugly buildings in the environment are what you might call concept-ridden. It might be a pyramid, or an upside-down pyramid, or a needle lying on its side, or a spiral. But basically it is some fantastically idiotic shape that everything has got to be crammed into.

I won't say that this is one hundred percent wrong. I would say it is about ninety percent wrong. In other words, there is a ten percent residue of good sense there which means, of course, that you need to have some global awareness of how the thing has got to be laid out before you start attempting to go into detail. And that of course the pattern language had to deal with. First of all there was the problem of getting people to be willing to let go of that function, so to speak, and to let that come to them rather than having them impose it on the matter. But from our side there was also a problem because we had not given enough attention to the need for this sort of global formation. There was still a certain mystery to the way the larger structure emerges. There was not yet enough generative material to actually give one the larger structure in a comfortable way. There were crucial patterns missing — like positive and negative outdoor space — and one felt as if one was skating on thin ice. It was not yet a nice, solid, comfortable process.

The true test of the generativity of the structure of the language would be in getting lay people to use it. They would of course not be bringing to the situation the same "conceptual" resources that a trained architect might bring. But in the initial experiments with lay people they tended to produce very sketchy, rambling designs which did have certain holistic properties but which were not yet clearly formed buildings or "proto-buildings" as Alexander calls them. The crucial experiment came when a set of twenty-four patterns were written to describe the generation of a Japanese Teahouse. Although the teahouse is an extremely simple building, it took quite a bit of time to give the sequence of the basic patterns a structure in such a way that when they were presented to someone that person would then form a complete image of a teahouse in their mind:

At one time I had a graduate student in computer science who was working on the mathematical problem of the teahouse after it was clear that the sequence of twenty-four patterns worked. The question was what was so great about that sequence. You could tell intuitively that it was great; but if one had made a cascade of the type we were studying earlier, what would have been the mathematical properties that got from that cascade to the correct sequence? That was a fairly difficult research problem and we worked on it for about six months before we solved it.

At that time Alexander had a teletype hookup to one of the largest computers on the Berkeley campus installed in the Center's office:

We put all the patterns that we had available to us at that point into the computer, connected them all up in cascade form, and wrote a whole series of programs attempting to extract sequences that actually followed the mathematical logic of what we believed a correct sequence to be. At that point there were still faint inklings that we would actually be able to offer this service. The way I ran the programs was based on the idea that a person would approach the teletype and punch in something like "house" and perhaps some other patterns and immediately get a language that was based on all those patterns, in the correct order, that would then be able to generate a building. Well, needless to say, we finally gave up all of that foolishness because it seemed too cumbersome and not very much to the point. And finally we discovered that, actually, it was possible to lay the patterns out in the form of a book that possessed the correct sequence in the sense that you could skip through the book and you would essentially be using them in approximately the right order.

Then, shortly after that, an extensive series of experiments were run with lay people to have them design their own houses:

We ran those experiments for more than a year — giving them the language, having them do the designs, and then we would look at what they had done and see how satisfactory it was to us. We would look at what they did, the houses that they had designed, and then we would say, "Well, if that is what people are doing with the language in its present form, then we need to change it in such and such a way." We spent certainly at least a year of solid work on experiments about just the format of the patterns themselves.

Let us say that there would be a particular format for the patterns. There was then the question of what is the best way to present them? And somebody would be working on nothing but that with lay persons. Even these sorts of matters, which normally might not be made the objects of experiments, were excruciatingly investigated. I just would not ever accept any particular format unless we had come to it on the basis of a series of experiments which showed us that that particular one was able to put the thing in a person's mind.

For instance, one of the crucial variables was, "Did the person feel it was theirs when they got through? In other words, we discovered that people had different attitudes to patterns, and sometimes you could present a pattern to someone and even if they agreed with it they would somehow feel that it was not coming from them. But there was another way in which you could present a pattern to someone and when they got through with it they would somehow connect it up with something they already knew. Basically they would walk away from it by saying that it was theirs; which of course is true. But that was a pretty crucial distinction. There were actually two

96

46

47

48

49

46. Pattern 180: Window Place.
47. Pattern 115: Courtyards Which Live.
48. Pattern 88: Street Cafe.
49. Matsushita-an Tea House, Kyoto.

PLATE XXI

50

51

50. Oscar Niemeyer, Project for an Art Museum, Caracas.

51. Oscar Niemeyer, National Assembly Building, Brasilia.

" . . . ridiculous assemblages, full of ego and fantastic images of giant concrete walls flying off in all directions."

PLATE XXII

people working on that facet for eighteen months, as well as Max Jacobson's study of the effects of the sequence in the way houses were laid out.

Then there was the whole question of the overall structure of the language if it was presented as a book. Even when we discovered that these sequences worked in certain ways, we thought at first that we would present the book more or less in alphabetical order, like a "treasure hunt." At the bottom of each page there would be instructions as to which patterns came next and according to where you were you would know which way to go. We tested that and it turned out to be quite cumbersome for people to work their way through. Finally, when it turned out that there was one sequence which, although it was not completely accurate, broadly represented the sort of structural sequences that typically came out of the individual sublanguages, we used that. But at the same time we were conducting an immense number of experiments on the patterns themselves.

These experiments ranged from real experiments — like going out and counting noses, doing things, and setting up situations — to just obtaining data in the most fantastic ways you can imagine. How do you figure out how many people it takes to support a small grocery? It turns out that you can look in the Yellow Pages and see how many groceries there are and correlate it with the population they serve and since you would of course miss a few, you would have a very rough but safe measure of the magnitude of the number of people it takes to support one of them. All it takes is a little bit of thought and in five minutes you can get an answer. A tremendous amount of what we did was like that. We were constantly trying to invent ways of checking things out. There is much more empirical substance to the pattern language than is even presented in the sense that there was this constant activity of experiments, and anything that did not make it through these experiments was taken out of the book.

Almost all these experiments on the generativity of the pattern language were in the realm of simulation. In other words, they had to do only with representing the structure of the environment in the mind or on paper. Although the earlier projects had all involved buildings of some kind — transit stations, a community center, an educational research facility, and public housing — these latest experiments were confined strictly to the laboratory. It was now time to test the results on the site.

Of particular concern was the sequence of patterns — once their format was established — in building up a complete form. Recall that a pattern is a generic description of something; it is not the actual thing. The object itself, according to Alexander, is made up of a complex ensemble of overlapping and interacting relations between all its components. A "pattern" is simply a description of the invariant properties of those relations when the object is well adapted. For example, the pattern "staircase as a stage" describes the interacting relations between the stairs and the room they are in, the walls and windows near or adjacent to them, the balustrade or hand rail, and the treads and risers between them. "Flaring out the bottom of the stair with open windows or balustrades and with wide steps so that the people coming down the stair become part of the action in the room while they are on the stair" is simply a description of the relations between several of the components at the lower part of the staircase that help make it a "stage."[1] But there are actually many, many different staircases that have these same invariant properties. And the *particular* staircase that might result from using this pattern would depend on the particular versions of the larger patterns that surround it and the smaller patterns that are contained within it. Using any pattern therefore involves a great deal of choice in deciding which particular version to adopt in the actual "thing" — but it is dependent on both the decisions made earlier and the decisions made later. Since in any one building several hundred such decisions are involved, the question immediately arises: How can the process of using patterns be flexible enough to permit one to reshape decisions on the basis of past and future decisions?

Part of this flexibility was provided by the *sequential* structure of the language itself: "each pattern is connected to certain 'larger' patterns which come above it in the language; and to certain 'smaller' patterns which come below it in the language. The patterns help to complete those larger patterns which are 'above' it and is itself completed by those smaller patterns which are 'below' it.[2] This sequence provides that enormous changes which might cancel out earlier decisions will not have to be made. Instead, the changes will get smaller and smaller as more and more patterns are built into the design. But still, since the design is built up one pattern at a time, the process needs to be kept as *fluid* as possible:

> As you use the pattern, one after another, you will find that you keep needing to adjust your design to accommodate new patterns. It is important that you do this in a loose and relaxed way, without

getting the design more fixed than necessary, and without being afraid to make changes. The design can change as it needs to, so long as you maintain the essential relationships and characteristics which earlier patterns have prescribed. You will see that it is possible to keep these essentials constant, and still make minor changes in the design. As you include each new pattern, you readjust the total gestalt of your design, to bring it into line with the pattern you are working on.[3]

Now the question is: In generating an actual building, what is the best way to do this? A building with fifty patterns in it is already more highly differentiated than the average "modern" building; and one with a hundred patterns might involve several thousand possible variations during the course of its generation. The process is far too complex to go on solely in the mind, where the upper range for keeping variables in focus is about seven to nine.[4] Drawings help enormously, but they cannot record or keep track of the full range of changing perceptual experiences that are involved in the actual building up of such a highly differentiated structure. This was the problem which Alexander faced in moving from simulation to the real thing. And the solution was, that at a certain point in the design process, one begins to lay the building out on the site itself — using string, cardboard, and wooden stakes. The opportunity to try this was in the design of a mental health clinic in Modesto, California:

Dr. Ryan, who was the chief psychiatrist and director of the clinic, played the largest role. But at first sight this seemed to him an amusing parlor game, and not a very plausible one at that — namely, that we were going to lay out a building together. We took four or five days to do it and it actually worked. It was a fairly large building — 24,000 square feet — and everything worked out. Several years later, when the building was actually built and occupied, he told us that the experience of laying out the building was one of the most important events that had happened to him in five years.

As a result, the process of laying out a building, in concert with certain patterns of construction that are compatible with the rest of the patterns, became a part of the pattern language and its implementation. Eventually it would open up the whole problem of construction, but for the moment it put the recently conducted experiments in the generative structure of the language on a solid footing. Although Alexander was deeply dissatisfied with the actual building (for reasons that will become apparent later on), the process of completing the design on the actual building site was workable.

At the other extreme however was the problem of testing some of the larger scale patterns — patterns dealing with the design of towns and which could never be built all at once. What kind of process would generate the correct growth of town and country, the layout of roads and paths, the relationship between work and family, the formation of suitable public institutions for a neighbourhood, or the kinds of public spaces required to support these institutions? The last formal "experiment" before a pattern language was completed was the design of a master plan for the Eugene campus of the University of Oregon in 1971:

We knew we wanted to use the pattern language but we did not know it was possible to create a planning process for an entire community. We knew in principle it was possible; but to do it was quite another matter.

The point of reference was Cambridge University in England and, in particular, the way that the individual colleges lie between the main street of the town and the river:

> Each college is a system of residential courts, each college has its entrance on the street, and opens onto the river; each college has its own boathouse and its own walks along the river. But while each college repeats the same system, each one has its own unique character. The individual courts, entrances, bridges, boathouses, and walks are all different. The overall organization of all the colleges together and the individual characteristics of each college is perhaps the most wonderful thing about Cambridge. It is a perfect example of organic order. At each level there is a perfect balance and harmony of the parts.[5]

This "organic order" is of course another description for "the quality without a name"; only here it is explained as a balance between the parts and the whole. And the question is: How did this order come about in the absence of a master plan?

> Somehow, the combination of tacit, culture-defined agreements, and traditional approaches to well-known problems, insured that even when people were working separately, they were still working together, sharing the same principles. As a result, no matter how unique and individual the pieces were, there was always underlying order in the whole.[6]

For Alexander, an explicit pattern language can play the same role that those shared traditions played in the past — it provides a unified morphological approach to making sure that individual building projects work together to create a whole. The idea is that only when the language is *shared* can everyone who enters into the making of the thing work toward a holistic vision of what it is going to be. Architectural experience confirms that, even within conventional practice, literally dozens of people are involved in making decisions that effect the actual shape and appearance of the final product. Most of the time one is attempting to explain to these people what the building is supposed to look like in order to get them to cooperate on the various phases of execution; but it is rare that a confluence of vision occurs. More typically, the building is only understood, as a whole, by one or two individuals. The others influence its evolution without really participating in the vision, or else they oppose it with conflicting versions. They are less likely, therefore, to contribute the same degree of care or concern for the outcome as would a craftsman who took pride in work he felt was his own. The same principle operates along a continuum of participation, from clients, bankers, and public officials to laborers firing bricks in a kiln or mixing mortar on the building site.

At a deeper level however, the sharing of a language is a prerequisite for its own articulation, development, and refinement. In Kuhn's model, unless consensus is reached on paradigms, the field cannot mature. Translated into architectural practice, as long as each act of design and building remains personal, private, and idiosyncratic, there will be little opportunity to profit from past mistakes, and the field as a whole will come to rest at the lowest common denominator of achievement. As Ruskin put it, "the architecture of a nation is great only when it is as universal and as established as its language; and when provincial differences of style are nothing more than so many dialects."[7]

The problem at Oregon consisted of developing a language within which the various members of a community of twenty thousand people could articulate their desires — and differences — in *spatial* terms. The adoption of a pattern language, therefore, was proposed as both a solution to the problem and an alternative to the conventional master plan. It was to be administered, on behalf of the community, by a single planning board composed of users, administrators, and a planning director. The users however, were to play more than a representative role.

They would not only initiate projects, but *participate* in their execution as well. User-design teams — based on the Modesto experience — would work with architects and contractors who would then implement the designs in coordination with the planning board:

> There are essentially two reasons. First, participation is inherently good; it brings people together, involves them in their world; it creates a feeling between people and the world around them, because it is the world which *they* have helped to make. Secondly, the daily users of buildings know more about their needs than anyone else; so the process of participation tends to create places which are better adapted to human functions than those created by a centrally administered planning process.[8]

Organic order, and user participation were the first two principles of the plan. The third principle was that construction undertaken in each budgetary period would be weighed towards small projects. The purpose of this principle was to stimulate *piecemeal growth* rather than large lump development, the reason being that well-adapted environments tend to have been generated that way:

> Any living system must repair itself constantly in order to maintain its balance and coordination, its quality as a whole. In the case of an organism, it is only the constant repair, the adjustment of chemical fields, the replacement of cells, and the healing of damaged tissues, which maintain the basic morphology of the organism.
>
> In the case of the environment, the process of growth and repair that is required to maintain morphological integration is far more complex. Repair not only has to conserve a pre-ordained order, as it does in an organism, but must also adapt continuously to changing uses and activities, at every level of scale. For environments, therefore, an organic process of growth and repair must create a gradual sequence of changes, and these changes must be distributed evenly across every level of scale. There must be as much attention to the repair of details — rooms, wings of buildings, windows, paths — as to the creation of brand new buildings.
>
> All the good environments that we know have this in common. They are whole and alive because they have grown slowly over long periods of time, piece by piece. The pieces are small — and there are always a balanced number of projects going forward at every scale. If one large building is being built, there are, simultaneously, many repairs and changes going forward at smaller scales all around the building; and each new building is not a "finished" thing, but brings in its train a long series of smaller repair projects. In such a way

102

buildings adapt to changing users and changing needs. They are never torn down, never erased; instead they are always embellished, modified, reduced, enlarged, improved. This attitude to the repair of the environment has been commonplace for thousands of years in traditional cultures. We may summarize the point of view behind this attitude by one phrase: *piecemeal growth*.[9]

Piecemeal growth is based on the idea of repair rather than replacement; it maintains those places which are working and have adaptive character rather than obliterating the past; it conserves resources rather than consumes. In Oregon, this was stimulated by an emphasis on small project funding and an annual repair budget for every building.

The fourth principle provided for the adoption and maintenance of *patterns* by a planning staff. The staff would modify the pattern language to meet local needs and formally adopt those patterns which have global impact on the community. The collection of formally adopted patterns would then be reviewed annually, at which time any member of the community could introduce new patterns, or revisions of old patterns, as long as it was on the basis of "explicitly stated observations and experiments."[10] At Oregon, thirty-seven patterns which had already been collected by the Center prior to the project, plus eighteen especially developed for the University, were adopted formally by the community. The rest were developed by users according to individual projects.

The fifth principle was the implementation of an annual *diagnosis* to insure that each project contributed to the larger whole, not by blueprint but by constantly monitoring its own internal state — as in a well-adapted organism, which is guided by the interactions of its own "growth fields" with the genetic code:

> The organism, from the very beginnings of its life, is constantly monitoring its own internal state. In particular, those parts of the organism where critical variables have gone beyond their allowable limits are identified. We may call this the diagnosis. In response to the diagnosis, the organism sets in motion growth processes to repair this situation. It is fairly certain that the broad framework of this growth is governed by the endocrine system, which creates a variety of chemical fields throughout the organism. These fields are created by changing concentrations of various hormones; and together these fields guide detailed growth, at the cellular level. These are the *growth fields*.
>
> The growth fields act chemically to encourage growth in certain

parts of the organism and to inhibit growth in others. At those places where growth occurs, the cells multiply. The detailed configuration of the cells which grow at these places is governed mainly by the genetic code, carried by every cell. This controls the exact development of the cells, and the arrangement of their growth, splitting, change and decay. In fine detail, this process is controlled by the interaction of the genetic code with the chemistry of the growth fields in which the cells are growing. This guarantees that local configurations of cells are not only intrinsically suitable but are also properly integrated with the whole.

We see, then, that global order within the organism is governed at two levels. First, the growth fields create the context for growth, and determine the location where growth shall occur. Then the genetic code carried by the cells controls the local configurations which grow at those locations, modified always by interaction with the growth fields themselves.

This process not only repairs the mature organism, when it is damaged, or diseased; it is also responsible for guiding the embryo during its earliest growth. It is thus responsible for shaping the mature organism, not only for repairing and maintaining it when it is finally complete. In short, the original global form of the organism comes from the very same process of diagnosis and repair which keeps it stable once it is mature.[11]

By means of a very similar process, a simple diagnostic mapping technique was developed to record places in the environment where patterns exist, where they nearly exist but where some repair is required, where they barely exist but are virtually unusable, and where they do not exist at all. The resulting maps defined a sort of "growth field" for each of the patterns, and the composite map for all the patterns could guide the growth and repair of the whole community. Like the patterns themselves, the map would be formally adopted by the planning board after discussion and revision in a series of public hearings.

The sixth principle was the *coordination* of the funding process by which projects were approved for construction through the planning board in conformance with the adopted patterns and diagnosis. In all, the six principles constituted an extraordinary document. They represented the direct translation of an objectively defined aesthetic phenomenon into precise, operational consequences — consequences often directly at odds with the existing paradigm, like the funding of small projects over large lump development. And yet, six years after its introduction, the

52

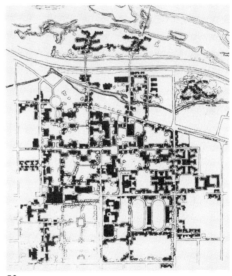

53

52. Existing Campus (1971), University of Oregon.
53. Proposed Growth during the 1990's, University of Oregon.

" . . . an organic process of growth and repair must create a gradual sequence of changes, and these changes must be distributed evenly across every level of scale."

PLATE XXIII

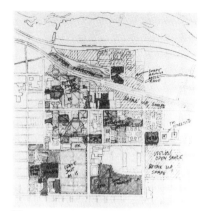

54

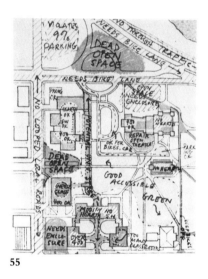

55

54. Example of Open Space Diagnosis, University of Oregon.

55. Detail of Open Space Diagnosis, University of Oregon.

A diagnostic mapping technique to record places where patterns exist, where they nearly exist but where some repair is required, where they barely exist but are virtually unusable, and where they do not exist at all.

PLATE XXIV

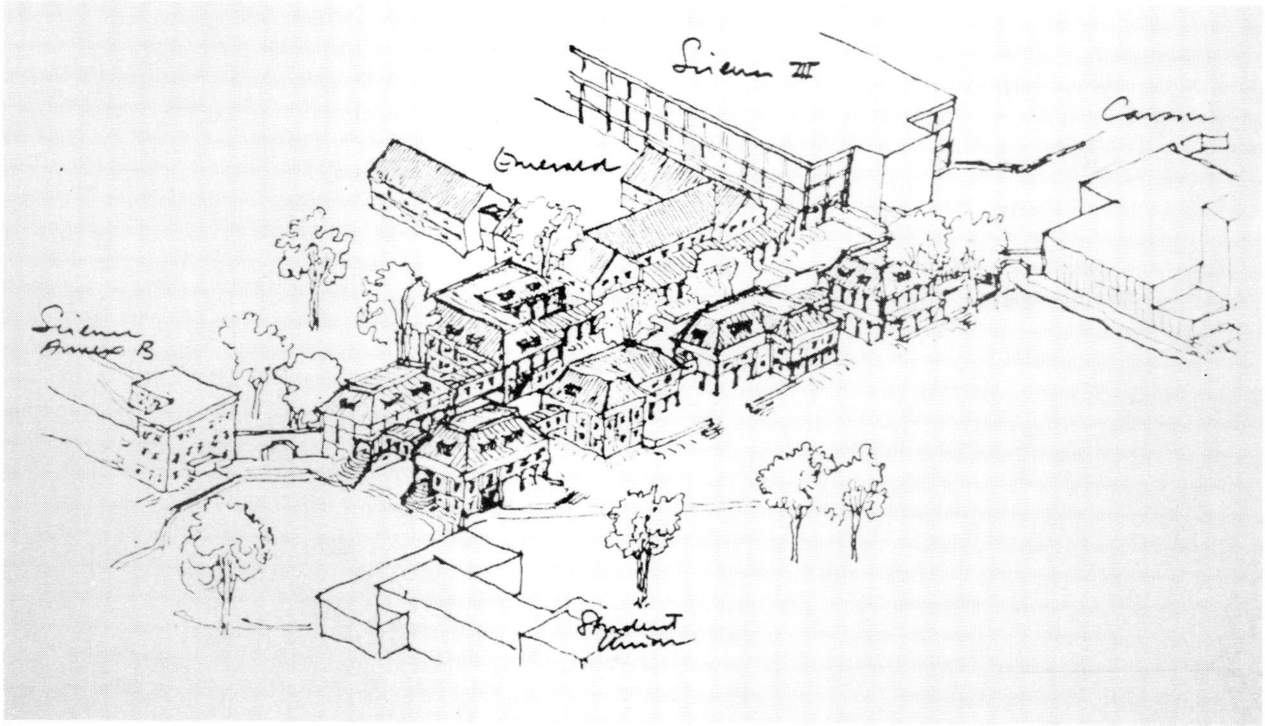

Example of Project Coordination Sheet, University of Oregon.

PLATE XXV

56

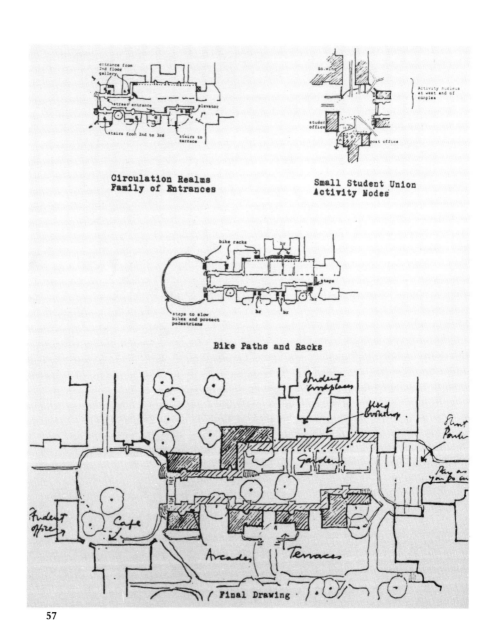

57. Detail of Project Coordination Sheet, University of Oregon.

PLATE XXVI

"experiment" was still in operation. In fact, in a post-evaluation study conducted in 1977, the success of the pattern language as a mechanism for user participation was cited as providing the University of Oregon with "the groundwork for a new 'tradition' in building."[12]

For Alexander, that was all that had really been achieved — the groundwork. Although some important questions were opened up — mainly in the realm of politics — the end of a long period of intense experimentation was coming to a close. It would soon be possible to see just how much more deeply he would have to go into the consequences of his discoveries before the real problem would be solved. In the meantime, there was the need to pull all of this work together before a progress report could be made. In addition to THE OREGON EXPERIMENT there was THE TIMELESS WAY OF BUILDING (which Alexander was writing by himself) and the completion of a A PATTERN LANGUAGE (which six people worked on together).

REFERENCE NOTES

1. A PATTERN LANGUAGE (New York: Oxford University Press, 1977), pp.637-640

2. IBID., p.xii

3. IBID., p.465

4. See George A. Miller, "The Magical Number Seven, Plus or Minus Two: Some Limits on our Capacity for Processing Information," PSYCHOLOGICAL REVIEW, 63 (1956), pp.81-97

5. THE OREGON EXPERIMENT (New York: Oxford University Press, 1975), pp.11-12

6. IBID., p.12

7. From "The Seven Lamps of Architecture," Chapter VII, in John Ruskin, THE LAMP OF BEAUTY, p.208

8. THE OREGON EXPERIMENT, p.40

9. IBID., pp.67-70

10. IBID., p.137

11. IBID., pp.148-150

12. Gilda Haas, "Public Money vs. Public Interest," unpublished M.A. thesis. Department of Urban Planning, University of California (Los Angeles: 1977), p.148

PART THREE

X

WORKING WITH OTHERS

The completion of THE TIMELESS WAY OF BUILDING and A PATTERN LANGUAGE occupied Alexander from the late 60's to about 1973. During this period, the Center for Environmental Structure consisted of a small group of people that varied between six and eight in number. At its core were Sara Ishikawa, Murray Silverstein, and Alexander. Others would usually be drawn in as an outgrowth of Alexander's classes at the University — which is how he usually made contact with potential colleagues. Under such conditions he would have the opportunity to work with someone for a few years before establishing a formal relationship, although during the early years the Center was a social world as much as it was an "office:"

Although we did not particularly spend any time together socially outside the group, there were always things going on that were social in character. We often went dancing, or to the movies, and every other day music was being played — usually by Denny Abrams or Ron Walkey. But perhaps the single most powerful and amazing thing about the Center, during the years from 1968 up until 1972 or 1973 was the fact that every day we had lunch together. And every day the lunch was cooked by another person, so that in the middle of the day there was about an hour of this communal meal which took on an incredible variety of forms and tastes. It was like a fantastic restaurant and each person whose turn it was tried to do their best.

When it came, one time, to discussing salaries, we had a two to three hour session in the garden where everybody said what they thought was a salary that made themselves comfortable. But they had to be totally honest about this comfort in both directions — that is, in terms of being too much or too little when compared with everybody else. It was almost like a family gathering; and that atmosphere was absolutely fundamental to the work, which was very intense.

The pattern language functioned during that period as the single force holding the group together. But since everyone was an architect, they all shared the immediate concern of making beautiful buildings. And in fact, everyone felt that what they were doing had reference to that larger task. But for Alexander, there were three different levels of understanding that task:

One level was to get the pattern language working so that the basic theory of it could be implemented. In other words, that people would use it to start making the environment for themselves and it would be alright. That was completely clear to everyone and there was no doubt everyone shared that. The second level, which was that these buildings could be really beautiful, was shared by everybody in the sense that if they were asked that question they would probably give you that answer. On the other hand, the extent to which that was, genuinely speaking, a deeply rooted and personal motive for each person varied considerably. But still, I would say there was a general awareness. Now the third level, the famous quality, I would say that was only dimly understood by most of the people. I would say that the only two people who understood it thoroughly at the time were Sara and Ingrid. I am not talking only about knowing that there was some such thing in the back of it all, but also in some sense being in contact with it and being able to be guided by it.

So the real unifying thing that held us together as a group was the desire to do the pattern language and the knowledge of the fairly enormous power this would have to do good once it was let loose and could work by itself. That seemed like an incredibly worthwhile goal.

It is obvious from Alexander's productivity throughout all of these years that he has relied considerably on group effort. The vast majority of the work is authored by several people and there are actually few projects undertaken by himself since NOTES. Aside from the fact that he is more comfortable hammering something out with someone else, there are the obvious benefits of collaboration:

There is no way that one person can be as strong as two or three who have the opportunity to thresh something out together. All of these people I have worked with are fascinating, brilliant people; and collectively we are just much stronger than if I had been alone. There is no question that the power of the work that came out of the Center in all of these years was completely governed by that.

But it is not only because different people have different strengths that makes it so fantastic. If you are dealing with material that is potentially true, if the subject matter is sufficiently objective, and you can constantly appeal to that objectivity, then it is viable. If one were attempting to work under circumstances that were not objective, you would just have a morass. Then you have to appeal either to authority or to democratic vote — neither of which is necessarily an appeal to truth. The real beauty of this group work has been that I have always been able to create circumstances where all of us were looking at the thing "out there" as the determinant of what is the right thing to do. If you can get into a framework where you can actually see that and focus on it strongly enough so that it is sort of telling you what to do, then the subjective element is removed. There is simply an appeal as to whether it is better one way or the other, whether in theory, practice, building processes, or patterns.

The power of the group, always, has been achieved because of the centrality and governing objectivity of the vision that all of us have been able to appeal to. And of course, since all of us, by our natures, have got various quirks of personality, subjectivity, and ignorance, which individually might make any one of us deviate from this thing that is true out there, they are able to correct one another's quirks, so to speak — so that work done by three or four people is just that much more likely to be more true than by one person simply because it has that much more quirkiness removed from it. But this sort of work hinges on the fact that there is a shared understanding and interpretation of what is going on.

This is not something that simply happens of itself. I have come to appreciate that I play a substantial role in making it happen. Obviously from what I have said, it is a steersman's position. There is no question of the real interaction that goes on in the group; but in order to set up the conditions for that, if one person is insisting on the questions, that is one of the major roles that helps these groups to function. In addition, I remember feeling at one time, that I had actually succeeded in welding two or three separate intelligences together into one mind, so to speak. It may sound a bit peculiar, but there was a tremendous unity of purpose and thought that was achieved several times, and it was just that much more powerful by having several intelligent people working together and always scrutinising what was happening. I think it is true that in some of the group work there has been a real loss of personal identity; but that is part of the reason why the work has been so good.

The question of the role played by Alexander, and the question of the loss of personal identity on the part of the members of the group, inevitably led to its dissolution in 1973. But from the standpoint of a research effort, this was a long time to maintain a fairly constant level of intellectual intensity on a single problem. From the standpoint of scientific investigation, it is also a measure of what Polanyi calls "the committment to transcend personal obligations to universal standards." But for Alexander it is simply a matter of stubborn persistence and single-mindedness:

I am continually occupied with only one question and refuse to let it go until it has been answered. To others I may appear as a maniac because I will hold onto a question for three or four weeks, four hours at a time, three sessions a week until it has been answered. To me this is a very natural thing to do. I feel comfortable with it. But the curious thing is that this is not something I can do by myself. In other words, its one thing to keep one's eye fixed on the target, and I do that a reasonable amount by myself. But the results we get come from the fact that I insist on keeping other people's eyes on the target as well. Now this involves an incredible amount of human energy which is very heavy for me and may appear totalitarian to others. But I refuse to allow deviation from the question. And it is because of putting myself and these people collectively through the ringer that we actually come up with the answer.

This is a characteristic of mine over and over again. The first seminar I ever gave on the pattern language (1966) had the same character. In that seminar we met four hours a day, five days a week, all year. It was practically like working full time — the same group of twelve or thirteen people every day. In the middle of this, people began to go slowly nuts. It was actually more than they could take. There began to be all sorts of personal problems, some obviously attached to the seminar, some having to do with me and my relationship to one or another of them. But yet the crux of it was this particular sort of single-mindedness. And by keeping everyone moving together on the same target I find that the most powerful thrust comes from that kind of situation.

I can remember times at the Center when we were working on the structure of the pattern language and we would arrive at a point where we felt comfortable and I would go home and think about it and become convinced, for example, that there was some fundamental flaw. So I would come in on Monday and say, "Listen. There is the following problem and we have got to start again." And of course there would be fantastic resistance to moving back to square one. They would inevitably feel that I am being a

112

damn nuisance and a sort of neurotic perfectionist. And so I would say, "Listen. Isn't such and such a problem? Isn't it true that there are the following peculiar contradictions, way, way under the surface?" So we would start to go into it, and then I would say, "Well then, isn't it true that we need to revise this concept in the light of all that for it to make sense?" And so finally we would all come around. But if you are working alone, that isn't necessary. So this has been a characteristic of mine throughout all of this work.

For Alexander, this kind of intellectual "stubbornness" is necessary if one is attempting to find answers to questions that have never before really been formulated:

Its very easy to give up and go on to something else. The stubbornness actually consists of knowing that an answer can be found, that its there waiting to be discovered. The weakness of heart lies in thinking that such a thing cannot be discovered. I don't even know why, for example, I was convinced that a process would be found which generates the geometric properties of this quality. At one point, in a seminar I gave on this topic in 1976, I said, "Lets try and write algorithms and find one that is capable of generating these properties." After a while it became clear that it would not work. An algorithm is a step-by-step procedure and somehow, in this particular problem, paying attention to the steps of the algorithm takes your mind so far off the quality that one is trying to create that you cannot create it. A fairly sensitive student would quickly appreciate that this is impossible and finds it intolerable that I insist we keep doing it for another couple of weeks; but I want to check out exactly what it is about the algorithm that doesn't work.

Of course one goes out on a limb when one says that such and such a process can actually be defined when it is not at all clear what that process really is. But if I had been making bad judgments about that I would long ago have been down and out. So it is not spurious or generic optimism; there is very serious judgment involved here. But most people are unaware of this dimension as an active component of doing this kind of work.

This is obviously what Polanyi means by "a confidence in one's ability to judge beyond the range of well formulated rules and a belief in the existence of an answer to one's questions before the answer is actually in sight"; but in Alexander's case this is considerably reinforced by working with other people. In terms of the intellectual benefits of group work — the intense hammering out of ideas — Murray Silverstein, Shlomo Angel, and Max

113

Jacobson played a large role in providing that kind of support. However, there is another kind of support which Alexander has received and which, for him, is both more significant and more subtle. It tends mainly to have come from women:

First of all, there is a certain way in which women's understanding of the environment has always seemed to me a little bit subtler, more delicate, and actually more to the point than the judgment of men. It is perhaps a bit gross to classify perception on sexual grounds, but in general terms it seems to me like that. Consequently, I have always gone out of my way to make sure that women are working with me and that there is a fairly equal balance of men and women in the groups that I have worked with. But that is still putting it in very pale terms.

When it comes down to the reality of the matter, I realize that several times in my life, the sort of emotional support that I needed in order to see one of these questions correctly came from a friend of mine or from someone I was working with who was a woman and who was able to put me into a position where I could have permission to be in touch with the correct answer. I am still talking about my own perception, but suppose that one has a certain matter, and suppose that in the world of men this matter would tend to be extinguished or eliminated. Take the question of where to put a seat in a garden. Suppose that there are some very subtle feelings associated with this. There is a certain tendency in the world of men that those feelings, although they may be felt, will tend to be ignored. But if I am working with a woman, who may feel the same feelings to start with but whose habit would be not to ignore them, then I will receive permission to continue feeling my own feelings about the matter; whereas if I was having the same discussion with a man, who would tend to give it more short shrift, I might more quickly lose touch with my own feelings. And I am not talking about rather obvious concrete matters like the example of the garden seat. Those are very important, and this kind of thing does happen a great deal with questions like that. But it also concerns slightly more complex and esoteric theoretical questions where the same issue might arise — where the real contact with feelings could not come about unless it was permitted to come about, and for it to be permitted to come about, there needs to be a woman's world at least as much as a man's world.

Certainly at this particular moment in history, environmental questions — whether they are practical or theoretical — tend to be decided by men. In that context, I think it is possible that the sort of matters that I am speaking about actually cannot thrive and therefore never really, in a sustained way, see the light of day. For me, this has had an immense immediate, and personal connection.

Ingrid is a very strong example. In talking to her over the years, there has never been any doubt that she was clearly operating in the emotional realm where all of this work leads. She might not have the strength of purpose to make a big song and dance about it, but as far as being oriented towards it and being rooted in it, that was absolutely clear. And I have been tremendously nourished by this. I am not talking about the kind of situation which you see in the beginning of books where someone says, "My dear wife made breakfast for me and I thank her from the bottom of my heart." I am not talking about that in the slightest. I am talking about something really basic and central, right in the interior of the work and which I do not believe I could have sustained my relationship to, or even recognized in the first place, if it had not been for the feelings felt by Ingrid, Sara, and other people that I was connected to and which I was therefore able to luxuriate in. This has just had a tremendous personal meaning for me.

Sara is a very experienced professional in the everyday sense. And of course, when we were dealing with matters where a sort of business-like attitude was required, she was very business-like. But whenever we began to enter a domain where there were some doubts about whether a particular idea was really adequate and where I had some faint misgivings, for example, the tendency would be that she also had these faint misgivings. And as we would begin to develop those misgivings, and the two of us would begin to talk back and forth, gradually these misgivings would flourish into a recognition that, indeed, we had been looking at the matter in the wrong way and that, really, it was this other way.

Inevitably this is a very personal matter because I think that a lot of everyday work that people engage in is not quite as close to the emotional domain as what I am talking about. So of course a very great depth of friendship was built up in these various cases. So although I am talking about it as something that has helped me very greatly from the point of view of an artist, or in terms of making a theory, it also just added a tremendous dimension, a tremendous fullness to my life which I could not conceivably have found in any other way.

Although personal, this particular dimension of Alexander's working relationships — the realm of sustained feeling — actually has a strong relationship to the work itself. Recall his discovery that the sense of being completely alive has a clear phenomenological counterpart in space — a particular quality in space that one can actually see as well as feel. The connection here is that Alexander's working relationships, particularly with women have sharpened both his own personal sense of "being alive" as well as his perception of its phenomenological counterpart in the environment:

Ingrid, for example, has a fantastic desire to sit in the sun. To some extent this is Norwegian. She comes from the far north and Norwegians love the sun, often at moments when someone else might not seek it. We might be having breakfast together and she will go to quite unusual lengths to take a deckchair and move it into the one patch of sun that is filtering into the garden. Or she will take a cushion and prop it up against a wall in the one place where, if we sit down there and have our coffee, we have actually got that little patch of sun coming down to us. And just from watching her going through the action of moving that chair, or that cushion, I have just been basking in this; and it is quite remarkable.

On the one hand this is the novelistic realm of human minutiae that the pattern language attempts to capture; but on the other hand it is the particular form of those details which happens to be very much in touch with what the central point of the work is actually about:

And it is quite certain that if it had not been for the tremendous amount I had been taught by various specific friends in that way, I do not think that I could have begun to see as deeply into the heart of it as I have been able to do. And to the extent that one might discuss masculine and feminine natures — which I am not particularly fond of doing — I think that a great deal of this requires the benefit of one's own feminine nature in order to come more fully in touch with it. But the personal version of it for me is that I think that without the love of certain particular people I could never have been stirred enough for this whole thing to come clearly into the center of my consciousness.

This bridging between the personal and the impersonal is characteristic of Alexander's working relationship with other people. But it also happens to be characteristic of the content of the work itself — namely the confluence of the elements of both art and science. According to Schopenhauer, the object of art is the particular that contains a universal; the object of science is the universal that contains many particulars.[1] Consequently, a work of art is successful in proportion as it suggests the universal of the group to which the represented object belongs. But in the case of paradigms, we are interested in the converse — namely, the extent to which a body of work can embrace all the particulars that constitute some universal . If the universal is some nameless quality, what kind of working attitude to the theoretical description of its actual consequences is capable of embracing all its manifestations?

According to Kuhn, this is as much a question of the shape and form of a theory as it is its actual content, especially in the early stages of paradigm debate.

REFERENCE NOTES

1. Cited in Will Durant, THE STORY OF PHILOSOPHY (New York: Simon and Schuster, 1961), p.254

F

XI

THE FORMULATION OF THEORY

The question of what is happening in a particular situation, and the attempt to describe it scientifically, are matters that relate to the *content* of a theory. But there are descriptions that are coherent, and simple, and deep — and which generate powerful results — and there are descriptions that are barely coherent, inelegantly formulated, and ultimately trivial. The difference has to do, in part, with the actual shape or form of the theory — its assessment in terms of aesthetic criteria as they are understood in science and its correspondence to some universal standard of applicability. In Kuhn's analysis, these are important signposts in the search for discoveries that eventually lead to paradigms. For Alexander, they actually play a large role in the formulation of the theory, quite apart from the question of content:

In mathematics and physics, the idea of aesthetic criteria is actually very concrete. It is not like it is in the arts where one does not really know at what level the term is meant. Its very clear, for example,, that a "nice" theory has a certain special coherence, particularly in mathematics where one is constantly making distinctions between a beautiful theorem, a trivial theorem, and a slogged-out theorem. There is also the question of how "deep" it is, which is not quite the same as whether it is nice. Its depth has to do with how much new mathematics is turned up as a result of this theorem — how large an area of the mathematical universe it exposes. In physics, there are similar questions, and as a working matter these criteria are absolutely basic. Everyone who is working in mathematics or physics is always appealing to them and they are constantly under discussion.

I think there is a sort of elegance about the theory of the pattern language which is similar to this everyday use of the word "nice" and "beautiful" in physics and mathematics. And that is just the way that it fits together as a theory. It is somewhat complete and it is very neat. In other words, you can

118

*have things that are complete in the sense of being an encyclopaedic catalog;
but in addition, it has to be simple. That creates a great sense of comfort,
because ultimately one wants everything to fit together in one place — so
you can understand it all.*

Elegant parts of the pattern language theory, for example, are
that patterns both describe the world and are elements of the
language at the same time that they are rules of the language; or, that
the hierarchy of human groups in a town can correspond with the
hierarchical structure of the patterns in the language. All of the ways
in which it is a "nice" theory, and the way it all fits together
compactly and beautifully, have to do with what is under discussion
in the "aesthetics" of mathematics and physics. For Alexander,
these concerns are absolutely fundamental:

*I use aesthetic criteria for the validity of a theory all the time. For
example, the theory of both "parts" and "patterns" — which we had at one
time — bothered me because the patterns had a clear logic to them and could
be accounted for; but the so-called parts were totally arbitrary. The idea at
the time was that you had these "parts" — like door, window, street,
etc. — and that the "patterns" were the relationships between them. But
the parts were totally arbitrary and came from nowhere. So until I had a
theory in which I could get rid of that awkwardness, I was not willing to
stand by it. And I use this sort of criterion all the time.*

*Let us suppose that there is an instinct about some kind of process, and we
are in a discussion, and somebody will say, "There doesn't seem to be one
process to do all of this. Perhaps we need one process to do x, y, and z, and a
second to do w and t." And I will respond by saying, "No. We don't want a
theory like that. It must be wrong because two processes for this are too ugly.
I instinctively feel that there must be one process here and we're going to
search until we find it." I use all this all the time, every day.*

This attitude toward scientific investigation obviously comes
from Alexander's training as a mathematician; but in what sense is it
related to his perception of these same qualities in buildings? In
other words, is the way in which a theory is "elegant," for example,
connected to the same sense of oneness, and simplicity, and life
which is essentially the *content* of most of his work?:

*I can see it to be the same human sense operating. You could say that one
kind of theory approaches the reality of these same qualities more closely
than another, and in that sense one could distinguish between different
theories. Its clear, for example, that some patterns approach that reality*

119

more closely than others; and I suppose that is true of entire sections of the theory as well. Probably one's sense of what is deep, and powerful and fundamental, and distinguishing that from more trivial theories, is the same sense that tells about buildings.

However, I do not really consider any theory to be fundamental. All of these theories are just like little crutches which attempt to project us into the actual reality; but they do not really have anything to do with the actual thing. The patterns, for example, are merely the shimmering outward forms in which one clothes one's understanding in order to penetrate to the actual reality. But the actual reality is wordless. I am not trying to be mysterious; it is just that any collection of words that someone uses to describe something is merely a description.

This detachment from theory itself may seem surprising, especially to those who have perceived Alexander to be essentially a "theorist" — a perception reinforced, perhaps, by his winning of the first medal for "research" ever awarded by the American Institute of Architects.[1] Since most people in the profession understand research to be an activity separate from design — and theory separate from practice — this is understandable, especially during a period of paradigm crisis. But Alexander has never really seen himself as a theorist in the sense that it is an activity separate from the actual experience of building. And it is the emphasis on the making of buildings that, ironically, permits him to make pogress with the theory — namely, the detachment necessary to reject inadequate formulations on the basis of "aesthetic" criteria. This combination is strikingly evident in the question of the coherence of a theory. For Alexander, it has to do with the making of "wholes":

It is normal working procedure for me to lay out a whole and look for what is missing purely according to the question of how coherent the whole looks. But I cannot know what is missing until I can see a whole. And it takes several cycles of that until something reasonable emerges. Making oneself vulnerable in throwing out incomplete wholes — presenting them to reality, and then accommodating them to reality — is the only way I know of to do a good job.

When I am working on a book, for example, the first thing I do is write a table of contents. By writing down chapter titles I get a sense of the whole. Then I rearrange or reshuffle them until I can see what is trying to emerge. And then I will write some chapters and look at it again. On a simple book — like THE PRODUCTION OF HOUSES — there might be thirty different versions. Some days I go through three or four in a single day. I look at the whole in all its unsatisfactoriness to guide me in its reconstruction. Its incredibly hard because of the fear that the whole will not be very good; and so the tendency is to put it off in the hope that it will emerge out of the individual parts. The assumption, often, is that if you can get a lot of material together the whole will emerge by itself. Consequently, the idea that you actually have to create the whole, and tear it up, and create it again, and tear it up — a hundred times — is not completely obvious. But I do that all the time. I assume that the various drafts of the whole will be bad. Its like a skeleton that keeps getting reconstructed as it is filled out with flesh.

The making of wholes is literally, for me, an everyday matter. I make up wholes and tear them up as fast as one can write down grocery lists. And I make them very vulnerable. I show them to people all the time. Brancusi once made an interesting remark about sculpture. He said he did not want to make a piece unless you could roll it down a hill without it breaking. I feel that way about a piece of writing. I am very, very rough on the things I write and I expose them to pretty violent assault on the assumption that when they are finally reshaped enough to withstand the assault they will be alright. But I do consider it to be difficult.

Eventually we will see how this idea of a skeleton getting restructured as it is filled out with flesh becomes a vital part of Alexander's conception of the building process; but the emphasis here is simply on the construction of theory. Of course he is aware that his approach to theory is unusual — but only in the sense that there is not really much contact between the people who have made up theories of architecture and the great tradition of theory-building which is commonplace in mathematics and physics. But the crux of the difference is not so much the question of a theory's elegance, simplicity, or coherence as it is its actual correspondence to reality:

The main characteristic of a real theory is that it actually illuminates the inner structure of a particular part of our experience in a significant way that ties it together for you. I think that most architectural theories, however, do not really do that.

Take Vitruvius, for instance — or Sir Henry Wooton: "Commodity, firmness, and delight" — or, in modern terms, comfort, structural soundness, and beauty. Well, in physics for example, if someone proposes a

121

division of the whole of a phenomenon into three categories, he must immediately ask, "Why this particular slicing of the cake? What significance do these three categories really have?" Is there something about the phenomenon itself which splits naturally into three parts. When you ask this question, you realise that there is not, and that "firmness/commodity/ delight" is a completely arbitrary way to cut up the cake of architecture. And so you know it is a very shallow theory. The difference between arbitrary constructions like this one, and constructions which are rooted in the reality of the phenomenon is fundamental. Its subtle but difficult. If you cannot tell the difference between a theory that is essentially related to reality and one that is just a bundle of words, by checking the structure of the theory against the structure of reality, and sort of constantly rehammering the theory, and cutting it and changing it, and going back and forth until the thing actually begins to have some reasonable capacity to mirror the reality, then you cannot make any headway.

When you are doing mathematics or physics you learn this sort of thing by osmosis, although it is never explicitly laid out. The "theory of theories" almost exclusively deals with what you might call the empirical side. In other words, the focus there is on the correspondence to experiments. But what I am talking about is much more basic, and unless you can get it right the empirical side is just nonsense. But its never really taught. You just gradually pick up the idea that you can assess a theory in terms of whether its structure roughly corresponds to the kind of structure reality might reasonably have. And you learn ways to go back and forth in order to extricate anything in the theory that could not possibly correspond to anything in reality and which therefore must be wrong.

Part of this comes from Alexander's training as a scientist and a mathematician. But it goes further than that. There has actually been a conscious effort on his part to continually test the evolution of his own theories up against the conceptual foundations of physics and cosmology — that is, theories about the way the universe behaves:

Although relatively little of my work connects up in any direct way to what is now considered to be part of physics and cosmology, there is a sort of question that I keep asking myself, which is whether all of this makes sense, fits together nicely enough, and fits together in the same general terms as the kind of things that people have said and thought about the very basic structure of the universe.

Consider patterns as an example. In chapter five of THE TIMELESS

WAY OF BUILDING I finally make the assertion that, insofar as there is a real discovery her, the discovery is that the basic elements out of which things are made are patterns. *That statement is a good example of what I am talking about here because it could equally well be made in physics, and conceivably in biology. And interestingly enough, it's the kind of statement that one would find on the frontiers of those fields where one is struggling to understand the universe correctly. In other words, the statement that it is all made of shifting patterns — quite apart from the truth or falsity of that statement — is completely consistent with the kind of thinking which both is emerging and is trying to emerge in physics. And so one could ask, "Is it deep enough to provide a reasonable conception of how everything is put together?"*

Alexander is certainly not claiming that he is doing physics. But what he is saying is that the tone of the work, the level at which the statements are made, and the way that they fit together, is consistent with the deepest and most interesting things that are being said or done in physics. And the reason is that when a physicist or a cosmologist thinks about things, he is conscious of the fact that what he is saying *has to apply to everything.* That is the crucial distinction for Alexander:

Suppose, for example, that an architect makes the statement that buildings have to be made of modular units. This statement is already useless to me because I know that quite a few things are not *made of modular units, namely people, trees, and stars, and so therefore the statement is completely uninteresting — aside from the tremendous inadequacies revealed by a critical analysis on its own terms. But even before you get to those inadequacies, my hackles are already up because this statement cannot possibly apply to everything there is in the universe and therefore we are in the wrong ballgame. And this kind of thinking is also the first level of intuitive check against anything I myself come up with as a possible account of what is going on. I immediately ask myself whether this is the kind of thing that could be true of everything. And that is what is so peculiar about physics and cosmology. Those two fields, above all the other sciences, are conscious that what they are dealing with is* everything. *And it requires a different attitude from what is common among architects. In other words, I actually do not accept buildings as a special class of things unto themselves, although of course I do take them very seriously as a special species of forms. But behind that is my desire to see them belong with people, trees, and stars as part of the universe.*

123

To understand how this attitude is a vital part of Alexander's work, consider several of the basic concepts already discussed. In addition to patterns, there is the question of generative processes, the question of differentation, the question of the possibility that there is an underlying geometry to space which has peculiar and special properties, and the question of uniqueness within similarities. In each of these conceptions, if just one of them were shifted slightly out of the context of architecture, it would immediately become much more general and profound. It is not just peculiar to buildings but is something that one could be concerned with on a general level and possibly begin to figure out the dynamics of how it fit together:

For each of these conceptions, you could imagine that one could say, "This is something important about the universe or the world that is not just peculiar to buildings." In that sense, the way in which I have always tried to deal with these matters shares something with the way physicists and cosmologists think. Because somehow, the mystery of the universe — which is being described in a very amazing way in those fields — is basically at the heart of my own inquiry. And so therefore, unless I do justice to it on an approximately equal level, or on a sort of similar footing, I am not going to be telling it right. It becomes a criterion for me as to whether I am actually making sense or not. I suppose I had the feeling or belief, from the very beginning, that if one was going to say something about what was a beautiful building, it better be serious enough that it could actually take its place along with physics and cosmology and not merely be some sort of half-baked theory that just applied to buildings. In other words, if it was going to be true, it better be serious.

But why should it be necessary for Alexander to seek correspondence between a theory of architecture and the standards of applicability of something as remote from the practice of building as physics and cosmology? Is it just his training as a scientist or has he drifted so far from the existing paradigm that the normal rules of practice no longer have any relevance? In Kuhn's analysis, such behaviour is typical of paradigm crisis. He cites Einstein who, during the period prior to his formulation of relativity, believed that there was "no firm foundation to be seen anywhere, upon which one could have built"[2]. And yet the breakdown of a paradigm and the blurring of its rules for normal research are themselves often sufficient to induce in someone a new way of looking at the field. Sometimes, in periods of acknowledged crisis, even the appeal of philosophical analysis is sufficient to weaken the grip of tradition upon the mind and to suggest the basis for a new one. For Alexander, physics and cosmology serve this purpose. Their appeal not only provides "a first level of intuitive check" against anything he himself might come up with, but they also serve as a means to expose the old paradigm in ways that isolate the root of crisis with a clarity unattainable in the laboratory. The deployment of such "extraordinary" procedures, as Kuhn calls them, is typical of the response to crisis and often proliferates new discoveries. In addition, they actually foreshadow the shape of the new paradigm. The resulting transition, therefore, is less likely to appear as a cumulative development; rather, it will take on the character of a complete reorganization of one's mental field. And this is part of the reason why the transition from one paradigm to another is such a highly charged event, often accompanied by prolonged debate. For if it is successful, the profession will have changed its entire view of the field, and consequently, most of its methods and its goals.

REFERENCE NOTES

1. See Don Conway, "Knowledge and Intuition in Combination," JOURNAL OF THE AMERICAN INSTITUTE OF ARCHITECTS (August, 1972), p.12

2. Thomas Kuhn, THE STRUCTURE OF SCIENTIFIC REVOLUTIONS, 2nd ed. (Chicago: University of Chicago Press, 1970), p.83; cf. P. A. Schlipp (ed.), ALBERT EINSTEIN: PHILOSOPHER-SCIENTIST (Evanston: University of Illinois Press, 1949), p.45

XII

HIATUS

The facts embodied in THE TIMELESS WAY OF BUILDING, A PATTERN LANGUAGE, and THE OREGON EXPERIMENT — that the actual substance of the environment consists of patterns, not things; that it is generated by language-like systems called pattern languages; that its successful adaptation requires an enormous number of minute local adaptations; and that, properly constituted, it has an objectively definable morphology — do not actually constitute a new paradigm in the sense of providing a new basis for professional practice. Although they change some of the field's most elementary theoretical generalizations — and thereby its paradigm rules — they do not really describe the full range of practical consequences necessary to solve the original, crisis-provoking problem.

For Alexander, this problem was that modern buildings are simply not beautiful and that even by pushing the existing rules to their limit, it is not possible to create a building as beautiful as those that have been built in the past. Consequently, it was necessary to discover new rules — which he has done. Now the question is, are these rules sufficient to solve the problem? Is it possible, working solely with these rules, to build a beautiful building? And the answer in the early 70's, unfortunately, was "no." As Alexander put it:

All the architects and planners in christendom, together with THE TIMELESS WAY OF BUILDING and the PATTERN LANGUAGE, could still not make buildings that are alive because it is other processes that play a more fundamental role, other changes that are more fundamental.

The nature of these changes, and why they are necessary, reveal the incompleteness of Alexander's work so far as well as an understanding of what is really meant by a paradigm shift. Recall that the transition to a new paradigm entails more than just changes in the field's most elementary theoretical generalizations; it is a total reconstruction, affecting many of its paradigm methods and applications. In science, it is inconceivable that the paradigm rules could change without fundamental changes in the actual methods of so-called normal research and practice. Anything else would constitute just extensions or modifications to the existing paradigm — which is, after all, the entire constellation of facts, values, and methods that directs the community of practitioners. In the case of architecture, it includes of course the actual processes by which buildings are built. And up until the Modesto Clinic, Alexander did not believe that the processes of building would have to be changed — that they would be compatible with the pattern language and the quality called for by TIMELESS:

Up until that time, I assumed that if you did the patterns correctly, from a social point of view, and you put together the overall layout of the building in terms of those patterns, it would be quite alright to build it in whatever contemporary way that was considered normal. But then I began to realize that it was not going to work that way.

The Modesto Clinic — although successful from the standpoint of using the pattern language to actually generate a building — was ultimately unsatisfactory to Alexander. The final product did not actually have the quality that was being sought, even working with an architect in Sacramento who was trying his best to fit into the vision that had been projected:

It's somewhat nice in plan, but it basically looks like any other building of this era. One might wonder why its plan is so nice, but in any really fundamental terms there is nothing to see there. There was hardly a trace of what I was looking for.

And it was not just in Modesto. During the same period, other people were beginning to use the pattern language with similar results:

Bootleg copies of the pattern language were floating up and down the West Coast and people would show me projects they had done and I began to be more and more amazed to realize that, although it worked, all of these projects basically looked like any other building of our time. They had a few differences. They were more like the buildings of Charles Moore or Joseph Esherick, for example, than the buildings of SOM or I. M. Pei; but basically, they still belonged perfectly within the canons of mid-twentieth century architecture. None of them whatsoever crossed the line.

But even more interesting was the fact that most of these people did not even realize that there wasn't any difference:

They thought the buildings were physically different. In fact, the people who did these projects thought that the buildings were quite different from any they had designed before, perhaps even outrageously so. But their perception was incredibly wrong; and I began to see this happening over and over again — that even a person who is very enthusiastic about all of this work will still be perfectly capable of making buildings that have this mechanical, death-like morphology, even with the intention of producing buildings that are alive.

So there is the slightly strange paradox that, after all those years of work, the first three books are essentially complete and, from a theoretical point of view, do quite a good job of identifying the difference but actually do not accomplish anything. The conceptual structures that are presented are just not deep enough to actually break down the barrier. They really do not do anything.

Faced with this "paradox," Alexander decided to embark on a second series of experiments and projects in an attempt to delineate precisely what still had to be done in order to solve the problems:

Its like taking a scalpel a complete layer further to actually lay bare what it is that has got to happen in order to produce this quality. And one way of looking at that task is that it essentially rests on the failure of the first phase of work.

But what exactly is the failure of the first phase? For Alexander it is twofold. First, that the work does not adequately convey, or describe precisely enough, the geometry implied by TIMELESS. This would account for why people working with the pattern language, even although they had read the book, did not understand what went wrong. The formulation was obviously not yet complete enough to cause the reorientation of the mental field that accompanies the recognition that the paradigm rules have changed.

As in science, the description of the consequences of a phenomenon is as critical, if not more, than the discovery of the phenomenon itself — at least if it is to succeed in the reconstruction of the field. Alexander had obviously not carried that description far enough. And yet geometry was a crucial consequence — perhaps the most crucial. His entire investigation had been concerned with

58

58. Mental Health Clinic, Modesto, California.
   ". . .there was hardly a trace of what I was looking for."

PLATE XXVII

59

60

59. Charles Moore, M/L/T/W, and Joseph Esherick, Sea Ranch Condominium, California.
60. I. M. Pei, National Center for Atmospheric Research, Boulder, Colorado.

PLATE XXVIII

geometry in one way or another. The golden mean, the cognitive studies, the diagrams, the tree and semi-lattice structures, relations, the mathematical representation of form, the quality itself and its comparison to the cardboard-like quality of modern architecture, patterns, the hierarchical structure of the language, morphological growth and repair, the laying out of the building on the site — practically every single point of inquiry so far has had a strong geometrical aspect. Yet the work does not adequately convey how crucial the geometry actually is. For Alexander, however, it is absolutely central:

You cannot produce a thing which has this very penetrating life in it unless you go to the roots and unless the geometry changes, also, as a consequence of what you do. You can use the geometry as a sort of litmus test, because the geometry will indeed change as a result of the life coming into it. Of course my basic concern is with the life coming into it; but one of the things I began to realize was that the geometrical consequences of that were not sufficiently spelled out. So that the majority of people who read the work, or tried to use it, did not realize that their conception of geometry had to undergo a fundamental change in order to come to terms with all of this. They thought that they could essentially graft all of the ideas about life, and patterns, and functions onto their present conception of geometry. In fact, some people who have read my work actually believe it to be somewhat independent of geometry, independent of style — even of architecture. But the geometry is one of the ultimate tests as to whether anything has really happened. It is indeed central. It is a particular kind of geometry which is completely different from the geometry which has been in people's minds for the last fifty or seventy-five years. It is quite similar in character to the geometry which has existed in many traditional cultures but it has nothing whatsoever to do with history. It is a geometry that has a definable character; and what I realized was that I had not precisely identified that character.

This would constitute one of the major tasks of the second series of experiments and projects — the precise geometrical identification of that character. But the second weakness of the work — and this was the failure of the Modesto Clinic — was the lack of a description of the procedural consequences in the process of building that are necessary to *produce* this character. It is one thing to identify precisely what that character is; but another to identify all the changes in the processes by which buildings get built that will produce it. For Alexander it involves a different level of understanding — more than just a cognitive shift:

There is one level of understanding at which you read something and you think it is fantastic; but actually, nothing in you changes. You think it is great, you believe yourself to agree with it, but in fact you do not change anything in yourself. All you do is add this material — whether it be TIMELESS, or the PATTERN LANGUAGE, or THE OREGON EXPERIMENT — you add it to your repertoire of what is going on; but essentially you are unchanged. The second layer of understanding essentially forces a change because it spells things out in terms which go so much further that you actually cannot do those things without fundamentally altering yourself and your activities as well as your perception of things.

In Kuhn's model of the structure of scientific revolutions, this second layer of understanding constitutes the resolution of crisis and the full emergence of a new paradigm. It is different from the period of transition which is characterized by the emergence of "extraordinary" theories and the reshuffling of the elements of the field. It is the most difficult phase in the evolution of a new paradigm, and the most volatile, because it entails major changes in the procedures and practices of "normal" research. But in the scientific community years, even decades, may elapse between the two phases — as in the case of general relativity theory and its only recent connection to quantum mechanics. In architecture however, the demands of societal urgency do not permit the luxury of a prolonged hiatus. For Alexander, it means embarking on a series of revolutionary projects having to do with construction, with politics, with the role of the architect, and with the social relationships in a community where building is taking place — because they impinge directly on the question of geometry.

These experiments and projects — starting around 1972-1973 — constitute the full emergence of the consequences of Alexander's discoveries over the preceding fifteen years of theoretical research when they are taken to their extreme. And they serve the same role in the resolution of a paradigm crisis as an "existence theorem" does in mathematics:

Suppose there is a postulate that certain kinds of mathematical structures are useful if they occur. The first thing you have to do is demonstrate the existence of what you are talking about. This usually happens when a new branch of mathematics is opening up. One of the classic examples are the Lobachevsky and Riemannian geometries at the beginning of the 19th century.

There was a vague disquiet about Euclid, especially regarding the axiom of parallel lines and whether or not they ever met. According to Euclid, they never meet; but there was no special reason among mathematicians for this axiom to be true. It seemed very arbitrary and people began wondering what would happen if parallel lines meet — once, twice, or even many times. Could there be such a geometry? So there is the need for an existence demonstration — an example of geometry in which parallel lines meet. All of the uncertainty cannot be settled until such an example can be given.

It turns out that you can give models of such a geometry. If you take the two-dimensional geometry of what is happening on a sphere, the axioms of Euclid are satisfied except that parallel lines do meet. If you have two great circles on a sphere, they are parallel locally but they also meet. On the earth, the meridians are obviously parallel but they meet at the poles.

At the time of Lobachevsky and Riemann, other models were given; but the effect was shattering. The whole of relativity theory is based on these geometries. But the point is that, at the time the demonstration is given, what is important is not the two-dimensional geometry of a sphere but the fact that if you can give one example of a geometry that is non-Euclidean, the whole paradigm falls apart. But one example must be found that can be relied upon.

Now, going back to my own efforts here, there is a similar disquiet and uncertainty among people who have read the theory. There are serious misgivings about the political dimension, the economic dimension, the industrial dimension, and the sociological dimension. Is it true that people want to be involved in the design of their own environment? Can it be done at a price comparable to the price of ordinary buildings? Is it compatible with the sophistication of modern industry? Is it compatible with the division of labor in the profession and on the building site? Is it comparable with local politics? And if the answer is "no" to any of those questions, what kind of changes are required in order to permit all of this to happen?

Of course the questions are asked tongue-in-cheek because, looked at through the eyes of the implementary apparatus that exists today, the assumption is that this is a complete dream. But if I can give one or two examples of processes where the politics, or the money, or the industrialization, or the social organization is actually changed, and is successful in the sense that it works on its own terms, then the criticisms fall apart. And you take the same sort of step out of our present views of industrialization, or politics, or economics of building as one takes by going from Euclidean to Riemannian geometry. You suddenly open up a completely new, possible world by giving a few examples.

I can talk forever about the fact that every part of a building needs to be slightly different — as I have done in TIMELESS, which constantly refers to it — but it means nothing unless I can show an integration between architect and contractor which permits this to occur and which enables the architect to earn a living. Or take the case of cost-control in a housing project under conditions where every house is different. Anybody who knows about housing — especially if you talk to people who are experienced in handling money, awarding subcontracts, or purchasing materials — is going to say that it costs more to make every house different than to make them the same, radically more expensive. When you get down to the line where the pennies get counted, these same people will attempt to standardize what it is being done in order to save money.

Its a fundamental problem. You can say as many times as you want that it would be better if every house was slightly different, or every part of every house slightly different, but there is an entire layer of people who are experienced in handling money, materials, and labor who will say that it is going to be too expensive. And until you can give these people a clear-cut model of how to handle cost-control in such a project, and show that it comes out costing the same or less than the conventional approach to cost-control — which relies on standardization of labor, plans, and components — there is a fundamental obstacle. Its not just a case of implementation. Major theoretical problems still need to be solved. You have to lay out a process which shows how it works. And for each one of these items of doubt or uncertainty — using the analogy of the existence theorem — a process needs to be worked out which permits this geometry to appear. But it turns out that in order for that to happen, some really immense changes need to be made in the way in which we conceive of the everyday events connected with building.

That immense changes are necessary in the processes by which buildings are made was a starting revelation — even to Alexander; but it is not surprising from the standpoint of the historical evolution of the current paradigm. For example: the transition from pre-industrial to modern architecture — which we perceive as a matter of style — was determined, in large measure, by changes in the processes by which buildings were actually built. New materials and methods of construction, new manufacturing and labor practices, new functions connected with an industrial society, and new values about the organization of people and activities in space were completely anomalous to the four-hundred year old tradition of building. Yet they are perfectly compatible with the new style — which we call modern. In other words, the resulting geometry was the product of a completely different set of processes. In fact, according to the evidence revealed by an analysis of the papers and manifestos written by architects during the period of transition (roughly 1890-1920), the stylistic innovations leading to the evolution of modern design were initiated as a somewhat creative and artistic response to these new processes.[1] Of course these responses, in turn, generated other new processes, so it was not an entirely one-way relationship; but the mold had essentially been cast by the societal-wide transition from the processes of a pre-industrial to an industrial order. Architects did not initiate that transition, which is why it is possible to say that the determination, of these processes, with the exception of the architects' individual interpretation of them, is largely *external* when compared to the previous (i.e., renaissance) paradigm and why, within the current paradigm, there is a relative absence of any cumulative, *internal* body of knowledge which describes their consequences. As paradigms go, it is either a weak one or else it is not yet a paradigm (and corresponds to the pre-paradigm period of development).

What the evolution reveals however is that, indeed, there must be changes in the process by which buildings are actually built for there to be a fundamental change in their corresponding geometry; but it also reveals a significant difference between the evolution of the current paradigm (or pre-paradigm) and Alexander's efforts to formulate the basis of a new one. And that is that, although the processes and the geometry must be mutually compatible, the processes are to be initiated *internally* — as a response to the desire to create a particular kind of geometry (just as the structural and constructional processes of a gothic cathedral were a response to the desire to create a particular kind of space). And as a consequence of that desire, the way in which one normally conceives of the making of a building needs to be radically altered.

REFERENCE NOTES

1. See Ulrich Conrads (ed.), PROGRAMMES AND MANIFESTOS ON 20th CENTURY ARCHITECTURE (London: Lund-Humphries, 1970)

PART FOUR

XIII

THE SEARCH FOR PROCESSES

One way of looking at the shift between the two paradigms — as well as the differences between the two phases of Alexander's work — is to understand the emphasis placed on the role of *process* in the creation of an object. Although this distinction was not even clear to Alexander in 1972, there is no question that the task of the second series of investigations and projects was to look in each of the different spheres of activity relating to building for the underlying generative processes that would do the work and make the geometry come out correctly. And although the task involves a different level of understanding of what is involved in the content of a paradigm shift — as discussed in the two previous chapters — it also involves a different level of understanding of the way in which such a change actually occurs:

I think that, in general, there is a failure among people who are concerned with making things, or who are responsible for things, to fully appreciate the extent to which what is done or what happens is a product of the processes that are governing events behind the scenes.

One of the extremely early examples of my own awareness of this is connected with D'Arcy Thompson's book ON GROWTH AND FORM. What Thompson insisted on was that every form is basically the end result of a certain growth process. When I first read this I felt that of course the form in a purely static sense is equilibrating certain forces and that you could say that it was even the product of those forces — in a non-temporal, non-dynamic sense, as in the case of a raindrop, for example, which in the right here and now is in equilibrium with the air flow around it, the force of gravity, its velocity, and so forth — but that you did not really have to be interested in how it actually got made. Thompson however was saying that everything is the way it is today because it is the result of a certain history — which of course includes how it got made. But at the time

I read this I did not really understand it very well; whereas I now realize that he is completely right.

In my own work, the idea of the pattern language as a generative process governed my approach to the problem for almost ten years. In fact, almost the entire first phase of the work rested purely on that kind of generative process — the pattern language as the fundamental genetic entity which would guide the process of design. But in the second phase, I have become concerned with a whole series of processes, each one of which bears the same relationship to its field of activity as the pattern language does to design.

After 1972, the critical generative processes in the history of an object for Alexander have to do with, in addition to design, the fields of money, politics, construction, and geometry itself. In the field of money there is the question of how different flows of money play a fundamental role in the way things get shaped — particularly in the relationship between the capital cost of a building and the mortgage process by which it is financed. In the field of politics there is the question of the relationship between the size and hierarchy of groups and the process of decision-making by which control is exercised over various domains of the environment — particularly in the domains between the privately owned house and the large-scale land use patterns of a town. In the field of construction there is the question of the relationship between the actual physical structure of a building and the process of building it — particularly the nature of the roles of the people involved, the sequence of decisions on site which shape the overall form of the building, and the specific operations which shape its individual, pattern-like components. And in the field of geometry there is the question of the relationship between the combinatorial processes by which an object is shaped and the properties it will acquire — particularly the properties underlying the unity of space:

If I place the pattern language and its relationship to design alongside each of these fields, the same kind of generative relationship exists. In each case, the fundamental assumption is that if you truly want to change things, what have to be created are new processes which can then be used millions of times over, by millions of people, to do millions of different things — as opposed to trying to shape a few dozen or a few hundred particular examples at which you could then say, "Isn't that nice." But in each case there is a jump in level.

Suppose, for example, you are trying to play chess very well. By

138

attempting to deal with every situation as it occurs on the board you are occupied with one level of thought. But at the time that computers came along and people started writing chess-playing programs, they were essentially involved with a different level of thought. They were not merely trying to figure out, as a player does in a particular game, "Shall I move my bishop or my king?" They were looking for an underlying process that would play chess well in every game. In other words, it is a level of depth and generality one step greater. And of course this is cumulative, so that by now there are chess programs that are capable of playing at close to master level. As a process, it is incredibly more powerful than playing one very good game. When you come up with one of these programs, and it reaches a certain level of tournament play, it remains at that level for anybody, all the time!

The same jump in level can be made in attempting to improve the environment, especially if you are trying to do it very well. The first and most naive level of trying to do something about the chaotic development in a town, for example, is to make a nicer plan for the town — a sort of Beaux Arts approach to planning. The second level of sophistication comes when you realize that what we see out there — in a town — is actually a product of the zoning ordinances. This, together with things like bank policies and investments, is the first level of process and it is foolish to only tinker with the physical thing because the zoning ordinance process is really governing what is happening. Now a third level of sophistication might be to realize that the zoning ordinances are themselves a product of the way in which zoning is administered and exists in the political structure of the town. It is not enough, actually, to try and tinker with the zoning ordinances because the exact rules of those ordinances — which govern that process — are themselves produced by the process by which zoning is administered. And unless you actually change the relationships between the zoning administrator, the city council, private enterprise, and public bodies, for example, you still won't be able to alter the zoning ordinance process in a sufficiently deep way because of this other process which is governing.

For Alexander, this kind of awareness of the role of process in the way something is shaped is not just important to the improvement of the environment; it happens to play a fundamental role in 20th century scientific thought:

On the one hand we have Whitehead writing a book called PROCESS AND REALITY, which is his cosmology and which essentially makes everything to be the child of process; and we also have modern physics, the

139

present stage of which is almost completely governed by what are called "Feynman diagrams" — each one describing a sort of alchemical process by which one or two particles of certain types and energies undergo transmutations — and which supports the view that the whole of physics is controlled by the interaction of certain processes.

In relating these ideas to architecture, there is nothing complicated about what I have just said. Its extremely obvious. However, it happens to be incredibly difficult to get people to accept it. Its one thing to say that, when we are talking about architecture, what we are really talking about is changing the processes by which buildings are made — not the "things" but the processes by which they are conceived and funded and regulated and constructed — and that that is ultimately where it all lies. But somehow, it appears to be an abstract idea. It's very, very hard for someone to actually get into it as a strategy for making something.

In architecture, the concept of process is almost anathema. There is a craft-like process in the laying out of a drawing — a process which someone who knows how to draw well understands. But in terms of the actual conception of a building, or its execution, the architect is very far from seeing it as a process, except perhaps in a business-like way. Even if he is process-minded, he will not actually see the processes as generative. In planning it is almost the opposite. The emphasis on administrative and decision-making processes of so-called policy planning has lost touch with the actual physical entity that the processes are supposed to be shaping.

But the crux of the matter is that in all of these fields or realms of activity that impinge directly on the shape of the environment — in design, in money, in politics, in construction, and in geometry — the processes that exist today are wrong; and unless one changes those processes, one is not actually changing anything at all.

Taken to its extreme, this view ultimately leads to a very simple but revolutionary concept of change. For Alexander, the crux of it has to do with a scientific understanding of genetics and how seriously one is willing to take the idea of generative process. At one level it is possible to understand that, although the structure of the natural world is teeming with an incredible profusion and variety of organic life, it is ultimately the product of a very small amount of information registered on the chromosones of a few species. At another level — only slightly more tenous — it is possible to understand that human culture is also essentially generated by a small amount of information which happens to take a language-like form rather than a chromosome-like form. At the extreme level, one understands that these kinds of processes are where the phenomena of the world really come from — and that to do something which is actually capable of changing the situation, or improving the situation, it is necessary to identify a relatively small number of processes and then alter them. For Alexander, "it is like working for years on a tiny little seed and then sort of dropping it into the pond and waiting for it to take root and then spread." But ultimately it depends upon an act of "empirical judgment":

It depends on the question, "Is that just fantasy or is that true?" In other words, it could be that this is just a pleasant semi-academic, semi-poetic myth or analogy — this generativeness. Its clearly true in the case of nature, only partly true in the case of culture, and in the case of architecture, it might be so faintly true that, actually, things do not really work that way. The other possibility is that, indeed, things really do work that way and that I have seen a fact which, although open to everyone's inspection, no one else has apparently picked up on and therefore have made efforts in different directions. What it hinges on is whether my judgment about that turns out to be correct or incorrect.

This is a general attitude about changing the phenomena of the world — with the accent on the process as a kind of seed. If I am right about this attitude, and the whole thing really works the way that organic nature works and the way that culture also works, then by dropping a few key processes into the pond the results will simply multiply and spread. But it is ultimately a question of empirical judgment. They will either work or not. The crux of the issue is not whether people will like the theory and will therefore surmount all odds. The crux of the issue lies in the question of whether these few processes actually have the genetic spreading power I think they have. The original theory, expressed in THE TIMELESS WAY OF BUILDING in relation to the pattern language, says they will. But whether it is really true still remains to be seen. The actual demonstration is the crux of it.

The question of whether they do or not belongs to the second phase of work — a five-year period from 1973 to 1978 dominated by the identification of these key processes in the realm of finance, politics, construction, and geometry, and by the alterations necessary to make them compatible with the production of buildings possessing the quality described in TIMELESS. This would then constitute the description of the full range of architectural consequences of Alexander's initial discoveries and complete the transition to a new paradigm. If successful, they would point the way to major changes in the methods and practices of building and, ultimately, to a complete reconstruction of the field — from the initial conception of a building to the nailing in place of the last piece of moulding. This is the final sense in which Kuhn says that after a paradigm shift scientists work in a completely different world.

XIV

THE FLOW OF MONEY

By 1973, Alexander had already begun working with a group of people different from those who had coalesced around the first phase of paradigm development in 1967 and who had begun to break up socially by 1972. Although there was a period of overlap between the two phases consisting of several years of completing remnants of projects connected with the pattern language — an "extended period of housecleaning" that lasted through 1975 — his efforts intensified upon a series of projects directly connected with the role of processes in shaping buildings.

The first of these projects focused on the question of financing and, in particular, the flow of money through the environment. The effort began during a seminar at the University of California in the fall of 1972 to explore the general social and economic conditions under which the pattern language could be implemented. The investigation very quickly became focussed on the role of the mortgage process in determining not only the cost of buildings but their actual shape as well.

The question of money and its relationship to piecemeal growth had already come up in THE OREGON EXPERIMENT. There it was discovered that, at the scale of a university campus, large-lump development worked counter to the slower, piecemeal growth process of an organically ordered environment. The solution was to emphasize small project funding — over a long time period — and the provision of an annual repair budget for every building — the idea being that organic order could only be achieved by an incremental, additive process of growth and repair. The connection to financing was that the flow of money needed to be as highly differentiated or modulated as the structure of the environment. If large lumps of money were invested for single projects at erratic intervals of time, rather than smaller sums being invested for many, simultaneous projects going on over a continuous period time, the environment could never achieve the finer more highly differentiated structure that was implicit in the pattern language. But the University of Oregon was a single, centralized client possessing enormous financial resources. The reallocation and modulation of those resources could be achieved almost exclusively within its annual budget (Cf. Omnibus funding package). Besides, the problem of the actual cost of building did not play a major role in the formulation of the principle of piecemeal growth on the Eugene campus. At the scale of a single building however, the problem narrowed down to the question of the mortgage process playing a major role in determining the flow of money, particularly in the case of housing.

For Alexander, the nature of the mortgage process plays the same role in the shaping of an individual building as large-lump development plays in the shaping of a university campus — only the consequences are far more drastic. The first of these consequences has to do with the cost of a building. In the case of housing, two-thirds of the cost of the actual building lie in the interest payments that are used to pay off the mortgage. A house typically costing $50,000 to build will end up costing almost $130,000 by the time the mortgage is paid off. The additional $80,000 is absorbed by the bank as its "fee" for financing the initial purchase. Although the reinvestment of this sum is purported to be beneficial to the overall economy, it has disastrous effects on the physical environment because it drives the price of housing up at the same time that it actually diverts the flow of money away from building.

Since very little of a homeowner's monthly mortgage payments are used to build up equity — beyond keeping up with normal inflation — the tendency is to try and make up the difference by increasing the resale price of the house. And since most of this money goes to the banks, very little of the total cash flow is used directly to improve the physical environment. In effect, only one-third of every dollar invested in the environment will actually be used to pay for the labor and materials necessary to shape it. And furthermore, any attempt to reduce the costs of labor and materials will, in turn, be cut by two-thirds.

This cost syndrome is well known to architects who have tried to compete with the mass-produced, standardized, and packaged home-construction industry; what is not understood however, is that the actual shape of the homes produced by that industry is one of the consequences of the mortgage process. For Alexander, it has to do with the commodity-like conception of a building which results from the way that process actually functions.

The mortgage itself is like large-lump development. It is based on a one-time, single investment in the capital cost of a finished building. There is nothing incremental about it. The advantage to the bank is that the initial investment for a complete, finished building is enormously high — much higher than the average homeowner can possibly afford all at once without significant debt. So rather than financing and building the house incrementally, over a longer period of time, and in proportion to existing assests, the mortgage process encourages that interaction between financing and building which results in the highest possible initial investment and, consequently, the greatest accumulation of interest. And in that interaction, the house is conceived of as a "commodity." It is built all at once, it is sold, it is used, and it is resold virtually unchanged. And as a commodity, it is of course subject to the cognitive manipulations of profit-motivated marketing techniques: high-volume sales achieved through built-in obsolescence, artificial scarcity mechanisms, changing fashions, image-induced upward mobility, and a disposable, throw-away aesthetic.

For Alexander, such a conception is formally static. It neither encourages nor permits the piecemeal growth process of a well ordered environment and leads directly to the sterility of the mass-produced, standardized, and packaged home. It diverts two-thirds of the total cash flow away from building, thus inflating the actual cost of building; it necessitates instant construction and results in a reduced capacity for labor and materials in any attempt to cut the inflating costs of that construction; and it ties up the homeowner's assets over a long period of time and inhibits the maintenance and repair necessary for any well-adapted environment, thus encouraging its absolescence and replacement. In the Berkeley seminar on the subject of the conditions under which the pattern language could be implemented, he summarized this problem:

We see, then, that the heart of "the housing problem" lies in the mortgage system — or, if you will, in that interaction between houses and money which treats a house as a commodity. People are persuaded that they must accept a house which someone else built; and persuaded that they must borrow money, huge sums of money, to get this house which someone else has built. Since they have to borrow so much money, most of their own money flows out of their pockets in the form of interest instead of flowing towards the land and houses themselves — where it could actually help to make the houses better: so, by accepting the idea that he must have this house which someone else has built, and must borrow money to get it, the owner also condemns the house itself to receive one-third of the resources in labor, care, and materials which it ought to get — so obviously the houses themselves get worse and worse with time.

There is no way to cut this cycle of cause and effect, except at the root. It cannot be cut by making more houses which are commodities; not by making better houses which are commodities; not by making cheaper houses which are commodities. It can only be cut when we stop treating houses as commodities altogether — and by our consequent refusal to accept the monetary side conditions which come with the house when it is seen as a commodity.[1]

"The Grass Roots Housing Process," which resulted from that seminar, is the attempt to define a building financing process which avoids the interest-cost syndrome of the mortgage process and which permits the incremental, piecemeal growth of the house to occur gradually, as part of its history. It is based on the conception of the house as an activity rather than a "commodity" — a conception which is congruent not only with the way in which natural growth occurs, but also with the observation that the environment is made of patterns rather than "things:"

> In this case, the life history of the house, and its relation to the people who live in it, and pass through it, is entirely different. The house is not produced at one time, and then used, unchanged, for years; it is created gradually, as a direct result of the living which is happening in it and around it. Building takes place in increments, day by day, year by year. The people who live in the house don't need to borrow money; they spend only what they can afford. The people who live in the house are the one's who design it, as they go. They do not necessarily build it with their own hands; but they may build parts of it, to help the builders. Each house is unique; it is the unique expression of a particular way of life, and of the particular history of all the people who have ever lived in it. Ownership of the house is not merely a way of making money, or a form of legal control; it is a vehicle for involvement, in the process of creating a suitable,

146

beautiful, environment.[2]

It follows from this conception that the way money flows
through the environment needs to be changed. "The Grass Roots
Housing Process" is Alexander's demonstration of a process that
attempts to change the flow. It hinges on the creation of two
innovative legal entities — the "cluster" and the "builder — " a
sponsor for their activities, and the use of the pattern language as a
sort of medium of exchange.

The sponsor may be any organization that has an interest in the
provision of housing and which has land that can be put in trust for
such purposes. It can be a group of individuals, a governmental
agency, a private corporation, an institution, or a non-profit
foundation. The cluster is a group of families, legally constituted as
a non-profit corporation. The sponsor sells the land to the cluster
under certain conditions and the cluster undertakes, as part of its
charter, to hold this land in perpetuity without speculation. The
families collectively own the land and the buildings on it and each
family has a share which entitles it to the private use of the portion
of the land where a house might be built. The builder is also a
non-profit organization that combines the functions of an architect,
a contractor, and a manager. The builder helps the group of families
design the houses and the common land between the houses,
supervises all construction on the site, provides instruction for
those families who wish to build for themselves, controls the
monthly payments from the families based on square feet of
construction, handles the seedmoney needed to start other similar
clusters and, in later years, helps the families and the cluster as a
whole to diagnose those deficiencies in their surroundings that need
to be repaired by new construction. A typical cluster of twelve
homes would grow to completion over eight years and the legal
relationship between cluster, builder, and sponsor would be
terminated after thirteen years — at which time the project would
be paid off and several new clusters generated:

> The families are expected to design their own houses and the
> common land between the houses as time goes on. As a part of their
> contract they will get all the help they need, in the early years, from
> the builder, using the pattern language. They have to put in a certain
> monthly payment based on the area of their house. The payment per
> square foot is very high in the first year and then declines quite
> rapidly and becomes very low in the later years. The purpose of this

is to discourage a large amount of construction in the early years and to encourage people to delay the rate at which they are building. Each family is entitled to sell their share at any time. They must sell it under specified conditions but they will be paid about eighty percent of what they have put in — which compares very favorably to about one-third of what has been put in under normal mortgage conditions.

Then there is the seed money which is provided by the builder. What happens is that every family gets twenty-five hundred dollars the day they start and which they are then committed to giving back. The most important reason that the builder has to be a non-profit organization is that he can make a public guarantee that this money will immediately be redistributed to other families in the same position. Each family which starts out with twenty-five hundred dollars of seed money is actually manufacturing seed money for five other families in the seventh, ninth, eleventh, thirteenth, and fifteenth years. We are interested in creating circumstances where every family is able to be an owner. We want to create this seed money and make it grow quite rapidly so that it can be distributed. If you generate seed money at the rate we are talking about, it grows at a fantastic rate. If you assume that you can find sponsors who are willing to make land available on the basis that I have described, one initial investment of seed money — about thirty thousand dollars for the first cluster — would generate the seed money for sixteen hundred clusters in fifty years. This is a kind of people's bank, but with very special rules that have quite dramatic consequences. For example, if you would invest seven million dollars in this way, half the housing supply of Egypt would be taken care of within thirty years.

Materials within this context are free. They are not literally free, of course, because they have to be bought with money that is coming in through the monthly payments. Each family is entitled to an unlimited supply of materials from the pool of materials that belongs to the cluster and is supplied by the builder. Anyone can make use of this material when they want to — but there is a catch because their monthly payments increase according to the amount of square feet that is built. However, embellishing a given amount of area with additional material does not cost anything — and the same is true for anything that is built in the common areas. The implication is that it is in everybody's interest to build. It is understood that it is in the general public interest for the cluster as a whole that everyone should be taking care of the environment — and this is the major incentive to encourage that. The expectation is that a tremendous amount of embellishment is continually taking place over a comparitively long time period.

The assumption is that the sponsor is making the land available on

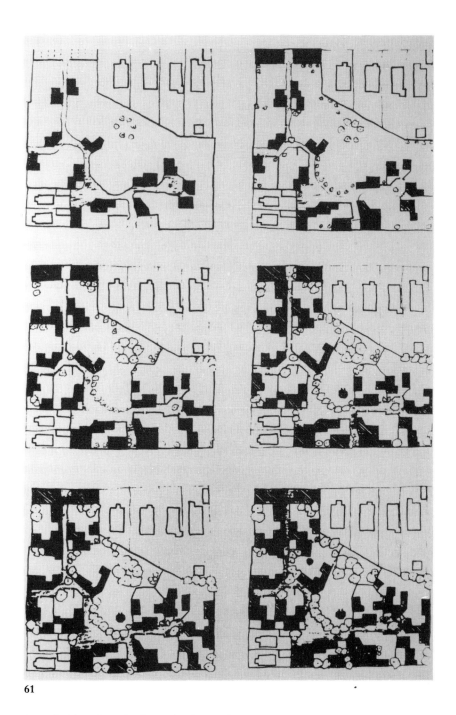

61

61. The Slow Growth of a Twelve-House cluster.

PLATE XXIX

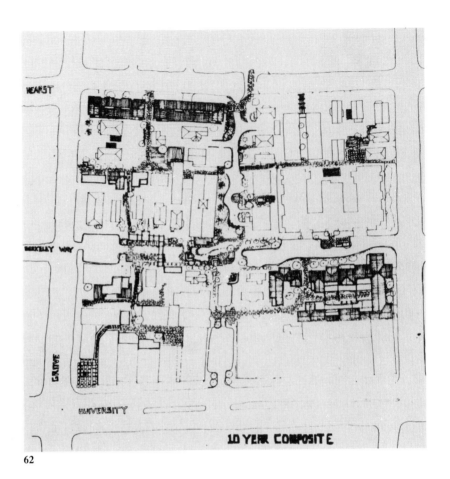

62

62. Plan for a Neighborhood after Ten Years, Berkeley.

"The simulations were necessarily schematic and couldn't fire up anyone's imagination very well. There was a tendency to dismiss what we were doing as sort of messing around with parking spaces. The idea that beautiful and coherent structures would begin to emerge in each neighborhood was not clear."

PLATE XXX

a delayed purchase arrangement. Consequently, the land is being paid for at a very low rate of interest. After thirteen years, in this example, it is completely paid off. The sponsor drops out of the picture altogether, the builder drops out in two more years, and then the cluster is completely in the hands of the individual families. But, within the range of payments being made, labor is not included. The builder provides the sevices that would normally be provided by a foreman. He will undertake to manage the trickier parts of construction, he will supervise the labor of the individuals, and help and teach and guide that labor — and all that service is relatively free. But it is up to each family to decide whether they want to provide their own labor or whether they want to buy it. The assumption then is that one builder together with two apprentices will work with one cluster, full-time, for one year, one-third time for four years, and then a visit of about a month per year until it is finally handed over. During the first year the families learn how to build and how to use the pattern language which is communally adopted by the cluster as a whole. In the next four years, when additions are taking place, there is still quite a bit of help going on. In the remaining years, the builder stays with the families and helps them to diagnose all the problems that are existing in the cluster. The builder is essentially making a committment to be in that situation for fifteen years. Consequently, there is a certain confidence built into the project that it is going to work and that he is going to make sure that it works.[3]

The "Grass Roots Housing Process" describes the legal structure of a cluster, the rate of construction and accommodation, the supply of labor, the experiences with user-design, the builder's tasks and fees, the payment schedule, the purchase of land, resale conditions, and the effects of inflation; but the crux of the demonstration is in the arithmetic of bypassing the conventional mortgage process through the gradual, piecemeal growth of the house:

Recognize first of all, that the very astonishing growth shown in this project, is in fact a phenomenon which is the normal back-bone of economic development. The only reason it is so unfamiliar in the form outlined in this project is that it is usually creamed off by the banks. Every month, Americans spend about six billion dollars on rent and mortgage payments for housing. Since even the rents are, for the landlord, most often mortgage payments, two-thirds of all this money goes to the banks in the form of interest. This means that, of the six billion dollars which people spend every month, four billion dollars goes straight into the pockets of the banks, and is immediately re-invested to make more money. If you stop and think about the incredible economic growth which has taken place in this country, over the last hundred years, and the vast riches that have been developing here, you recognize, indeed already know, intuitively, that the paychecks of people coming home from work month after month, can create enormous wealth. Imagine simply that the *entire* six billion dollars which people spend on housing every month goes into the land. This is essentially what this proposal does. It channels money in such a way that *all* the money people spend on housing actually goes into the land — not just a small part of it. In short, the vast, explosive economic growth which has created such untold riches in this country, is being rechanneled so that it benefits the land and the people who live on it, instead of the banks.[4]

Although the emphasis in this project was on the flow of money through the environment — and the demonstration of a process which could make that flow compatible with the implementation of the pattern language — the political implications for the control and regulation of land in a community would soon have to be faced. In addition, it was not, as far as Alexander was concerned, a very careful piece of economics:

I went through this whole thing like a child. I had just naively set up the problem of how you reduce the price of building. And the logical answer is to find a process which does not involve the interest. So after we had worked out a process which succeeds in doing that, someone in the seminar asked me my views about Marxism and I said I did not really have any. And this person said, "You mean you do not realize that the basis of Marxism is what you have being doing in this seminar — which is to challenge how capital is used to produce interest?" I had just come to it in this childish way without really having any political intent. But obviously the way that money flows is crucial.

Alexander's political naïveté would soon be tested in his exploration of the political processes necessary to implement the ideas already developed; however, in addition to the piecemeal growth process, two new and important concepts had emerged in exploring the flow of money that were not immediately deducible from the first phase of work. One was the idea of the house cluster as an actual social entity exercising control over the land it uses in common. In the search for political processes compatible with the pattern language, this would lead to the conception of the nesting of territories in space — an extremely sophisticated and highly differentiated political structure. The other was the idea of the architect-builder. The image that emerged was of a group of professional people taking responsibility for both design and construction — essentially managing the pattern language, helping people use it, allowing them to participate in the construction to whatever extent they wanted, but taking responsibility for building and for helping all of the patterns to emerge. This idea would eventually lead to a major investigation of the actual processes of construction. The second phase had only just begun.

REFERENCE NOTES

1. "The Grass Roots Housing Process," (Berkeley: Center for Environmental Structure, 1973), pp.11-12
2. IBID., p.12
3. "The Economics, Politics, and Implementation of the Pattern Language" (Stockholm: Royal Institute of Technology, 1973), pp.16-19
4. "The Grass Roots Housing Process," pp.54-55

XV

POLITICS

Kuhn shows in his analysis of the Copernican Revolution that the emergence of paradigm crisis is as much a response to anomalies in the field as it is to the social and intellectual milieu within which the paradigm is practiced. Paradigms are a function of the questions which seem important for the community of practitioners to answer at any given moment; and insofar as there are new questions to answer, the social and intellectual climate will encourage the rise of new paradigms. This is why the Copernican theory became the focus of controversy in so many fields outside of astronomy, including economics and politics. In Copernicus' time, astronomical concepts had become strands in a much larger fabric of thought and, as Kuhn puts it, "the non–astronomical strands could be as important as the astronomical ones in binding the imagination of the astronomers."[1]

In architecture, the relationship to questions of economics and politics would seem more direct; and yet, in the case of politics specifically, the relationship seems to elude definition. Most of the literature on the subject treats either the political influences or context within which particular architects have worked, or the way in which the symbolic content of various political systems or movements have influenced architectural style.Rarely however is one able to establish a direct link between political structure as a system of societal relationships and the actual *form* of a building or town — although the literature is rich in utopian schemes for social reform through geometry.

For Alexander, the relative amorphousness and lack of differentiation in the built environment is intimately connected with the political character of advanced industrial society — that is, with the lack of a rich structure of societal relationships between the individual and the State. The connection comes from the fact that between the individual home and the vast public places of a town there is a relative absence of any control over those parts of the environment which are used in common: paths, sidewalks, alleys, streets, squares, plazas, parks, as well as the vast realm of intermediate, interconnecting open and closed spaces that make up the traditional palette of urban design. In other words, there are no socio-political groups with decision-making controls that correspond to these parts of the environment. Consequently, they acquire an undifferentiated character based on the ad-hoc decisions of people who have a competitive rather than a common interest in their use. The contrast is striking when compared to the obviously richer character of pre-industrial environments like Amsterdam, Venice, or the Greek Islands, for example, and which correspond to a more *communal* process of management. This is really the critical distinction — the presence or absence of a communal structure to society. Alexander agrees with Martin Buber's postulate of an "organic" society: that without the common and active management of what it has in common, it *cannot* exist:

> At whatever point we examine the structure of such a society we find the cell-tissue "Society" everywhere, i.e. a living and life-giving collaboration, an essentially autonomous consociation of human beings, shaping and reshaping itself from within.
> ..... it is not an aggregate of essentially unrelated individuals, for such an aggregate could only be held together by a "political," i.e. a coercive principle of government; it must be built up of little societies on the basis of communal life and of the associations of these societies; and the *mutual* relations of the societies and their associations must be determined to the greatest possible extent by the social principle — the principle of inner cohesion, collaboration and mutual stimulation.[2]

For Alexander, it happens to be the characteristic of *any* living system that all the parts in its internal structure are mutually well adapted to one another. In the case of society, this means that there must be a process whereby people exercise local control over the parts they use in common. And furthermore, since urban society is a very complex system, the process of control must be differentiated according to the various scales of use that determine its overlapping, interconnected structure. This means that there must be substantial changes in the amount of local control that people now have if the society is to be well adapted to their needs and, in passing, acquire the physical characteristics of a richer environment.

These connections emerged for Alexander between 1972 and 1974 — the period following the Oregon Experiment, the Grass Roots Housing Process, the Swedish Seminars, and the attempt to implement the results of the Oregon Experiment in the town of Berkeley:

To me, the most fundamental issue in politics has to do with the size of groups and the hierarchy of groups which are making decisions and which have control over various domains. The central issue of all this is the one which says: each person inside the house has a room of his own, and then each member of the family has some communal space which is jointly controlled; each house has its own territory which it controls and, together with a half-dozen or a dozen other houses, forms a house cluster which has common land; and that group is, again, a social entity called the "cluster," and then let us say that there are ten clusters which make up an identifiable "neighborhood" of about five hundred people that has common land belonging to it, and it is a legal and corporate entity with control over its common land and partial control over the house clusters; and then you have a community of approximately five to ten thousand people and perhaps a dozen to twenty neighborhoods in it, and again there is common land, outside the neighborhoods, but owned corporately by the community; and then there is a township which does the same thing at the next level, and so on. And at each one of these levels there is common land that is controlled specifically by that group and each group sends a representative up to the next level. All that is required is to elect a representative and that automatically forms the political structure by means of which each level takes care of the patterns that are appropriate to that level and the territory that is owned jointly at that level and then each level gives some sort of incentive to the next level down in order to help produce the larger patterns required by that level.

In other words, the cluster — say a group of ten families — is a political entity and has a board which consists of one member from each family. Now that board, as an entity, may say that they want certain patterns at the cluster level to appear and they have responsibility for making them appear. But they don't actually have to build them themselves. In other words, the way they can manage that is to create certain incentives which encourage individual householders to help those larger patterns to occur. I believe that,

63

63. American Settlement Patterns, California.

PLATE XXXI

64

64. Italian Hilltown, Positano.

Buber's postulate of an Organic Society. "...it is not an aggregate of essentially unrelated individuals; it must be built up of little societies on the basis of communal life and of the associations of these societies."

PLATE XXXII

to some extent, these incentives have to be monetary and so it is presumed that there is some sort of taxation on every single level. It might all be collected at the State level — in order for it to be progressive by income, for example — and then a certain portion of the taxes would be distributed to each level in the form of a budget. Each level would then use that budget in the form of incentives to encourage certain things to happen. For example, a cluster may decide to buy the materials for a brick path on its common land with the understanding that any householder who is willing to do that portion of the path outside his house will be paid for the materials. The crux of the matter is that there is always this reciprocal and mutual relationship between the two levels.

A neighborhood, of course, would be more concerned with neighborhood scale patterns. They would be more likely to say to a cluster: "Where your cluster is we need a gateway to the neighborhood so we would like your cluster to help in the construction of this gateway." Or there might be a problem in the road pattern within that neighborhood and this particular cluster is needed to somehow modify that pattern. The cluster would then have the burden, in part, of that effort — again, receiving some monies down from the neighborhood insofar as they would be willing to help.

The assumption is that it is never paid for totally by the level above. In other words, as in the previous example, the cluster would never pay for the paths entirely because the assumption is that the path needs to be done in such a way that it is for both the individual house and the cluster. In this particular case the cluster might pay half with the assumption that it is equally beneficial at both levels.

There is an incredibly important principle throughout all this which does not really exist in modern urban society as we know it, and that is that at any level, the individual is not only responsible for taking care of his own needs, but also for contributing to the needs of the larger group to which he belongs. I would say that, on a social level, this has almost completely disappeared from present-day urban society.

Within what I am talking about it is an absolutely basic assumption that every act that you perform has fifty percent of its value to you, personally, and fifty percent of its value to a larger human group. Part of it has to be managed by incentives and part of it by responsibility. It's not quite "voluntary" — which makes it sound like it might not get done. These are all matters of necessity and so they will certainly be done. There is a difference between today's voluntary associations — which actually accomplish very little because they have no money — and the system I am talking about where these associations would all have money. That's the fundamental point; and it is a piece of politics which is deeply ingrained in what all of this implies.

What Alexander means by politics then, are the decision-making processes that have to do with the control and maintenance of land at all levels of scale as well as the legal, regulatory, and fiscal mechanisms that would permit those processes to operate as a "nesting of territories" in space. But it is a basic political structure which does not exist at the moment:

To give an example, at this point in American law, specifically in California, the local streets within a neighborhood are not within the jurisdiction of that neighborhood. At the moment the City, and sometimes the State, sets ordinances that determine such things as parking laws, the surfacing of streets, drainage, what is permitted or not permitted to occur in the street, and so forth. The peculiarity of American law is such that if the City or the State has ordinances governing the conduct of those streets, the neighborhood cannot be empowered to do so. In other words, the laws set by the larger body automatically prevail over any laws that the lower body might try to create. It can delegate temporarily; but it cannot actually give up its authority. Consequently, genuine decentralization is very difficult. There are certain examples of it that are possible, because there are mechanisms for setting all of this up; but I'm pointing out that if you take this seriously, it goes to the root of what a political structure really is.

The opportunity to precisely define such mechanisms occurred in 1974. The impetus came from a seminar which Alexander conducted between 1972 and 1973 in an attempt to simulate what would happen to a city like Berkeley if it followed the principles laid out in the Oregon Experiment (organic order, participation, piecemeal growth, patterns, diagnosis, and coordination), with a specific focus on creating neighborhoods which would operate as "self-sustaining, self-governing" political entities. The results would lead to Alexander's own involvement in local politics, the creation of a citizen's advisory group to the Berkeley Planning Department, and the Center for Environmental Structure being commissioned to prepare a report on the neighborhood concept for incorporation, through referendum, into a revised master plan for the city. The report took the form of a book entitled PEOPLE REBUILDING BERKELEY:

This experience moved us into another dimension altogether. This was serious, practical politics. It started out just as a simulation of several neighborhoods; but then after having worked that out, we decided to actually try to implement it. So we began working with about a half dozen Berkeley neighborhoods — working with people, explaining how the pattern language worked, trying to get them to initiate processes that were actually real in the physical sense. We came close to being arrested several times. For example, we would ask a group of people what they needed on a particular street. Let's say that a children's play area was needed. Suppose then that we simply remove a parking space? If there was consensus on that then something would actually be done, physically, in that part of the street. But then the Public Works Department would instruct the Police Department to come and break it up. The local television stations eventually picked up on the fact that there was this weird activity going on — that there was a group of people in Berkeley that were building things in the streets — and that we were the ones behind it.

It is important to understand the context of all this. In 1972 and 1973 there was a lot of radical activity in Berkeley and we became involved in trying to put on the ballot an ordinance which would call for a participatory planning process in the city. We were the major initiators of this ordinance. Several people at the Center decided that we were going to do this and so we took it to some people who had a bit of political know-how in the City and they actually got this thing on the ballot. Although altered substantially, it was actually an ordinance that put a moratorium on all construction in Berkeley for two years with the idea that in the meantime the Council would appoint a citizen's commission to look into the creation of a new master plan that would be a participatory planning process. That ordinance passed on the ballot.

At that point we hooked up with the citizen's commission to write a new ordinance which would actually create all of the various mechanisms for the process to occur. It's a very complicated ordinance which involves decentralizing public funds, describing precisely the mechanisms by which they could be administered without fraud, and making sure that it would be compatible with existing ordinances at the same time that it would allow people to take control of their immediate public land and do something with it. The Commission was friendly to us, not because they were our creation but because they liked what we were talking about. But in writing the initial ordinance which created that commission we made a blunder. The provision was that there would be this commission of eighteen members — two for each councilman — and a budget for two professional staff members.

But what happened was that the staff completely took over. They were appointed by the City Planning Department upon the innocent request of the Commission, but their basic mission in life was to oppose what we were talking about and they succeeded in manipulating the Commission to an incredible degree. They basically ended up redefining a master plan in the classic sense, although they did do one rather radical thing. They coordinated with the Traffic Department to help in setting up traffic barriers to close off certain streets. It was participatory in the sense that the Traffic Department went around and asked people which streets they thought could be closed without causing local problems. But of course it constituted virtually nothing of what we had proposed.

Although the Commission failed to adopt Alexander's proposal, the experience provided the opportunity to look at the whole idea of a neighborhood in a very serious way. The notion of an area of two to three city blocks in diameter as a self-governing political entity with precise controls over its streets was what was important:

We definitely succeeded, for ourselves, in beginning to sketch out quite an amazing process and we began to appreciate a great deal about the dimensions of the problem and exactly what legal structures would be necessary to implement that process. We also gained enormous encouragement from the beauty of the simulations, although they were not presented very well in the report. I think very few people truly understood what we were trying to do. The simulations were necessarily schematic and couldn't fire up anyone's imagination very well. We also found that it took quite a bit of time to convey a vision of what this might actually be like. There was a tendency to dismiss what we were doing as sort of messing around with parking spaces. The idea that beautiful and coherent structures would begin to emerge in each neighborhood was not clear. That is one of the major reasons why we failed practically. Since that wasn't clear, there wasn't enough to get a hold of for the people on the Commission to find it worth opposing the staff for. Another reason simply had to do with the difficulties that are involved in trying to change people's basic attitudes toward their environment.

The street is an embedded fact in our lives. We accept the idea that it is owned and managed by some very large organization outside our immediate ken. But for a person who has experienced what it is like to live in traditional cultures — as I have — the idea that the common land between the buildings is actually the basic arena in which social events take place,

65

66

65. Pattern 53: Main Gateways.

66. Housing Cluster, Santorini.

"...at any level, the individual is not only responsibile for taking care of his own needs, but also for contributing to the needs of the larger group to which he belongs. On a social level, this has almost completely disappeared from present-day urban society."

PLATE XXXIII

67

68

67. Pedestrian Street, Vicenza.

68. Royal Bazaar, Isphahan.

"The idea that the common land between the buildings is actually the basic arena in which social events take place — and is clearly being molded all the time to conform to that activity — is not very real in a modern American city."

PLATE XXXIV

and is clearly being molded all the time to conform to that activity, is very real. But in a modern American city it is not very real at all. And so the idea that we were actually challenging the current existence of the street — although in fact we never quite put it in those terms — was interpreted as having to do with parking spaces and street furniture. So the real crux of the matter is that no one understood the vast differnece it would make. But what actually happens as a result of this process is fundamental human change. Of course the thing is physically different, but it also psychically quite different. Its a completely different experience to live in such a place and be in such a place. It causes genuine political and emotional change — to an enormous extent. And its quite clear to me that the people we were speaking to in Berkeley had absolutely no idea that this thing could possibly have those kinds of consequences. To them it was basically aesthetic.

Nevertheless, in discussing changes in political and fiscal structures, budgetary and legal processes, and in addressing the role of by-laws and the problem of zoning and the extent to which individual rights interact with collective rights in a neighborhood or in a community, PEOPLE REBUILDING BERKELEY outlines a direct relationship between the socio-political structure of a town and its physical form. It also provides the opportunity — as does the "Grass Roots Housing Process" — of changing the implementary apparatus of the existing paradigm. But the "political" problems Alexander encountered in attempting to implement such changes only confirmed his own perceptions of the frustration and agony of paradigm shift. Recall his statement that the shift does not just concern architecture, that it is fundamentally in the culture: "The shift that is involved here, because it transforms words [like 'street' and 'neighborhood'], necessarily and ultimately transforms the whole of society on a fundamental level."

This should come as no surprise to urban designers who have admired the high points of urban history and yet have had to struggle within the constraints of contemporary urbanization. Perhaps in no other field of environmental design is the discrepancy between the standard of the art and the possibilities within practice so great. More than in the case of a single building, the design of a town is almost totally dependent upon the forces at work on a societal level. And yet, it is at that level where the possibilities of transformation are today most likely to be felt. It is in the far-reaching decentralizing tendencies of post-industrialization that the meanings of 'street' and of 'neighborhood' are likely to be different than they are within the current, advanced industrial paradigm. In that sense, the idea of self-governing neighborhoods is much more in tune with the "global village" of Marshall McLuhan than with the affluent suburbs of post-war industrialization.

For Alexander, PEOPLE REBUILDING BERKELEY[3] showed that it was possible to lay out a coherent structure of political changes that would be congruent with the processes suggested by the TIMELESS WAY OF BUILDING and the PATTERN LANGUAGE. It demonstrated, with a precision few designers have attempted, that in the political sphere there is a model which deals with the large issues of implementation — provided someone were willing to go along with it. Like the financing model of the "Grass Roots Housing Process", it was a step closer to the "existence theorem" so essential to the evolution of a new paradigm — namely, a systematic and precise description of the consequences of the theory when they are pushed to their extreme.

REFERENCE NOTES

1. Thomas Kuhn, THE COPERNICAN REVOLUTION (Cambridge: Harvard University Press, 1975), p.77
2. Martin Buber, PATHS IN UTOPIA (Boston: The Beacon Press, 1949), pp.133, 14, 80
3. PEOPLE REBUILDING BERKELEY, Center for Environmental Studies, Berkeley 1975

XVI

CONSTRUCTION

Perhaps the most severe criticism which can be levelled at an architectural theorist is to ask, rhetorically, "But what does he know about building? What has he built?" The question presupposes that the nuances of theoretical speculation (such as whether the structure of a problem is "tree-like" or semi-lattice") are meaningless next to the actual process of making (and financing) a building, in modern urban society.

Of course, if time, labor, and materials were in relative abundance — as they were throughout most of architectural history — it might be possible to argue the details of theory; but until then, the mere achievement of a clearly defined (and standing) building, regardless of content, will always command the attention and respect of the architectural community. For in the final analysis, it comes down to the building; and knowing how difficult it is to actually build a building, and how many costly decisions are involved — decisions in which matters having only the remotest relationship to the question of beauty often decide the outcome — one can easily imagine the authority which architectural practice commands.

Alexander's first experience with actual building construction was in connection with the Modesto Clinic. There, it was assumed that the pattern language was compatible with normal construction procedures; the only difference being that the final design was prefaced by the staking out of the plan on the site. But after final adjustments were made, a standard set of working drawings were made from which a contractor undertook construction. From that point on, the building began to be shaped by a set of forces and constraints having little or nothing to do with the original conception but, rather, with the availability of materials and the

161

division of labor of standard building practice: shop drawings, specifications, change orders, and so on. For Alexander, the design became so altered and so rigidified that, although all the patterns were present, there was hardly a trace of the quality he was hoping for. To him, the construction process needed to be much more gradual, more responsive to the individual spaces of the building and yet still have a structural unity and integrity of its own. Recall his analogy of a skeleton that keeps getting restructured as it is filled out with flesh (Chapter XI). This meant that not only was current practice incompatible with the pattern language but that the problem could not be dealt with by turning it over to someone else — a distinguishing feature of the separation between design and construction that is considered normal within the current paradigm. The problem, however, is not just Alexander's; it is anomalous to the paradigm itself:

A major problem in architecture today is the basic question of what is the structure of a building? In every architectural period you might say that the discovery of an appropriate structure for its time is a major preoccupation of architects. That has been true in the recent period and I think that unsatisfactory answers have been given. A lot of buildings today are more or less "cardboard architecture" and I think that even the most architectural of architects are rather uncomfortable with the fact that there is not a more profound connection between the engineering structure of a building and its actual social form.

In looking back over the recent past, one could argue that the existing paradigm attained a peak of development in the steel-and-glass cage office building. However one might today fault the structure (in terms of cost, efficiency, and energy) or the social form (in terms of habitability, function, and image), there is a direct if not profound relationship between the modular system of support and span and the bureaucratic organization of a large corporation. But insofar as this form is today anomalous — even within current practice — there is certainly the question of an alternative. For Alexander, the question takes the form of a search for a construction process which lends itself to user-design, hence uniqueness and variety (i.e. non-modularized and non-prefabricated); which is based on long-term, incremental, piecemeal growth (i.e. not instantaneous or large-scale); which is dynamic, more like sculpture, and permits gradual stiffening and forming; which permits the engineering to be optimized and is therefore efficient and relatively inexpensive; and finally, which maintains continuity between design and construction (in fact, which permits them to occur as a single activity).

Although the Modesto Clinic was built in 1972, Alexander had already begun thinking along these lines two years earlier. The Clinic only served to magnify the problem and to confirm his intuition. However, in 1970 he conducted seminars at both M.I.T. and Berkeley in an attempt "to derive the optimum type of structure for a human building from first principles."[1] The focus was on a structural system that was congruent with the kinds of generic arrangements of spaces, planes, and lines that would typically occur in a socially responsive building — a sort of internally coherent space-structure morphology:

Spaces: Rectangles, near rectangles and occasional polygons in plan, with straight sides; flat floor; varying ceiling height; the upper triangle between wall and ceiling filled with structure.

Overall arrangement of spaces: A close packing, at any one floor. In three dimensions, corners of any space must come over walls of lower spaces; how to pack variable ceiling height spaces in three dimensions not yet determined.

Columns and walls: Columns at the corners of spaces (unless they form arcades); straight line walls with 'columns' or stub walls built into them frequently along the length.

Roofs and floors: Vault-like structures, which start with what amounts to triangular box-beams, running along the edge of spaces, starting six feet above floor — the roof/floor itself braced with ribs same as the walls — and the whole thing geometrically rigid and redundant. (sic.)

Windows and doors: Frame is part of structure; upper corners of openings chamfered off to give continuity.

Foundations: Mainly point foundations, in which colums splay out into the ground; but also lesser strip foundations, in which the struts buried within walls do the same thing.

Materials: As far as possible, continuous materials in all directions, i.e., if possible not an assembly of components, but a more continuous "woven" structure, where columns, beams, skins, run continuously through each other.

These ideas were of course tentative; but after the Modesto Clinic and a few limited-scope construction experiments (including the contracting of the remodelling of a portion of a sleeping-bag factory in Berkeley), Alexander decided to actually construct a building by himself. At the time (1973) the Center for Environmental Structure was located in a house on Etna Street in Berkeley and the land behind the house seemed suitable for a small cottage and workshop. He ran this "experiment" as part of a ten-week class at the University:

It was completely illegal of course. It would have taken ten weeks just to get permission if we followed normal procedure. Luckily, we managed to get the building almost completely finished before anyone found out about it — although we were finally stopped within days of completion and had to wait another three months before we were able to paint it and put in the light bulbs. But it was actually built.

I designed the building and that literally took two to three days. But the crucial part was the construction — which of course was completely new and, in light of my extreme inexperience as a contractor, an incredibly daring structure in a sense. I knew all of the construction details we were going to use, but more than fifty percent of them were experimental. I knew in principle what we were supposed to do, but there is a difference between thinking about it and doing it. I'm not talking about the difficulties which are always attendant upon building a building. I'm talking about deliberately putting myself out on a limb so that the pressure of having to get off that limb forces a solution — something I do repeatedly and which many people do not understand.

The project however was very successful and the building beautiful in its way. But above all, what mattered most, was that it started to prove that it was possible to do what I thought — namely, to start building from a set of stakes in the ground. It also began to establish, much more strongly than even the Grass Roots Housing Process, how absolutely critical it was that there be one person doing this all the way from design to construction and that, because of the number of decisions we were making every day, there was no way that it could be turned over to someone else.

The workshop cottage was really the first attempt to not only lay the building out on the site — which had already been attempted in modified fashion with the Modesto Clinic — but to not use conventional building systems. Instead, the focus was on

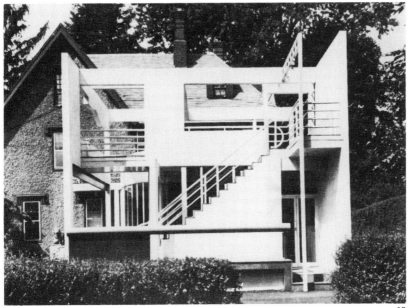

69

70

69. Michael Graves, Benacerraf House Addition.

70. Ludwig Miës van der Rohe and Philip C. Johnson, Seagram Building, New York City.

> *"A major problem in architecture today is the basic question of what is the structure of a building? In every architectural period you might say that the discovery of an appropriate structure for its time is a major preoccupation of architects. That has been true of the recent period and I think that unsatisfactory answers have been given."*

PLATE XXXV

71

72

71. Workshop Cotttage, Etna Street, Berkeley.
72. Form work for Vault, Housing Project, Mexicali.

PLATE XXXVI

developing an on-site production process using ultra-lightweight reinforced column, beam, and vaulting techniques with gradual stiffening that permitted modifications and changes to be made in the exact size and position of doors, windows, interior columns and vaults, alcoves, closets, minor spaces, and in the extent of openings in interior positions. To Alexander, these characteristics could best be attained by experimenting with reinforced concrete:

What interests me about concrete is that it is the ideal, generalized building material that can take any shape which, ideally, a particular member of an element of a building should, for whatever reasons, be they structural or constructional or in terms of the way it looks. The vaults we have been building are merely an example of that.

In other words, here we have developed this technique where you make a different vault over every room and it takes a unique shape according to the shape of the room. It is made by spraying the concrete, or hand-applying it, over a basket. The vault is incredibly thin — only two inches thick. It has a very delicate wire mesh in it. But in general, if you look at a particular room from a pure point of view and you want to support a ceiling with vertical supports, and you start imagining exactly where each element ought to get thicker and thinner according to the distribution of forces and according to the way the windows work, and so on, then what starts to emerge is a very rich form — not ornate, but rich in terms of subtle changes in size at every point. So I am very interested in developing hand-applied concrete as a sort of extremely fluid and flexible building material which might bear the same relationship to building as pencil does to drawing.

However, the concrete code is only worked out for what you might call the traditional building techniques for concrete. That is, for standard pre-stressed or poured-in-place elements, which are very massive and very expensive. But you cannot afford to build concrete like that. It's massive and consumes vasts amount of steel and cement and it's quite ugly. Whereas the kinds of structure that I'm talking about consume much less because they are so stiff and because they work in so many different directions that the material does not have to be that thick. But there are no codes that permit this or that have been worked out for it. On the other hand, it's very expensive and difficult to work out all the structural calculations each time. A simple house like this might easily involve three or four thousand dollars worth of calculations because of the very complicated engineering that is required to analize the three-dimensional interactions of the forces of these elements when they're all working together. And that is prohibitive and

165

essentially means that no one will do it. I can hardly even afford to do it experimentally; and certainly no one else will do it, and I'm not interested in it if its just me that's doing it. So the question arises of how to come up with a generic approach to the engineering which sets up rules that clearly govern what you can do and what you cannot do in a manner that permits this thing to be developed in a very rich and fluid way and knowing that it will be structurally sound provided that it conforms to those rules.

This is essentially equivalent to writing a code for a new kind of building process — which is what we have actually embarked upon.[2] The ideal conclusion of it would be a book which would describe in a very general way how one could build in concrete using all of these thin-shell techniques and be legitimate so that a building permit can be issued. That's essentially what it amounts to.

There is a real sense in which, at the moment, buildings are shaped, to an extreme extent, simply by available techniques of putting materials together and not at all by generalized considerations of a more idealized form. In the paper "From a Set of Forces to a Form," I gave an example of a cantilever. It happens that there is a mathematical solution to the general problem of having a cantilever with a point load at one end and determining the optimum shape of the cantilever. There are not many engineering problems where you can give an exact solution, but there is in that case. It turns out that the optmum shape of a cantilever is remarkably like a leaf. That is, in plan, it has a very pointed tip where the point load is; it sort of swells in a kind of reverse curve back toward the point of support; and before you get to the point of support, the width of it suddenly goes in so that at the actual point of support it is quite narrow again. In section, it is very thin at the end and, in a parabolic curve, is actually getting thicker and thicker towards the stem — all of which has to do with the analysis of the bending moments. It's a good example because nobody knows how you could possibly build such a cantilever in a way that would even be faintly competitive with a simple box-beam that's just stuck out there. Although the leaf-shaped cantilever has less material in it, the construction techniques we have are so limited and so crude that, for us, the most economical shape is some crude rectangle. But that's just because of existing forming techniques.

So the point of what I am trying to do with concrete and with these very generalized shell structures has to do with actually trying to begin to move in the direction of what you might call genuinely "optimum structures." And the point about these techniques that I'm so interested in is that they actually, for the first time, begin to make it at least imaginable that one could shape things that come close to the optimum design.

As time goes by I become more and more interested in concrete construction. I believe wood to be a very limited building material. Its very good for certain things, like windows, but not very good for building in general. There are only a few parts of the world where it's even possible. Even though you can farm forests, there are serious ecological problems. And also, beyond that, to me a building is a more stable thing than can be made out of this very green, kiln-dried lumber. If you're working with 10 × 10 oak members, then you can build a building that will last five hundred years, even although its made out of wood; but to be making buildings that will have to be torn down in forty or fifty years is ridiculous. Consequently, I am generally more interested in concrete and concrete-wood combinations, than in all wood buildings. And beyond that, concrete is an incredibly rich building material which, to my knowledge, has never really been correctly used because most of its use has been governed by some very crude forming techniques. In other words, its either pre-stressed, pre-cast, or poured into forms which are massive and crude and not at all delicate in their detailing and certainly not at all flexible in the kinds of forms that you can create.

This is certainly something that people like Pier Luigi Nervi were striving towards; but you have to be a superb engineer to even attempt it. I'm talking about a situation in which that would actually become general. At the moment it is very complex to form such buildings. There aren't any simple techniques available for producing these complex shapes in a simple way. Even the forming techniques that are available are incredibly primitive and fantastically expensive. They cost more than the concrete.

Neither the analysis nor the production is available to the average lay builder or lay architect. There are currently computer programs for finite element analysis — a technique known for quite some time but which goes much deeper than the classical techniques of analysis. It is still a bit cumbersome to use, but if you could actually just punch in the configuration of a building in such a way that it would immediately be subjected to finite element analysis, and immediately get back a complete read-out of all the stresses developed in the different parts of the building, that would bring one much closer to all this.

Alexander would develop and test these ideas further in several projects between 1973 and 1976: a shopping center proposal in Walnut Creek, California; a proposal to the Spanish Ministry of Tourism in Andalusia; an apartment house proposal in France; and a housing complex in Mexico.

The Walnut Creek Project mainly provided the opportunity to simulate the process of incremental growth at an architectural scale. The Andalusian project involved describing, in some detail, the role of the architect as a builder and the kind of production organization that would make this a viable professional activity — including the operation of builder's groups, local builder's yards, and the training and replacement of architect-builders as first suggested in the Grass Roots Housing Process[3]. But the French Apartment House offered a chance to synthesize almost all of the ideas developed during this period into a complete, pre-construction simulation.

The project was initiated by Francoise Choay — a prominent urban theorist and historian and editor of the French translations of Alexander's publications with Oxford University Press in Paris. She had been involved in an analysis of the poor quality of the mass-produced, standard apartment houses currently being built in France and invited Alexander to explore opportunities for developing alternative solutions to the housing problem. Eventually, the Director of one of the new towns on the outskirts of Versailles became interested and the Center was commissioned to do a study of a large group of four-storey apartment houses. For Alexander it was the opportunity to put together the ideas of the user-oriented house cluster, the neighbourhood group, incremental financing, the architect-builder, and the model of a dynamic construction process within the constraints of actual cost-control. But the first real opportunity to put all of this into practice was in Mexico in 1975.

Under the sponsorship of the University of Mexico, Alexander and a group of colleagues and students from Berkeley were contracted by the Mexican Government to spend a year in Mexicali to set up a process for the design and construction of low-cost housing. The individual houses — which were eventually built according to this process — have an area of sixty to seventy square meters, are arranged around common land owned jointly by the families, and were designed by the families that lived in them so that each would be different from the others. During construction, the houses were made from interlocking cement blocks produced on site, with ultra-lightweight concrete vaults built over lightweight woven wood baskets, at a cost of about US$3000 each:

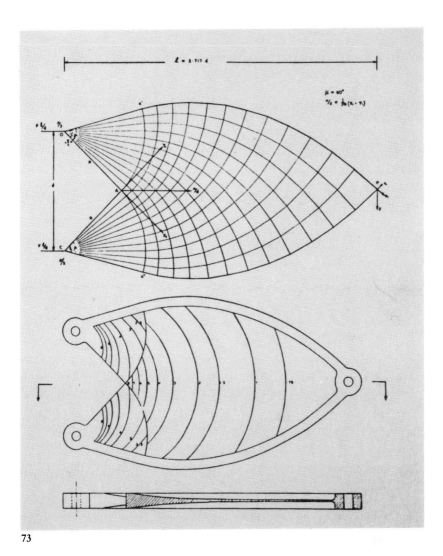

73

73.   Drawings for Optimal Structures.

PLATE XXXVII

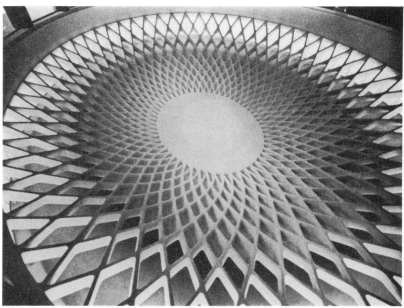

74

75

74. Pier Luigi Nervi, Festival Hall, Chianciano.

75. Pier Luigi Nervi, Aviation Building, Orvietto.

PLATE XXXVIII

The Mexican project was simply the first opportunity we had to put the ideas that had been developed during this second phase of research and experimentation into practice. In other words, we had the opportunity to get the architect-builder working in a full-fledged way, to get the families operating as a social group and not just users of the pattern language, to have a small amount of success with the flow of money, and even to be able to change land tenure in the sense that we were able to have cooperative ownership of public land as well as private ownership of private land, and of course to implement the construction system we had been developing. This was the first opportunity to actually put that into effect in a serious way. And we did it. It actually all works and we have written about it in THE PRODUCTION OF HOUSES.

In spite of the incredible hassles we had during that year, and in spite of the fact that many of the people working on the project were somewhat traumatized by the experience — challenging the existing order on so many fronts at once — I believe the project to be a success, particularly from the standpoint of the testimony of the individual families who were involved.

Its very curious. It isn't as if the families did not experience any hardship. They were working very hard and they had to work several months longer than was anticipated. But somehow, in spite of those difficulties, I think the process was so rooted in their reality, or it made so much sense to them, or it tied so closely with their feelings and their desires, that they actually experienced no problems whatsoever. We checked this out very carefully. The fact that the administrators or my students were traumatized just made life uncomfortable for us and I was sorry about it; but in the long run, if the families had begun to feel that way it would have been terribly serious, because it was for them that we were working. But they didn't. They felt wonderful from beginning to end. And that's curious and important. It indicates something that I do believe to be true: that all of this, every part of what I have spoken about, including all of the theory developed in phase one and all of this material in phase two, speaks directly to the human heart as it really is and actually goes to archetypal necessities and realities that exist in people. And therefore, to put it somewhat overdramatically, there is almost a recognition of something that was part of you already and which, in spite of the heaviness of paradigm shift, is not traumatic from the point of view of the person who is benefitting by it.

These experiences brought Alexander much closer to realizing his original goals than any of the previous projects. The Mexican Project, especially, demonstrated that the major theoretical problems connected with implementation had been resolved. The buildings were still imperfect, but not in any fundamental way that further experimentation with reinforced concrete and with the basic structural systems could not straighten out. It seemed as if it were just a matter of fine-tuning; and yet, although it was clear that a plateau had been reached, certain observations suggested that there was still something missing:

There was one fact above everything else that I was aware of, and that was that the buildings were still a bit more funky than I would have liked. That is, there are just a few little things that we built down there that truly have that sort of limpid beauty of things that have been around for ages and that, actually, are just dead right. That's rare; and it occurred in only a few places. Generally speaking, the project is very delightful — different of course from what is generally being built, not just in the way of low-cost housing — but it doesn't quite come to the place where I believe it must.

This is very important because here we have the question of the quality again. That is always my reference point, and I ask myself, when all is said and done, after a lot of us have spent a year building these buildings, to what extent has this timeless quality actually manifested itself?

Part of the reason for the whole of the work of phase two was that I noticed that when other architects were using the pattern language they were still making the same old architecture and saying that it had the pattern language in it. And that of course led to the whole analysis of phase two — all of those fundamental and sweeping economic, political, and procedural changes that are needed to make this happen correctly. But what I am saying now is that, given all of that work (or at least insofar as it came together in the Mexican situation) and even with us doing it (so there is no excuse that someone who doesn't understand it is doing it), it only works partially. Although the pattern language worked beautifully — in the sense that the families designed very nice houses with lovely spaces and which are completely out of the rubric of modern architecture, so that there is no problem on that level anymore — this very magical quality is only faintly showing through here and there. So of course I began to think about this more and more.

We were running several little experiments in the builder's yard. There is an arcade around the courtyard with each room off of the arcade designed by a different person. Some of the rooms were designed by my colleagues at the Center and they also had this unusual funkiness — still very charming, very delightful, but not calm at all. In that sense, vastly different from what

76

77

76. Housing Project, Mexicali.
77. On-Site Construction, Mexicali.

PLATE XXXIX

78

79

78. Courtyard, Mosque of the Yeni Camii, Istanbul.
79. Housing Project, Mexicali.

PLATE XL

is going on in four-hundred year old Norwegian farm where there is an incredible clarity and simplicity that has nothing to do with its age. But this was typical of things that were happening. Here is this very sort of limpid simplicity and yet the pattern language was actually encouraging people to be a little bit crazy and to conceive of much more intricate relationships than were necessary. They were actually disturbing. Yet in all of the most wonderful buildings, at the same time that they have all of these patterns in them, they are incredibly simple. They are not simple like an S.O.M. building; — sometimes they are incredibly ornate — so I'm not talking about that kind of simplicity. There is however a kind of limpidity which is very crucial; and I felt that we just cannot keep going through this problem. We must somehow idenify what it is and how to do it — because I knew it was not just my perception of it.

The problem is complicated because the word simplicity completely fails to cover it; at another moment it might be exactly the opposite. Take the example of the columns. If you have the opportunity to put a capital or a foot on it, it is certainly better to do those two things than not — which is different from what the modern architectural tradition tells you to do. Now, in a peculiar sense, the reasons for it being better that way are the same as the reasons for being very simple and direct in the spacing of those same columns around the courtyard (i.e. approximately equal along each side). I'm saying that, wherever that source of judgment is coming from it is the same in both cases. And the question is, "Where is that coming from? What is it that makes the column spacing want to be so simple and yet the colums want to have capitals and feet?" The word simplicity is obviously not the relevant word. There is something which in one instance tells you to be simple and which in another tells you to be more complicated. Its the same thing which is telling you those two things. And I became aware of this over and over again in that building project — that there were things like this going on and that I had a reasonably clear intuition about it but that it was very difficult to make explicit and absolutely beyond my capacity to explain to anyone. In spite of all my efforts at trying to explain it over the past ten or fifteen years, I just could not explain this matter — although I knew what I was feeling about it and knew that it had nothing to do with me personally.

That was the first observation. The second observation concerned Alexander's own attitude toward construction. It was one thing to say that design and construction are sufficiently interdependent or interrelated to justify the logic of having one person do both; but it is another thing to realize that the act of construction is itself as important as design, and not just a matter of implementation":

I gradually began to realize that I was not taking the problem seriously enough and that I had a very casual attitude to construction. I thought that if one followed a set of operations which were defined by the patterns — actually they were more specific than patterns because they refer to particular versions of patterns — then that was enough. But what I realized was that the craft element was crucial.

I began to be aware that the actual craft of building in itself was as gigantic and fascinating, in its own way, as the whole of the pattern language. I had no idea of that. I had taken it much too lightly. And of course there is no way that one is normally taught that. For an architect, building is considered to be a sort of semi-automatic procedure. It is not something that you actually put any emotion or effort into. Somebody else basically does it. So you never have any opportunity to find out how fascinating and how complex it really is. Although there is nothing shattering here from a theoretical standpoint — even Gropius wrote about this and was convinced that the architect ought to be a builder — the point is that the whole of modern construction is taken for granted. I think that I myself was just laboring under the delusion of not realizing how well it has to be done — not just in the formulation of the rules, but in their execution as well. It wasn't so much that I thought this was mere implementation and that I was going to rush through it. Its just that I had a very inadequate conception of how fascinating and complicated it really is.

Only recently have I begun to realize that the problem is not merely one of technical mastery or the competent application of rules — like trowelling a piece of concrete so that it's really nice — but that there is actually something else which is guiding these rules. It actually involves a different level of mastery. It's quite a different process to do it right; and every single act that you do can be done in that sense well or badly. But even assuming that you have got the technical part clear, the creation of this quality is a much more complicated process of the most utterly absorbing and fascinating dimensions. It is in fact a major creative or artistic act — every single little thing that you do — and it is only in the years since the Mexican project that I have begun to see the dimensions of that fact.

These observations — that the actual decision-making process in the resolution of the details of construction had not been made explicit, and that the process itself required a level of mastery not accounted for by the previous work — would lead Alexander into

80

81

80. Interior, Housing Project, Mexicali.
81. Hjellum Farm House, Vang, Norway.

PLATE XLI

82. Gateway (under construction), Mexicali.
83. Veranda detail, Ise Shrine, Naigu.

PLATE XLII

the last and perhaps the most fascinating series of experiments of the second phase of his research: the precise identification of the geometrical properties of the unity of space. It would also bring into focus his little-known research in cognitive psychology at Harvard under Bruner and bring him full circle back to the original questions he posed as a student at Cambridge twenty-five years earlier. In the meantime, however, his experiments in construction would prove to be the decisive ingredient in forcing a confrontation with the existing paradigm.

REFERENCE NOTES

1. Published in Edward Allen (ed.), THE RESPONSIVE HOUSE (Cambridge: MIT Press, 1974), pp.22-32. See also "Specifications for an Organic and Human Building System," Allen, OP. CIT., pp.33-51 and selected papers and discussions from "The Shirt-Sleeve Sessions in Responsive Housebuilding Technologies," Department of Architecture, Massachusetts Institute of Technology (Cambridge: May 3-5, 1972)

2. "The Construction of Thin Shells," unpublished manuscript (Berkeley: 1976)

3. See also "The Architect-Builder: Toward Changing the Conception of What an Architect Is, "SAN FRANCISCO BAY ARCHITECTS REVIEW (September, 1977), p.4

XVII

THE BATTLE LINES ARE DRAWN

Kuhn points out that the differences between paradigms constitute more that a disagreement about the behavior of the world. They are directed not only out towards the nature of reality but also back upon the field that produced them. And since paradigms are the source of the methods, problem definitions, and standards of solution accepted by the field's practitioners at any given moment, the reception of a new paradigm will often necessitate a redefinition of the corresponding field.

For Alexander, the attempt to discover new processes by which buildings are made now places him in a radically different posture vis-a-vis the current paradigm. For the first time since NOTES, his work can no longer be mistaken as paradigm extension or modification, but rather, as a completely different conception of building. It entails the realization, for example, that to produce the particular geometry called for, the building itself needs to be in a constant state of creation:

It involves a dynamic process where you need to be constantly modifying the design while you are building it because it is only while the building is going up that you appreciate exactly *how to make certain details. It includes the idea of working without drawings, by and large, and it includes the idea that a set of construction processes are specified rather than drawings and that these processes take off where the pattern language stops. In other words, you use the pattern language up to a certain point, you lay out the building, and then you initiate a set of processes, you carry these processes out, and when you finish carrying them out you have a building. Its a completely dynamic conception of the translation of a design into an actuality as opposed to having a set of working drawings which are complete and finished and describe a building which somebody then figures out how to construct. This is a completely different idea. It is more like sculpture in the sense that one is constantly reacting to the last operation they just performed and deciding if it is correct.*

As a consequence of this conception, fundamental changes in the methods and practice of building are necessary. The way contractors work and the way architects relate to contractors needs to be altered. An amalgamation of contracting and designing needs to occur in which the architect is also a builder. And because the building is to be constantly built and rebuilt during its lifetime, the relationship between the architect-builder and the environment needs to be on a relatively permanent as opposed to a temporary basis — resembling the traditional family physician's relationship to his patients. It actually calls for more rather than fewer architects.

It entails a shift in understanding of what is going on in a building site — that there needs to be a confluence of a series of very simple processes. It is analogous to understanding that, although every spider's web is different and every piece of every web is different, there is only one process that produces all the webs as opposed to only one component out of which many webs are made. It requires corresponding changes in manufacturing and industrialization and even in structural engineering because the materials compatible with such processes would need to be slightly different — more labile — than those which are used in current practices.

It requires alterations in the flow of money through the environment, particularly how large the sums are to be handled and how distant is the place where such sums are approved. And finally, it requires modifications in the structure of land ownership and local politics so that there is a fairly differentiated hierarchy of responsibility for the built environment between the private home and the large public spaces in town

The demonstration that such changes are possible, and practical, constituted the task which Alexander faced in the second series of experiments and projects after 1972-1973. But it is clear from the onset that, although the task was completely dependent upon and congruent with the preceding work, it is radically different:

I believe that this second phase is actually harder to grasp than the first. You might say that the first took more of an intellectual achievement than the second; but it is easier to accept because, even although it is perhaps shattering to one's cognitive beliefs, you still do not fully appreciate the break that you need to make with present day notions about how to build. In the second phase you make a completely sharp break and are projected into a future where one is just operating and making things in a completely different way. It is really two parts to one paradigm. I think the first body of material is most crucial intellectually, but the second body of material is actually more crucial in the sense of bringing somebody to terms with what this paradigm really is. But it is not true to say that I knew this in 1972. All I knew was that I was embarking on a whole new series of projects and investigations.

And yet the difference between the two phases of work was already foreshadowed by events prior to 1972, events which suggested that the final break with the old paradigm was just beneath the surface. For example, as compatible with the existing paradigm as NOTES actually was, there was also a sense in which people found it disturbing, even threatening — and that was the tacit assumption on Alexander's part, conveyed through the tone of the book, that one could (and indeed should) be much more precise about the subject of design than was considered normal or acceptable within the profession. Even if one disagreed with its thesis, one had to overcome a sort of mental laziness that was endemic to current architectural thought in order to dispute its content. Then there was the BART study which, although it appeared just as an attempt to solve an unusually complex problem, involved several firings and rehirings over the question of what was actually being done. And during the Multiservice Center project, the architectural firm in New York that was to do the final design for the building eventually had to be replaced. There was also the fact that the jury for the United Nations competition on the Peruvian housing project was seriously divided between those who felt Alexander's scheme should get first prize and those who did not understand it or approve of its implications. And then there was the OREGON EXPERIMENT, which drew serious protests from the American Institute of Architects (AIA) in Portland and caused several misunderstandings about the real purpose of the project — even among its most ardent supporters:

In the OREGON EXPERIMENT we were rather careful to include the conventional model of the architect in our definitions and procedural discussion. There was a limit to how far we could go, particularly with material we could not support at the time. So we said that the architect should take over after the users had designed the building and that he should be constrained to produce a building according to what they had done. We wrote it that way because, in the light of reactions we had already invoked from the AIA, we felt it was the most realistic statement that could be tolerated by that community at that time. But we knew, even then, that there was a more extreme version in which the conventional architect did not appear at all. However, it was ridiculous to even try to go into that because we wanted the project to be implemented.

Bob Harris, then Dean of the Architecture School at Oregon and the person most responsible for us getting hired, understands this work to an incredible degree — but he took our statement at face value. He really thought that the existing process was completely fine. In other words, given the fact that the users had laid out the building, at that point you just called in an AIA architect, you put the constraint on him that he must work with the layout that the users have made, he must know the patterns, and he must be willing to work with the users in the development of the building. But basically, at that point you have a conventional architect taking over control of the job. And from Bob Harris' perspective, this meant that the experiments we were doing in construction at that time were incomprehensible and slightly bizarre. (We were already conducting experiments in the actual construction process which did not follow the normal route of working drawings, contractors, and so on.) I think he found those experiments bizarre and alarming and he became actively doubtful about the possibility of our involvement in the actual process of building on the Oregon campus.

But I had already had the experience with the building of the clinic in Modesto and I knew it was not the architect who was at fault but the process that the architect normally has to follow. I did not want to repeat that experience and I did everything I could to convince him that there was a fundamental theoretical problem here. I tried to describe the differences to him between having a set of working drawings from which the thing is built and what we were exploring as a dynamic process of construction, but he had accepted the OREGON EXPERIMENT as a document and did not realize that it was the first sentence of a rather long paragraph. All sorts of matters still had to be addressed in the proper formation of the environment, but that was all he could take.

It was all most people could take. There was even serious disagreement among Alexander's colleagues at the Center over the direction the work was taking. Independently of the fact that the group was already breaking up as a social entity, several of its members did not feel it was necessary to explore changes in the process of construction:

I remember that the construction patterns disturbed people quite a bit, apart from the fact that Murray and Max did not want to work on them. For instance, there was the Swedish architect Johannes Olivegren. He was very much taken by the pattern language and tried to work with it and teach courses in it in Sweden. In fact, as a result of his interest in all of this, we undertook a planning project in Sweden. But one time, he was visiting San Francisco, and he wanted to see our latest work. We showed him a draft of the construction patterns we were working on and he became quite upset. He was actually a very successful architect in Sweden and he had been treating all of this as information. Suddenly, with the construction patterns, it was quite impossible to say this was just "information." Here this thing was actually beginning to clearly project the physical form of things, albeit with quite a large possibility of variation; but nonetheless, it was clearly not only starting to rule out skyscrapers — which some of the other patterns did — but it was actually ruling out particular forms of construction and indicating others. And I remember that he was quite white when he came through reading it and he said that I was making a terrible mistake — that I was getting locked into architecture when this stuff was such beautiful information!

Reactions like these were directed at the now obvious *architectural* direction of Alexander's work and represent a tendency to regard him as essentially a theorist who, although perhaps brilliant analytically, does not qualify him to seriously enter the domain of building. In part, this tendency originates in the deep split between theory and practice within the existing paradigm. But part of it originates in the confusion over the identification of Alexander with the so-called design methods movement of the late sixties.

NOTES ON THE SYNTHESIS OF FORM had become one of the basic texts for a number of architects in the academy and, later, in professional practice, whose primary concern was in improving the rationality of the existing process of design — particularly with regard to the functional requirements a building was supposed to satisfy. Because the book had provided a fairly explicit and rational model for analyzing and talking about the activity of design, and because it was one of the first attempts to use a computer in the service of an architectural problem in a fairly significant way, it quickly provided the basis for a number of independent but similar inquiries into the application of various scientific problem-solving techniques to the existing paradigm.[1]. Foremost among these, in addition to computers, were operations research, mathematical modelling, and general systems theory. Coupled with a growing interest in the research tools and findings of the social and behavioral sciences, these attempts to rationalize the existing process of design commanded the interest and attention of architectural debate into the early seventies; but few if any results emerged from this school of thought, except perhaps a sharper critique of the existing paradigm and a deeper sense of crisis.

Alexander however became identified as one of this movement's leading proponents, in spite of an article he wrote as early as 1965 on the limitations of computer applications to architectural design, and in spite of a rather forceful disclaimer in the preface to the second edition of NOTES in 1971. The "design methods" label would remain for a long time and serve to prevent serious consideration of the non-theoretical consequences of his work.

At the same time, however, somewhat more serious difficulties with various and specific individuals developed. It was as if the battle lines were finally being drawn:

Serious fights began to develop between us at the Center and people in the School of Architecture at Berkeley. In other words, my work and the work of the Center appeared completely supportive of the general framework of architecture as it was then being built — up to a certain point. NOTES architects felt they could eat like mustard on their sandwich; it just made things a little spicier for them. The patterns also, especially in their early years, were considered a solid basis for what many considered to be a generally positive direction in the evolution of modern architecture. This was certainly Roger Montgomery's position when he favourably reviewed our early efforts. But the whole notion that there was actually an objective reality here, and that it was not just a matter of whatever you said was right was right, but that there is really something which is right and there are other things which are wrong, began to cause tremendously acrid disputes.

Roger Montgomery would eventually not talk to me for several years, not exactly because of all of these things — ostensibly for other reasons; but actually, in a large way, I think, because after his initial enthusiasm for what we were doing he began to feel more and more uncomfortable about where we were heading. He eventually began to see where this was going. What happened, for several people, was that it suddenly started to appear

179

on the horizon as a concrete alternative — not merely a happy alternative that is going along with other stuff, but one that is specifically confronting it and saying, "Stop that garbage. This is something else." Of course it was also, I think, the tone — both in my writings and in my dealings with people — which is one of my serious shortcomings as a person. But the situation is such that, as a result of the paradigm that exists today, the whole beautiful earth is being made into a horrible mess, and I have a tremendous amount of rage about it. It makes it very difficult for me to enter into these debates on a perfectly neutral level because I am too angry about what has been happening and I hate what is going on. As a result of all this, my situation has become completely switched around. Originally I was sort of this intellectual protege that was going to put the mustard on the sandwich, whereas now the situation is such that I am the only licensed contractor on the faculty of architecture (at the University of California in Berkeley).

What is this confrontation really all about? Obviously, from what has already been said, more than a simple clash of opinion over the definition of the problem is at stake. What is actually being debated is the definition of the field and, as Kuhn has shown, the proponents of competing paradigms — once the distinction has been made and acknowledged — will inevitably talk past each other. Because they see different things when looking in the same direction, they will disagree about the problems that each candidate must solve. This is why the acknowledgment of crisis — which Alexander has consistently and unhesitatingly invoked time and time again in his critical assessment of contemporary architecture — plays such an important role in the emergence of a new paradigm. There either is or is not a crisis; and certainly little is gained by being polite about the seriousness of its consequences. But more is involved, however, than the incompatibility of standards. Since a new paradigm often develops out of pushing the old one to its limits, it will ordinarily incorporate much of the vocabulary and conceptual apparatus that had been previously employed in the existing paradigm — *only it will use them in a new way.* "Within the new paradigm," says Kuhn, "old terms, concepts, and experiments fall into new relationships one with the other. The inevitable result is what we must call, though the term is not quite right, a misunderstanding between the two competing schools."[2] For Alexander, this "misunderstanding" constitutes one of the

180

most frustrating and ultimately painful aspects of such a confrontation:

The work of Benjamin Whorff and the whole tradition of linguistic anthropology partly explains how the actual structure of words captures you. Whorff's classic observation was during a fire insurance investigation. He was analyzing a fire that had taken place when someone had thrown a match into an empty gasoline drum. "Empty" has the normal connotation of safe; and "full" has the connotation of pregnant with danger. Yet actually a full drum, being sealed, is relatively safe; while an empty drum, being full of gasoline vapor, is extremely dangerous. The words give you a 180° misreading of the situation. It was a typical example, for Whorf, of how words could trap one into an incorrect perception of things.

Because of this sort of Whorffian effect, most of the major concepts that have to do with the environment, such as the word "planning", the word "architect," the word "budget," even possibly the word "building," the word "bylaws," the word "zoning" — every single one of these words, certainly including "design" and, as we have discussed, the word "beauty" — is actually one of these explosive little traps. Structurally, each one is in a certain position and, in their present state, each is congruent with the others — that is, they all fit together to create precisely the situation which we have in the environment today.

Now one way to discuss the paradigm shift and how painful and how difficult and how drastic it is, at the same time that it is so subtle, is to imagine that every one of these words is invalid. Either that the word cannot be used because it is structurally connected up to the others in the wrong way, or, that its structural connotations would have to undergo profound changes, changes so great that they may not be able to be achieved and therefore you have to abandon them — so that the basic map of the world that we have about these concepts is completely messed up. The agony of such a change is excruciating. It almost amounts to a surgical operation.

Consider an extremely simplified model of the brain in which you have a large number of neurons connected to certain others. Although this is totally inaccurate, imagine that each neuron stands for an idea. Now what is happening in such a model is that each of these words or concepts or ideas is essentially defined by a certain collection of connections that it has to the others. The word "zoning" is connected to "enforcement," and it's connected to "categories" of "land-use," and to the "board of appeals" at the city level, and to various other words. And according to the picture I have been painting, every one of those connections is incorrect. So what is going on here is literally like going into that brain with a scalpel and actually severing every single one of those connections and growing new ones. It's literally that violent. But what is so complicated about it is that it actually does not appear violent. It appears incredibly subtle — and that is what is so frustrating and agonizing. And the reason is that this paradigm shift does not just concern architecture. It's fundamentally in the culture. It's not just architects who have these connections between words. That is the way those words are in today's culture and in the language of today's society. And the shift that is involved here, because it transforms words, necessarily and ultimately transforms the whole of society of a fundamental level.

Alexander is aware of the fact that no theory stands in isolation to the intellectual circumstances of its context in society — a fact which is as true for science as it is so obviously true for art. Kuhn for example, in his study of the Copernican Revolution, shows that Copernicus lived and worked during a period when "rapid changes in political, economic, and intellectual life were preparing the bases of Modern European and American civilization."[3] His theory of the motion of the planets and of the sun-centered universe was only part of a wider shift embracing more than astronomy. Although initiated as a narrowly technical, highly mathematical revision of classical astronomy, as Kuhn puts it, "The Copernican Theory became one focus for the tremendous controversies in religion, in philosphy, and in social theory, which . . . set the tenor of the modern mind."[4]

Part of Alexander's sense of frustration and agony comes from this awareness — that although the focus of concern appears so highly specialized, it is actually part of a major transformation of thought that embraces more than just architecture. This is why Kuhn compares a change of paradigm to a "revolution." Like the choice between competing political institutions, that between competing paradigms proves to be the choice between incompatible modes of community life — and of course, political revolutions aim to change political institutions in ways that those institutions themselves prohibit. The search for processes that effect such changes constitutes this second phase of experiments and projects in Alexander's attempt to delineate precisely the full consequences of his discoveries — when they are pushed to their extreme.

REFERENCE NOTES

1. See Geoffrey Broadbent and Anthony Ward (eds.), DESIGN METHODS IN ARCHITECTURE (London: Lund-Humphries, 1969); J. Christopher Jones, DESIGN METHODS (New York: John Wiley, 1970); and Gary Moore (ed.), EMERGING METHODS IN ENVIRONMENTAL DESIGN AND PLANNING (Cambridge: MIT Press, 1970)

2. Thomas Kuhn, THE STRUCTURE OF SCIENTIFIC REVOLUTIONS, 2nd ed. (Chicago: University of Chicago Press, 1970), p.149

3. Thomas Kuhn, THE COPERNICAN REVOLUTION (Cambridge: Harvard University Press, 1957), p.2

4. IBID.

PART FIVE

XVIII

THE BEAD GAME

We come now to the intersection of two observations: the first, by Banham, that the "precious vessel" of handicraft aesthetics — the chain that goes back from Gropius to Morris to Ruskin to Blake, etc. — is dropped and broken with the modern-industrial movement; and the second, by Kuhn, that the ideas upon which new paradigms are based may often be — as in the case of Copernicus — long-held or ancient ideas rediscovered in a new, more precise way.

The tradition of thought which is being called upon here is the search for a universal formative principle — a search which goes beyond Ruskin and Blake to Leonardo, Brunelleschi, and Alberti. In fact, it was Alberti who believed that aesthetic judgment was not a matter of personal opinion but something which came, rather, "from a secret argument and discourse implanted in the mind itself."[1] The idea that form — and its perception — is not merely representational, but is active in the deepest sources of cognition, has been evident to many great philosophers since Plato; but only recently has there been any recognition of the argument within the scientific community. This rapprochement was summarized in 1951 by Herbert Read:

> The increasing significance given to *form* or *pattern* in various branches of science has suggested the possibility of a certain parallelism, if not identity, in the structures of natural phenomena and of authentic works of art. That the work of art has a formal structure of a rhythmical, even of a precisely geometrical kind, has for centuries been recognised by all but a few nihilists (the Dadaists, for example). That some at any rate of these structures or proportions -- notably the Golden Section -- have correspondences in nature has also been recognised for many years. The assumption, except on the part of a few mystics, was that nature,

in these rare instances, was paying an unconscious tribute to art; or that the artist was unconsciously imitating nature. But now the revelation that perception itself is essentially a pattern-selecting and pattern-making function (a Gestalt formation); that pattern is inherent in the physical structure or in the functioning of the nervous system; that matter itself analyses into coherent patterns or arrangements of molecules; and the gradual realisation that all these patterns are effective and ontologically significant by virtue of an organisation of their parts which can only be characterised as *aesthetic* — all this development has brought works of art and natural phenomena on to an identical plane of inquiry.[2]

For Alexander, this is the "Bead Game Conjecture," an allusion to Hermann Hesse's great imaginary game in which all forms — musical, mathematical, historical, social, physical, chemical, biological, and visual — can be represented in a single way. The conjecture:

> That it is possible to invent a unifying concept of structure within which all the various concepts of structure now current in different fields of art and science, can be seen from a single point of view. This conjecture is not new. In one form or another people have been wondering about it, as long as they have been wondering about structure itself; but in our world, confused and fragmented by specialisation, the conjecture takes on special significance. If our grasp of the world is to remain coherent, we need a bead game; and it is therefore vital for us to ask ourselves whether or not a bead game can be invented.[3]

The problems posed by the Mexican project only served to magnify this challenge; however, they constitute only one of several sources for what was to become a major investigation into the geometry of spatial form. The first was the recognition of a general lack of formal order in the buildings that Alexander had built so far:

I had been watching what happens when one uses pattern languages to design buildings and became uncomfortably aware of a number of shortcomings. The first is that the buildings are slightly funky — that is, although it is a great relief that they generate these spontaneous buildings that look like agglomerations of traditional architecture when compared with some of the concrete monoliths of modern architecture, I noticed an irritatingly disorderly funkiness. At the same time that it is lovely, and has many of these beautiful patterns in it, its not calm and satisfying. In that sense its quite different from traditional architecture which appears to have this looseess in the large but is usually calm and peaceful in the small.

To caricature this I could say that one of the hallmarks of pattern language architecture, so far, is that there are alcoves all over the place; or that the windows are all different. So I was disturbed by that — especially down in Mexico. I realized that there were some things about which the people putting up the buildings did not know — and that I knew, implicitly, as part of my understanding of pattern languages (including members of my own team.) They were just a bit too casual about it and, as a result, the work was in danger of being too relaxed. As far as my own efforts were concerned, I realized that there was something I was tending to put in it in order to introduce a more formal order — to balance this otherwise labyrinthine looseness.

The other point is that even although the theory of pattern languages in traditional society clearly applies equally to very great buildings — like cathedrals — as well as to cottages, there was the sense that, somehow, our own version of it was tending to apply more to cottages. In part, this was a matter of the scale of the projects we were working on; but it also had to do with something else. It was almost as if the grandeur of a very great church was inconceivable within the pattern language as it was being presented. Its not that the patterns don't apply; just that, somehow, there is a wellspring for that kind of activity which was not present in either *A PATTERN LANGUAGE* or *THE TIMELESS WAY OF BUILDING*.

The second source for this investigation was a growing awareness, over several years, that very few people understood TIMELESS on a *geometrical* level. Even chapter twenty-six, which describes the fact that a certain geometrical character manifests itself when all of the processes are followed, did not succeed in bringing home this critical point:

I've known from various readings that the book has had, that most people do not fully understand that chapter. Its just too short and it does not fully explain itself — although I was aware that in that book I just could not do the topic justice. In other words, I became increasingly aware of the fact that my own understanding of this, among other things, existed at a very highly developed geometrical level and that all of what THE TIMELESS WAY OF BUILDING was about — all of its human psychological and social content, and all of its political and constructional content — could actually be seen in the geometry. That is, there was a particular morphological character that exists in buildings which have this quality and which does not exist in buildings which lack it — and furthermore, that this geometrical

189

character is describable and quite clear. But although I knew that to be so, and thought that I had written about it, I actually had not. I thought that chapter eight — which has to do with the morphological processes in nature — together with the patterns, and together with chapter twenty-six, must make this clear. But in fact they do not.

For Alexander, this character includes, for example, a certain kind of roughness — where things are approximately but not precisely equal. It also includes such features as having something large and then right next to it something smaller, and then something smaller still. These very general phenomena are hardly developed in modern architecture and it appeared to him that they were very much deeper than patterns themselves. It was almost as if they were what the patterns were all about insofar as these themes keep recurring in the patterns and yet no one pattern is about them — except possibly the pattern "positive outdoor space.'" The lack of positiveness of space, especially outdoor space, is certainly one of the most conspicuous errors of modern architecture, but again, that appeared to him to be a general phenomenon:

The point is that I was aware of some sort of field of stuff — some geometrical stuff — which I had actually had a growing knowledge of for years and years, had thought that I had written about or explained, and realized that, although I knew a great deal about it, I had never really written it down. And this was quite different from observing in Mexico that something didn't work. Here was something I had been aware of for years and years and had simply not succeeded in getting people to understand that I was saying this. But not only did they not understand that I was saying it, they did not understand that this was actually a crucial and important distinction between good buildings and bad.

In a diagnostic sense, I can say that if this geometrical field is not present in something then there is something wrong there and I can assess that fact within a few seconds. If I then go back into it, and examine it functionally, I will find out that I'm right in the same way that a physician or a biologist who knows his field can go in and do that.

So that was the second source — an increasing awareness on Alexander's part that he knew a great deal about this subject but had never taken the trouble to recognize this knowledge as being important and was tending to dismiss it as ancillary. It was almost as if he went to great lengths in several of his books and discussions to *not* mention this topic. This tendency of avoidance, however, is understandable in the context of his critique of modern architecture — namely, that it is *too* geometrical: "It is essentially made to be looked at. It is not made to be a living, breathing thing." In a sense then, Alexander's avoidance of specifically dealing with the question of geometry stems from the fact that, for him, the geometry of modern architecture constitutes that paradigm's most revealing anomaly. That he should confront it head on only towards the end of his research is not surprising in light of Kuhn's observations that "sometimes the shape of a new paradigm is foreshadowed in the structure that extraordinary research has given to the anomaly."[4] It is only by completely restructuring the conception of geometry and its relationship to building that Alexander is able to deal with it.

The third source for the investigation however, appeared to be totally irrelevant to his work and stems from one of those peculiar events that just seem to happen in one's life. For Alexander it happened to be rug collecting. Between 1970 and 1976 he had been collecting rugs — particularly religious Turkish rugs — and at one point actually became a rug dealer:

I was extremely innocent when I started out. I simply liked them. My main concern was actually in their color. I was completely absorbed by the question of color but never thought it would have any serious connection to my work. Also, I had never thought of my interest in these rugs as having to do with geometry. Sometimes I felt I was in the grip of a psychosis, or under the influence of a powerful drug. My heart would start pounding when I was contemplating buying a rug. It was like an insane compulsion. I would spend far more than I could afford and get myself into all sorts of financial difficulties. But in the process, I saw tens of thousands of rugs and fairly quickly assembled a collection of some very beautiful ones.

Operating within a very small and closed community of rug dealers and collectors in the San Francisco Bay Area, Alexander had acquired an unusual reputation. Most people who are interested in Turkish rugs tend to have a special interest: perhaps from an ethnographic point of view, or an historical point of view, or from the standpoint of weaving, or monetary value. Alexander's interest, however, did not fit any of the standard categories. Each rug he collected might correspond to one or more of the categories; but taken as a whole, it seemed impossible to identify a common point of view — except to say that there was a certain "something" in all of the ones he had acquired:

When people started telling me this I began to look more carefully to discover that there was indeed something I was attracted to in a half-conscious way. It seemed that the rugs I tended to buy exuded or captured an incredible amount of power which I did not understand but which I obviously recognized.

In the course of buying so many rugs I made a number of discoveries. First, I discovered that you could not tell if a rug had this special property — a spiritual quality — until you had been with it for about a week. (This of course would infuriate most dealers because I would insist on taking the rug home with me before deciding. However, because large sums of money were involved, there was a lot of pressure to be accurate.) So, as a short cut, I began to be aware that there were certain geometrical properties *that were predictors of this spiritual property. In other words, I made the shocking discovery that you could actually look at the rug in a sort of superficial way and just see if it had certain geometrical properties, and if it did, you could be almost certain that it had this spiritual property as well.*

This discovery — that certain reasonably definable geometrical attributes should actually correlate in some sense with the spiritual power that an object possessed — seemed just fantastic to Alexander because it was not to be expected from anything in A PATTERN LANGUAGE or THE TIMELESS WAY OF BUILDING:

Actually, the rugs never entered my mind as having anything particularly to do with other matters until I decided to give a course on geometry [in 1976]. In some sort of curious way I was instinctively led to describe this course not only in terms of geometry but in terms of religious buildings. The more I thought about it, the more I realized that these geometrical properties were especially evident in religious buildings. I also realized that the kind of purity and simplicity and complexity and the whole weird mixture of things that I was deriving my sense from was most highly developed in religious buildings — whether a Japanese temple or a Gothic cathedral or an Islamic mosque. In the extreme sense, you could probably say that three-quarters of the great architecture of the world happens to be religious. Anyway, I just decided I was going to give a course on this and when I looked around for ways in which I could explain all of this I realized that showing these rugs to people would be one of the fastest ways in which I could get a person to appreciate the fact that there really was something going on.

84

85

84. Positive Outdoor Space: Town Square, Rouffach, Alsace.

85. Kazak Rug, Caucasus.

PLATE XLIII

86. Kazak Rug, Caucasus.

PLATE XLIV

So I decided I would try to educate my students in what I was talking about by showing them my rugs. I was trying to show them that there was one property that the really remarkable rugs possess and that this property is what I had been very loosely calling "oneness." But instead of being a rough word for some vaguely perceived beauty, it turns out that one could actually identify this oneness in terms of specific geometrical properties. The correlation is in fact remarkable.

When Alexander uses the word "remarkable," he is actually using it in the same way a research scientist would in describing a previously undetected causal relationship. This is not to say that the passion isn't there — only that it is grounded in the fact that, whatever else he may be doing, he is always trying to conduct a scientific inquiry. And this brings us to the fourth source of the investigation into geometry — Alexander's earlier work at Harvard's Center for Cognitive Studies under the direction of Jerome Bruner — one of the pioneers of cognitive psychology:

I went to see him initially because he was interested in perception. He invited me to take some of his courses — which I did — and then very soon afterwards gave me a job as a research assistant. I worked for him doing research on various experiments in cognition and also taught a section of his and George Miller's psychology course at Harvard College. Eventually I was given a lab of my own at the Center for Cognitive Studies.

Bruner was a fascinating person. Although he was a very respected scientist, a number of his friends were artists and he was always willing to try to ask precise questions about obviously woolly subjects. For example, the question "How does a painter paint a picture?" would have been a perfectly legitimate question to attempt to answer in his lab. So he and I hit it off very well because there was considerable mutual interest in such questions.

Alexander's research at Harvard combined his training in mathematics and his studies in aesthetics at Cambridge with the experimental techniques and procedures of Bruner's laboratory. And the driving force behind all of this was his intuition about the ability to demonstrate that when a thing appeared pleasing, or beautiful, a mathematical event was occurring which was therefore describable in unmistakable terms.

In "The Universe of Forms" — the burnt manuscript mentioned in Chapter V — he sought to describe mathematical structures that could represent all geometric forms on a comparable footing — in

193

the way that a computerized eye could distinguish between a rabbit, a glass of water, or a human face for example. To do this, it has to categorize these objects correctly — which means that it has to calculate the geometrical invariants of each input and, because it does not know in advance what the input will be, it has to describe those invariants in a single language within which each input will appear as a possible variable. Alexander was interested in what the mathematical structure that provided such a single "language" looked like. But he was especially interested in knowing whether certain forms occupied any particular location within that structure — namely, those forms that are perceived as simple, coherent, memorable, or beautiful.

In "A Result in Visual Aesthetics" (1960) he wanted to find out the different ways in which an observer naturally looks at forms, whether there is a connection between his liking for those forms and the ways in which he looks at them and, if there is a connection, the nature of its structure. The experiments consisted of mapping the perceptual responses of numerous subjects onto a matrix of space to see if they tended to fall in certain places and not in others. Alexander's hypothesis was that the complete structure of "The Universe of Forms" could be compared to a celestial galaxy and that the most coherent, memorable, or beautiful forms would tend to fall into the least dense and most isolated parts of the space. Although the results in "A Result . . ." were not that fascinating, they did encourage the notion that one might eventually be able to construct a theory along these lines.

In "The Origin of Creative Power in Children" (1962) he discussed how the source of creative talent can be understood in terms of the child's developing ability to visually discriminate by forcing forms apart from one another. In other words, just the act of distinguishing one scribble from another is a process of isolating, or de-densifying that parallels the hypothetical structure of the "Universe of Forms" — and that such a process will result in producing something coherent.

In "On Changing the Way People See" (1964) and "Subsymmetries" (1968) Alexander discussed the results of a long series of experiments dealing with the visual perception of 35 black and white linear patterns (each pattern consisting of a horizontal arrangement of three black and four white squares). The most interesting results grew out of the experiments which had respondants arrange the patterns on the basis of similarity on one hand and simplicity on the other.

The first of these two papers attempts to construct part of the "Universe of Forms" — the space within which the various patterns were embedded and how close they were to each other. Unlike "A Result in Visual Aesthetics," where the space was purely abstract, the space here was actually laid out by placing the forms with respect to one another. The emphasis in the paper however was on the differences between perceiving the patterns sequentially (by cataloging) and figuratively (as 'wholes'). It was important for Alexander to focus attention on the results obtained during holistic perception because he regards that as more "real" than other forms of perception:

There is a certain sense in which the holistic perception actually corresponds more closely to the real structure of the thing being perceived. But just saying that raises a very interesting topic. I know that this is one of the reasons why some people dislike my work. They say he's so dogmatic; or what does he mean by "real" and "not real?" After all, we have people seeing this thing in such and such a way and how could he dare say that what they are seeing is not real? And this is sort of typical of the kind of criticism which is very often levelled at my work. However, we happen to be caught up in this weird sort of nominalist period of philosophical history at the moment where someone will say that however you choose to see something is the way you see it; or however you choose to name it is the way you name it. And of course that coincides with pluralism and is a genuine reaction against positivism. So what do I mean when I say that there is a certain perception of this that is more real?

I am actually making two different statements: one of them is psychological and one of them has to do with physics. The psychological statement that I am making is that the fundamental neurological processes and the deep-seated cognitive processes going on in the brain are actually taking place in the holistic way and that the sequential way is secondary and constructed out of it — as a cultural superimposition. Thats the first thing that I mean when I say that one is more real than the other. I mean that it is real in the brain; it corresponds to the basic cognitive structure out of which other structures are built.

Now the second thing is that when I say it corresponds to physics, I mean that the holistic perception is congruent with the behaviour of the reality being perceived. As an imaginary example, assume a flowing stream of water and just consider the hydrodynamics. You have the flow, which is relatively viscous at the edges, and in the middle it is more rapid and turbulent, and let us assume that there are whirlpools and so forth. Now, in the sequential perception the eye would start reading from left to right and therefore would start with the viscous flow of the left bank. The holistic eye would immediately pick out the overall gradient across the stream and the whirlpool, not as the only configurations, but certainly as the salient and important ones. In other words, in the flow, there is not a great deal going on at the bank. In fact, at the very edge the molecules are static. The big picture of the way the flow is working is happening more in the larger configurations. From a hydrodynamic point of view, the person who is seeing the thing holistically is actually seeing what is congruent with the behaviour of the thing and not just its physical geometry. He is in a position to see the physics correctly; whereas the person looking at it sequentially is just not seeing what is really happening. In other words, there is a gigantic connection between functional perception and geometrical perception — so that when you are seeing something correctly, your perception is congruent with the actual behaviour of the thing.

In these experiments, Alexander found that figurative or holistic perception can be brought to the surface by the simple technique of confronting someone with such a difficult perceptual task that the superimposed, sequential processes will no longer work — a sort of laboratory version of phenomenological "bracketing" or "causal efficacy."

In the "Subsymmetries" paper the focus was on rank-ordering the 35 different patterns according to four experimental measures of coherence. Once this was obtained, it was possible to look at the spaces laid out in the previous experiments in order to see where these particular patterns occurred:

If you look at one of the layouts in which the patterns are figuratively or holistically arranged, you will see that those patterns that are considered simple or coherent and that scored very high in the "Subsymmetry" paper happen to be in very isolated spots in the structure of the space, whereas those patterns that happen to be clustered together with others in the space are the same ones that were scored very low. In other words, the hypothesis of "The Universe of Forms" is actually exhibited in that example in a very clear way by comparing the results of the two papers.

But one particular question had surfaced — namely, what was it

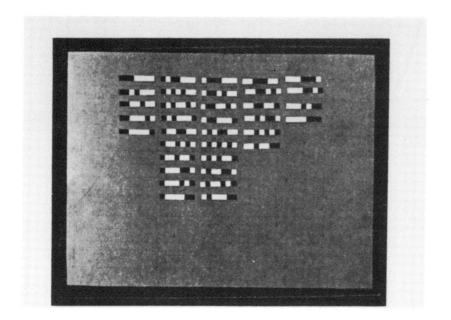

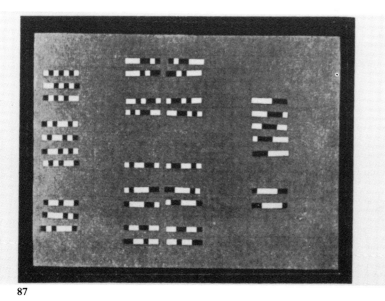

87

87. Sequential (top) and Figurative (bottom) Arrangements of Black and White Linear Patterns.

PLATE XLV

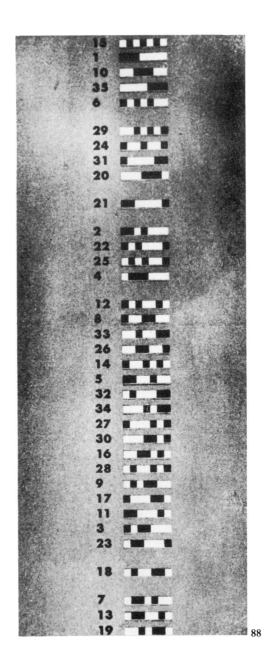

88. Rank Ordering of Black and White Linear Patterns.

PLATE XLVI

about the patterns that scored high that accounted for their perceived simplicity and coherence as forms?:

I got the experimental results and they correlated five different ways. The question was, "O.K. How do you explain it? Why are some of them more coherent than others? Its an amazingly simple problem, but it took me two years to find the answer. Here I am with 35 little strips, each one composed of three black squares and four white ones, and I have a particular rank order on them which means, according to the lab results, that the ones at the top of the order are perceived as coherent and simple and the ones at the bottom of the order are perceived as uninteresting and confused — and I cannot find any obvious reasons why that should be so. There are plenty of reasons available which explain why some of them are coherent and why some are confused; but I couldn't find a reason that explained why all of them were ranked where they were.

The answer — in the case of these particular two-dimensional patterns — turned out to be that those patterns with the greatest number of internal symmetries of the segments within the pattern were perceived as the most simple and coherent. This property — which Alexander called "subsymmetries" — is considerably more subtle than ordinary symmetry which is often proposed in aesthetic theories as a measure of simplicity. In "Subsymmetries," the focus is really on the "subobjects" of a thing:

The fundamental idea in "The Universe of Forms" was that the structure of any object is, in some sense, the structure of its subobjects. Now that of course is compatible with NOTES and it is compatible with "The City is not a Tree" and all of those kinds of structures that I have been interested in from the beginning, including pattern languages. But the question is, "What are the subobjects of a thing?" In particular, I was wrestling with that question in the case of a simply drawn outline. In other words, suppose that I draw a circle on a piece of paper. What are the subobjects that give it the structure of a circle? What are its pieces?

There are millions of ways that you can think about that. I can make smaller circles that completely cover it with a ring of smaller circles round the edge; but why should they be its relevant pieces? Certainly they have a characteristic structure in the sense of their overlap and how they fit together, which is typical of the circle. Or suppose that I am looking at the letter "L." Its obvious that in some sense it has two major pieces which interlock at the corner of the L, so that naively I could say that it basically has two big pieces and three small pieces, the small pieces being the ends of

197

the L and the corner of the L, and there is a certain characteristic way they overlap. Yet even that isnt enough to define the L because it doesnt explain what it is that makes it an L rather than an open ∟ with 135° in the angle instead of 90°. And to answer that I have to say that there is sort of an imaginary white rectangle that is half enclosed by the L, and in order to understand the structure of the L completely I have to include that as being one of its parts and its relationship to the whole.

By pursuing that kind of line of thinking one can hope that the purely interlocked structure of the components, if you pick the right components, will actually give the structure of the object. But what are the right components? And is there such a possible thing?

I spent a great deal of time working on the problem in that way and it occurred to me that one of the most natural kinds of components that one thinks of are symmetrical ones. Even in the examples I've just given, the things I've called the main components all happen to be symmetrical. One does not typically choose assymetrical things to be components. So at some point in looking at those 35 little strips I simply decided to take all of the symmetrical components and count them. And after some quick arithmetic I got a 95% correlation with their rankings. I was both very happy and somewhat amazed because the most simple patterns had the most number of subsymmetries. In other words, how could something very simple have the most of something rather than the least? A simple structure would presumably be one which is very simple to represent in the mind. It suggests that, somehow, there is an inversion and that actually this way of looking at it is not, even now, the correct way — that actually its a by-product of some other phenomenon.

It was that "other phenomenon" which was so attractive to Alexander's persistent curiosity. These studies only hinted at its existence and demonstrated that, if it did exist, it could be analyzed in precise terms. But what was it? Everything seemed to point to a kind of geometrical field of relationships that comes into focus under certain conditions. The single most powerful property of this field is the way everything in it — all the parts — work together to create a whole. The feeling of "oneness," or unity of space is the dominant impression.

Alexander's rug collection served as a constant reminder of the existence of this phenomenon; the shortcomings of the buildings in Mexico served to focus his motivation and energies on this last missing ingredient; and his work and experience at the Center for

198

Cognitive Studies had given him the knowledge and confidence to try and unravel the mystery. If he was right, that the structure of any object is, in some sense, the structure of its subobjects, then the structure of this field, this "oneness," could be understood in the same sense — by an analysis of its geometric properties.

REFERENCE NOTES

1. Edward de Zurko, THE ORIGINS OF FUNCTIONALIST THEORY (New York: Columbia University Press, 1957), p.51; cf. THE ARCHITECTURE OF LEON BATISTA ALBERTI, trans. by James Leoni, Book II, p.85

2. Herbert Read, "Preface," in Lancelot Law Whyte (ed.) ASPECTS OF FORM (New York: Pellegrini & Cudahy, 1951), pp.v-vi; see also Lancelot Law Whyte, ACCENT ON FORM (New York: Harper and Brothers, 1954)

3. "The Bead Game Conjecture," LOTUS, 5 (Milan: 1968), p.151

4. Thomas Kuhn, THE STRUCTURE OF SCIENTIFIC REVOLUTIONS, 2nd ed (Chicago: University of Chicago Press, 1970), p.89

XIX

GEOMETRY AND COLOR

The various sources and motives for an investigation into the geometrical properties of the unity of space, or "oneness," came together in 1976. The Turkish prayer rugs became merely its experimental point of departure:

You cannot go in a single afternoon to the Alhambra, Chartres, and the Ise Shrine. Even if you could, their physical presence is so overwhelming that they would be very difficult to analyze comparatively. You cannot just keep looking at them the way you can look at rugs. The rug is small. You can look at it, rather intensively, and you can look at twenty in a single day. Indeed, by their very size and number they invite comparison. They have a kind of laboratory nature which a building cannot have.

So I was drawn to use the rugs in this way — which is somewhat different from saying, "Lets make a building which is like a rug," as one might try to make a building which is like a vanDoesburg. The rug simply happens to embody at a very small scale, but as powerfully, the actual quality that these buildings have. Unfortunately, the circumstances of the prayer rugs as the origin of these properties do not compare favorably to the incredible research that went into the origin of pattern languages.

Nevertheless, Alexander did set up a workshop similar in intensity to the 1966 seminar on pattern languages. The goal was to make objects — not necessarily buildings — that had the same attributes as the rugs. His first concern was to communicate their essential geometric character to others and to demonstrate the correlation between this character and the spiritual power they possessed. The investigation went through three phases: the identification of about a dozen geometrical properties — of which "subsymmetry" was only one; the search for generative processes capable of producing these properties — including their relationship to pattern languages; and finally, the attempt to relate these properties and processes to the question of color and light. As with almost all of Alexander's research, the record of this investigation took the form of a book which would eventually be called THE NATURE OF ORDER:

> The central thesis of this book, is that there is a specific archetypal structure, which I shall call the "one" for short, that exists in a thousand forms, but that is always at the bottom of all art and all building which lives and breathes.
>
> This "one" is a geometric structure, which can be defined in precise mathematical terms. It is an invariant structure, a "presence" which manifests itself in anything which lives, or which is "one."[1]

The geometrical properties of this structure are described below. Since no single property works alone — indeed, they all interact to create a unified spatial field — there is no particular order implied by this summary.

1. *Many levels of scale:* Every part has smaller parts and every entity is a part of some larger entity. (The jump in level of scale cannot be too great, i.e., 1:7) (Helps to establish overall proportion and scale.)

2. *Good figure:* Every part has good figure, is a strong entity, and displays regularity — as opposed to amorphous blobs, vague shapes, etc. It is (a) distinct from what surrounds it; (b) possesses closure and a sense of concavity; (c) roughly compact (between 1:1 and 1:2, with exceptions up to 1:4); and (d) possesses a high degree of internal symmetries and subsymmetries. In addition to simple points, the following configurations can be used as elementary figures in creating space:

> The circle (column)
>
> The square (column again)
>
> Dash
>
> Arrowhead
>
> Hook
>
> Triangle
>
> Row of points alternating with space
>
> Rosette (cluster of circles)
>
> Diamond
>
> S-shape
>
> Half circle
>
> Star

Steps

Cross

Waves

Spiral

Tree

Octagon

Hexagon

Rhombus

3. *Solid boundaries:* Every thing has a boundary, and every boundary is a thing (an entity, i.e., solid). The ratio of the boundary to the thing it is bounding cannot be too small (e.g., a two-inch border cannot hold a three-foot field; thirty inches of wainscotting between floor and wall is more pleasing than four-inch trim).

4. *Ambiguity:* The "thingness" or solidity of the boundary should create ambiguity between itself and the thing it is bounding. (Helps establish interlock and figure-ground reversal.)

5. *Repetition:* A structure which has many of the same things repeated over and over again has a special sense of order (e.g., the fibers in a woven basket, the repetition of blades of grass in a field, the ten thousand knots in a rug, the ceramic tiles of Isphahan, the stones of a cathedral, rows of columns in a colonnade, the incredible degree of repetition in music etc.) There cannot be too many varieties of repetition, and what repeats may also be intervals, relationships, or patterns rather than just "things." (Helps establish echoes and resonance.)

6. *Alternation:* Oscillating gradients of repeating things is more pleasing than simple repetition (e.g., ordinary bond brickwork is more satisfying than stacked bond). The alternation should include the repetition of the things between the things that are repeating (e.g., the mortar between bricks, the spaces between columns, the pauses between notes, etc.) (Helps establish rhythm.)

7. *Positive-negative:* This is the same as figure-ground reversal. Every entity has, next to it, other entities which are also positive entities and which are shaped, in part, by the things which lie next to it (e.g., as in the Yin-Yang symbol.)

8. *Interlock:* Interlock unifies two areas and makes them inseparable (e.g., latchooks). Can be understood as an extreme case of negative-positive. (Also helps establish ambiguity.)

9. *Contrast:* Contrast creates differentiation (e.g., between light and dark, empty and full, solid and void, and between colors). Contrast can be emphasized by boundaries or borders (e.g., hairlines between colors; or the thickening of edges around windows or

doors).

10. *Centers:* The identification of a locus of relationships — a nodal point or area — which affects the rest of the organization and which radiates out in a hierarchy of levels. (Helps establish a sense of sequence.) Contrasted with a homogenous space which doesn't have much structure.

11. *Slight irregularities:* Within overall symmetries and configurations, slight irregularities hold the differentiation of the field. (e.g., a hand-drawn line — if it is good — always looks better than a machine drawn line; hand-sewn fabric — with its very slight imperfections — looks better than machine-sewn fabric, which is just too regularized.) There is a relaxedness which results from slight irregularities, but it must come from necessity rather than from the desire just to have a bit of irregularity or else it will appear too selfconscious, primitive, or "funky" (e.g., as in the rustic imperative of neo-Californian whole foods restaurants with a great deal of deliberately rough hewn cedar, old wagon wheels, and straw flowers). Natural irregularities, on the other hand, result from local adaptations to the external environment, or from the nature of the process or from other properties.

12. *Inner calm and balance:* Finally, there is the relationship between the pre-differentiated Void and the intensity of activity created by the interaction of the other properties. A field consisting entirely of alternating levels of repeating interlocks of contrast between solid and void, for example, would be too busy, too intense. There needs to be a balance of calm and emptiness with the fuss and delirium of detail for the unity to establish itself and take hold.

The emphasis of the investigation was not just upon identifying these properties but, more importantly, on describing the many ways they interact to produce a single quality, even although the combinations of interactions, in a million different versions, are never twice the same. The overall character of these interactions is a very highly differentiated, high density spatial unity — a sort of maximum saturation of ordered interconnectedness, analogous to a poem which achieves, with the bare minimum of elements, the highest possible degree of meaning:

Even in the early part of the investigation, these properties were already very amazing and extremely powerful. It was clear that their presence or absence almost entirely determined the spiritual depth that an object possessed. But the most remarkable thing was that it was as if they lay beneath the patterns.

After having identified these dozen properties, I realized that all of the patterns in A PATTERN LANGUAGE have these properties — or that every one of the patterns is essentially an embodiment of one or more of these properties. Thats where their ultimate power in the geometric sphere comes from and it also serves to distinguish them from other patterns which certain people occasionally create and which may be functionally very sensible but which do not have this underlying geometrical substance.

Obviously the question arises: what is the connection between these properties and the patterns in A PATTERN LANGUAGE? It turns out that, on the one hand, if you do follow these geometrical properties, you almost create the patterns without having to know about them. Its as if you could actually solve functional problems without trying to. On the other hand, it suddenly makes you look at the pattern language in a new light. You realize that the pattern language, for all that it does in functional and generative terms, is also bringing these properties into being and that that is an explanation of its power which was never given by me or anyone else.

The discovery of these properties thus served to resolve two dilemmas that had plagued Alexander for several years. First, it provided an explicit basis for distinguishing between patterns which are obviously creative and those which seem trivial and uninteresting. Secondly, it established a direct, physical connection between patterns and the elusive "quality without a name." All previous explanations had focused on the functional and social situations — the life of a place — that patterns could induce; this now tied them to geometry. All that remained was the question of how one could produce these properties in a building:

In the second phase of this work we began to study what kind of processes could produce these properties — because you just cannot produce them by knowing about them. If you have a set of patterns, you can generate a thing that contains those patterns; but if you have these twelve properties, you cannot necessarily generate a thing that has them. So these properties are more mysterious and actually more difficult to deal with because even knowing about them does not put you in a position to produce something which possesses them. So the question is: what kind of processes are capable of generating them?

The attention of the workshop focused on the search. At first it was thought that an algorithm — a step-by-step sequence — could be written. Out of that effort one property emerged as having more power than the others in organizing the geometrical field of "oneness" — the property of centers. From that realization

89

89. Kazak Rug, Caucasus.

PLATE XLVII

90

90. Ceiling detail, Palacio de Comares, Alhambra, Granada.

The structure which is created is essentially a structure of centres and the process by which this structure is created is one operation which is performed over and over again.

PLATE XLVIII

emerged a reiterative centering process that actually produces all the other properties and, at the same time, complements the processes described in A PATTERN LANGUAGE and THE TIMELESS WAY OF BUILDING.

The fundamental concept is that of a center — defined not as a point but as a whole, a shape, or an area. In many cases the middle itself will be void, but the whole, by virtue of its overall organization, creates a focused core with at least one axis of symmetry. The structure which is created is essentially a structure of centers and the process by which this structure is created consists of one operation which is performed over and over again. It consists of making, elaborating, strengthening, or completing some center which exists, or begins to exist, or has the potential to exist.

The process assumes that at any moment, the thing which is being created, has in it a large variety of centers defined at many different levels and in different degrees of articulation as suggested by the structure which exists at the time. The fundamental operation, whether it is applied to a blank, unformed sheet of paper or building site, or whether it is applied in mid-process to an emerging ornamental design or building structure, consists of taking one of its emerging centers and developing it or elaborating it — in short, differentiating it. This operation is then expanded outwardly, to some larger center in which the first center is embedded; inwardly, to some smaller center or centers within the first center; and laterally, to other centers of similar size which lie next to the given center. In that sense, it is identical to the generative process of pattern languages in which each pattern is part of some larger pattern, has smaller patterns within it, and relates to similar patterns next to it.

In order to keep performing the operation over and over again, it is necessary to have a complete and precise idea of both the constituents of a center and its relationship to the other geometrical properties:

> In general, a center needs to have more material towards its edge than in the middle. The overall shape of a center needs to have at least one axis of symmetry. The outside boundary of a center will often be imbricated, so that there is interlock with its exterior. In the same way, the center will often be most powerful when it is so formed, at its edge, that there is some ambiguity with the adjacent center, or with an overlapping center. The boundary of the center needs to be

formed in such a way that its shape creates additional, smaller centres and differentiates the larger center from its surroundings. The actual boundary of the center needs to be made up of smaller centres itself, which both unite and distinguish the center from what lies next to it.

Each center needs to have a color which is complementary or contrasting in value with the adjacent color. Each center needs to be made by lines and colors which come from the same family as the other centers near it. At the same time, the boundaries which form the smaller centers between any two given centers must be of colors which both unite and distinguish the neighbouring colors. Finally, each center must create other centers — or an alternating sequence of centers — contrasting in color but equally strong in shape.[2]

The question of color and its relationship to geometry — which appeared to be important to the centering process — constituted the third phase of the investigation:

Of course color is an integral part of any ornament. Its also very clear that in some of the rugs, and in some ornaments, and in some buildings, there is a very miraculous color phenomenon that occurs — an almost heavenly inner light. Curiously however, this color phenomenon is actually enhanced by the geometry that I have described. In other words, one of the things that we discovered is that the way the color works is completely contingent upon this geometry, and vice versa. But the whole question of color poses problems of a very strange nature.

For example, it is possible to start studying color from the point of view of the quality without a name. There are certain instances, whether in ornaments, buildings, rugs, color in nature, or in painting for that matter, when color approaches this quality more closely than at other times. It has to do with a very special color realm which is at the same time very, very soft and very intense. In other words, its not brilliant in the sense of sharp, primary colors; but it is brilliant in the sense of a sort of underglow, even although the colors are almost muted — not grey, just pale essences of color that work together to create an almost unbelievable quality.

When you start looking carefully at many examples of this quality, and separating them out from other examples of color phenomena, and begin to ask, again, what are the properties, what are the features that are typical of those colors, it turns out that it is much harder to do and be objective about than in the realm of pure geometry. And yet, these properties or features parallel almost exactly the geometrical properties of the "one."

For example, one of the geometrical properties calls for slight irregularities, or roughness — that is, when things are repeating they do not repeat perfectly, and there are oddities which are sometimes brought in to make the thing whole. Now in the realm of color it turns out that if you have a perfectly even-toned color it isn't nearly as alive as it is when it is varying slightly within itself. In other words, it parallels the phenomenon of slight irregularities in the geometrical sphere. However, because these properties do not have any obvious functional connection to the color, it isn't really clear where the parallelism is coming from.

On the other hand, it turns out that the geometrical properties actually intensify the color. When you start asking what it is, really, that you are trying to do when you produce color — and what this quality in the color is — one way of describing it is that in some sense it feels like light. And the more you focus on this, and begin to be able to detect it and become precise about when it is occurring and when it is not, the more you begin to see how the geometrical properties are responsible for this color phenomenon.

For example, interlock and negative-positive — which are very important in the geometry — crucially affect the way that the color works. The presence of boundaries — which is very important in the realm of geometry — appear in the realm of color in the form of hairlines. Their presence has a crucial effect on the whole color phenomenon. In addition, you get the very curious observation that the more the centering process takes place in the geometry, the more that this light-filled character appears in the color. I would almost go so far as to say that you begin to vaguely suspect that the color may be the ultimate purpose of all this. In other words, if you were forced to name one thing which is the center of all that is going on there — beyond the many social and functional events — it would be the color; and that rather than a minor adjunct to things — such as painting something to make it alright — the whole organization of a building ultimately dissolves into the color that is produced by it.

Of course it's incredibly difficult to get colors to work in that way — much more difficult than geometry. To actually succeed in getting a group of colors to work together so that they actually melt into each other, and yet are apart, so they produce this sort of inner light, is really very hard. I think anyone who has ever done anything serious with color knows it to be an incredibly tricky domain. In my own case, it is as though I have been looking very carefully at colors in rugs for several years but only just recently — in connection with the centering process — have begun to do anything with them.

Alexander's observation, that the whole organization of a building ultimately dissolves into the color that is produced by it, is very similar to Ruskin's statement that "everything that you can see in the world around you, presents itself to your eyes only as an arrangement of patches of different colors variously shaded."[3] For Alexander, however, this observation can be misleading:

The quality without a name described in TIMELESS is still the crux of all this. And that, of course, essentially has to do with living things; whereas color and light are slightly abstract. At the same time that they are so beautiful and reach so deeply down into us, I find that they remove one slightly from life in a way that music, for example, does not because it is so physical and connected with dance and movement. But color: I actually feel it to be even dangerous to become too preoccupied with it because it is so abstract. So its very peculiar that at one and the same time my intuition is that this thing is somehow very central but also, in the moment of being central, it is also very divergent from the thing that I actually have been searching for all of these years.

It was the centering process, however, that was really the crux of the investigation, and as soon as its operations were understood, it became clear to Alexander that — in addition to color — there were very strong implications for building construction, particularly in terms of the formal shortcomings of the Mexican project:

It turns out that even the knowledge of the actual procedure of construction that we used in Mexico, for instance, does not go quite deeply enough. In order for this centering process to occur, you actually need to be working on the building details in a manner which technically requires a slightly different set-up. What it means is that there is a certain freedom which is needed in the production of detail in order for this centering process to occur. There are some construction processes which permit that, and others which do not; and that is a distinction we had not been aware of at all.

According to Alexander, most acts of construction in current practice are mechanical in the sense that the tasks are fragmented — they are part of some whole but they do not actually complete any particular whole at the time they are performed. Secondly, during the actual construction, one is not really free to concentrate on the emerging centers and to develop them spontaneously. The details are usually all worked out in advance. And finally, the process itself is usually not absorbing or fascinating or active enough to capture one's emotion sufficiently to engage in the creation of detail at the time the building is going up:

With this in mind it should become clear that if we do succeed in making a building process, it will be quite different from the kind of process we normally engage in during construction. It will be a process where at each moment, we are actively, and creatively, completing some center. This implies that the building is, to us, psychologically, just like ornament while we are making it. It is filled with centers and made only of centers: each joist, each space between joists, each connection, each little piece of wall, is a solid entity in itself, which becomes a center in our eyes — and our control over the act of making and building is great enough so that we can transform it, improve it, make it more of a center while we are building it.[4]

One is reminded here of Ruskin's famous and often misunderstood statement that "ornamentation is the principal part of architecture." Famous, because it provided Ruskin's critics with "proof" that he placed too much emphasis on ornament at the expense of an understanding of the true nature of building; and misunderstood because, as John Unrau has pointed out, it has seldom been noticed that Ruskin usually implied a much wider definition of "ornament" than the modern reader tends to expect:

First of all, Ruskin is using the term "ornament" in an unusually broad sense. Depending upon the distance of the viewer from the building, almost any major subdivision of structure might be considered ornamental. Ruskin would, it appears, regard as ornamental all elements of the building which, at the specific distance from which one is viewing it, are treated in such a way that they contribute to its aesthetic articulation. Secondly, even the smallest details must be considered visually in relation to the larger schemes of ornamental subdivision within which they are comprehended; which, in turn, must be considered in terms of the total effect of the building as viewed from varying distances . . . . If architectural ornament is to be considered subordinate to the total effect of the building, it follows that, to be successful, it must be designed as an integral part of the composition, not added to a building after the large-scale masses and structures have been determined. This is in fact Ruskin's position . . .[5]

This is obviously Alexander's position as well — except that he is going a step further. The ornament must not only be designed as an integral "part" of the composition — it *is* the composition. And in order for this to be true, certain changes in the processes of construction — in addition to those specified earlier — need to be made:

Obviously, for example, we cannot consider the creation of a piece of wall as an act of centering if the wall is a prefabricated panel over which we have no control while it is being made, and no opportunity to make it a center *with respect to what is around it while it is being made*. This, therefore, rules out the use of large-scale prefabricated components. But it is also true that not all small-scale components and processes meet this requirement. Thus, for example, if a process works in such a way that it would be necessary to make the sill and sides of a window frame, but not place the top part until later, it would violate the centering process — even if done by handcrafting — since it would give the builder no opportunity to *complete* the center of the window frame, at the time that he makes it. In short, it must be a process which allows us to feel the emerging centers at every stage, it must be a process which we can think of, conceive, and feel as a process of successive center-making.[6]

Thus, in the light of the implications for building construction which are suggested by the discovery of the centering process in "The One", Alexander's experiments with hand-applied ultralightweight concrete and structural engineering take on wider significance. In fact, all of his experiments in building can be seen as attempts to make the construction process much more finely tuned to the actual differentiation of form than modern techniques permit. Far from fostering a return to medieval craftsmanship — as Ruskin may have envisioned — Alexander's work is much more attuned to a post-industrial society than most of his writings would suggest:

When someone says that the idea of people designing their own buildings, or the idea that every part in a building has to be unique according to its locus in space is fine but impossible because we live in an industrial society, I find that to be an extremely naive view of industrialization. In fact, you can say that we are really only at the end of the first one hundred years of industrialization. The idea that industrialization has a central relationship to mass production is not true —— although it has appeared to be so in the recent past. It is certainly true that the wonders of technology make it possible to produce all kinds of things very quickly, efficiently, and cheaply — but that does not imply that all the things that are made have to be the same.

Imagine a science-fiction technology in which one sketches out a hypothetical building, together with all of the patterns and properties which are supposed to guide its construction, and then suddenly it is built out of an imaginary spider-like machine weaving a web out of some unknown

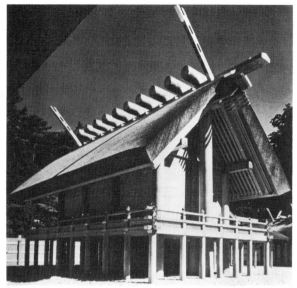

91

92

91. Ise Shrine, Naigu.
92. The Hôtel-Dieu (Hospital), Beaune, Burgundy.

PLATE XLIX

93

93. Linz Cafe, 1980.

PLATE L

materials. This would obviously be a technological advance of a much higher order than being able to manufacture thousands of refrigerators which are all identical and quite crude by comparison to the building. Industrialization certainly means very rapid, very efficient, and very inexpensive production — but it does not mean that objects need to have this dead and unbelievably ridiculous and identical character that they now have. This is just the first phase of industrialization. There is a much more sophisticated kind of industrialization possible whose stirrings are already visible right now. Its not that I'm going to invent it — just that people have not focused in on it before or known how to use it.

The second point is that industrialization is a social concept which, at the moment, tacitly implies an obnoxious form of human organization.But there is, again, nothing about the wonders of technology that tell us we need to have a sterile and inhuman form of hierarchical organization. There is, on the horizon, the complete reorganization of human production processes in accord with this very highly sophisticated technology which will emerge. So there are two issues in industrialization: one is understanding the nature of production from a mechanical and technical standpoint; and the other is trying to understand how to reorganize production so that it is actually a satisfying and profound human experience.

Indeed, it is the realm of human experience — at once satisfying and profound — that is most important to Alexander. There is, for him, a danger — already hinted at in the discussion of color — that the analysis of the "one," for all its architectural implications, can become somewhat removed from human experience because it seems to lie so much in the realm of pure form:

> Contrast the purely geometrical side of it with the life-seeking, life-giving quality described in THE TIMELESS WAY OF BUILDING as the quality without a name. That quality is completely down to earth. It happens when we are free in ourselves, running down the street, chasing the rollers in the ocean, sailing a boat, riding a horse, dancing, singing, drinking a glass of water, eating an omelette, or just breathing deeply. All that goes to the heart of life. But an object, no matter how beautiful, how much it touches us, in its formal self — how can it possibly be like that, life-giving, making us free in ourselves?[7]

In the end, this is the question posed by the analysis of the "one" — and possibly by this analysis of Alexander's work. For him, there is one way in which the two realms — geometry and human experience, form and function — are one and the same:

On the obvious level, as living, they are different. But both put us directly in touch with the one greater self that we become a part of when we give up ourselves. When we are splashing, running, laughing, we are alive, because we no longer hold onto ourselves, no longer clutch at our precious person, or own ego, but instead give up ourselves, and let go...

And when we are making an object, a thing which has this oneness in it, we must abandon ourselves too — again, we must let go, because we know that this "it," this quality which manifests itself, can only come into the thing we are making when we get rid of ourselves, abandon ourselves, and let the process, the larger self which we cannot control, take over and make the thing for us.

And it is perhaps not too much to say that when we are in the presence of a thing which has this quality, then too, we are made light, the wind blows through us, because, once again, we feel a little of that contact with the greater self behind our individual selves, we feel a little of this abandon in which we can let go, of our small selves, relinquish our control, this thing that we are in, or next to, looking at, comes so clearly from this realm of the greater self, the one self, that we let go of our small selves, and to that extent, this work helps us to reach for contact with the larger self, of which we are a part.

And this explanation perhaps adds something to our knowledge of the one — because it teaches us, that finally we can judge a thing, an ornament, a building, just to the extent that it releases this abandon, this letting go, to the extent that it can whisper to us, and help us to let go of our foolish selves, and join the one...but of course, this is a very special whisper, a very special quality — and we can feel that, and use it as our criterion....[8]

REFERENCE NOTES

1. THE ONE, unpublished manuscript (Berkeley: 1977), p.1; this will eventually be published as THE NATURE OF ORDER by Oxford University Press.

2. IBID., pp.191-192

3. Cited in Robert L. Herbert (ed.), THE ART CRITICISM OF JOHN RUSKIN (Garden City: Anchor Books, 1964), p.2; cf. Ruskin, "The Elements of Drawing" (1857)

4. THE ONE, p.278

5. John Unrau, LOOKING AT ARCHITECTURE WITH RUSKIN (Toronto: University of Toronto Press, 1978), pp.67-68

6. THE ONE, p.278

7. IBID., p.292

8. IBID., pp.292-293

XX

SYNTHESIS

The progression of steps in Alexander's work over the twenty-five year period beginning with his formal study of architecture at Cambridge, and culminating in his discoveries in the realm of geometry and color, constitutes a unique preface to his more recent career as a practicing architect and builder. It is unique not only because of the amount of time spent in preparation for such a career, but because of the depth and scope of its content.

First, there is the logical sequence of often startling discoveries that touch base with many of the most important and interesting lines of 20th century thought. Secondly, there are the very strong parallels between Alexander's work and the evolution of a new paradigm in the structure of scientific revolutions as described by Kuhn. Thirdly, there is the fact that this body of work both illustrates and attempts to resolve the conflict between art and science — the outcome of which has implications far beyond the practice of architecture. And finally, there is the running commentary — between the lines of analysis — which parallels and describes one man's search for freedom and personal liberation.

The sequence of Alexander's discoveries began with his recognition of the shortcomings and absurdity of most of modern architecture. During the early years of NOTES ON THE SYNTHESIS OF FORM, in his experiments at the Center for Cognitive Studies, in his awareness of Gödel's Theorem, in "The Revolution Finished Twenty Years Ago," and in the unfinished manuscript on beauty, he acquired the conviction that all of architecture was potentially objective.

In his analysis of building requirements he established a precise definition of "function" in minute particulars; in COMMUNITY AND PRIVACY and in his work with computer programs, the

Indian Village and highway interchange diagrams, and the BART stations, he realized that it is the individual components of a building — its subobjects — which matter most; in "Atoms of Environmental Structure," the highway route location project, "Relations for a House Entrance," and in "The City is not a Tree," he demonstrated that the components are pattern-like and that the environment is made up, essentially, of patterns.

In "The Urban Rule System," the Indian village proposal to the Government of Gujurat, his lecture on "The Genetics of the Environment" at Berkeley, and in "Systems Generating Systems," he showed that form comes from a generative process. In the first seminars at The Center for Environmental Structure he arrived at the idea of a generative language of patterns and the first draft of A PATTERN LANGUAGE; and in lay experiments with pattern languages and in the projects in Peru, Modesto, and Oregon, as well as in the Osaka World's Fair Exhibit, he demonstrated the importance of user design in the generation of adaptive forms.

In "The City as a Mechanism for Sustaining Human Contact," he broke with the idea of scientific neutrality on the question of value and established the centricity of the realm of feeling; and in THE TIMELESS WAY OF BUILDING he described the phenomenon of spatial unity — "the quality without a name."

The realization that "process" is fundamental characterized a long string of experiments and projects. In the last chapters of A PATTERN LANGUAGE, and in the Peruvian Housing and Modesto Clinic projects he realized that current systems of construction need to be changed; in PEOPLE REBUILDING BERKELEY, and in the Swedish and Berkeley Seminars it was taxation and land ownership; and in "The Grass Roots Housing Project" — as well as in THE OREGON EXPERIMENT — it was the flow of money.

In the workshop cottage, the Andalusian project, and in the Canary Islands proposal, the idea of the "architect-builder" emerged; in experiments with concrete and in computer simulations of structural forces in thin shells he acquired a new attitude towards engineering; and in THE PRODUCTION OF HOUSES — based on the Mexican Project — he realized that the overall process of production was at stake.

And finally, in "The One", he realized that ornament is

214

fundamental and that the rules governing geometry and color are central to the unity of space and underlie all patterns.

In all this work he has come in direct contact with the theories, methods, and facts of an extensive body of thought: operations research, statistical design theory, information theory and computer programming, cognitive and gestalt psychology, psychophysics, morphogenetics, linguistics, classical aesthetics and color theory, structural engineering, social and human ecology, macroeconomics, public administration and local politics, and a great deal of mathematics and philosophy, including existentialism, evolutionary humanism, phenomenology, and zen. And yet, what reads like a vast intellectual odyssey parallels, almost exactly, a very carefully defined sequence of steps and events that lead out of one disciplined world-view and into another.

In Kuhn's model of the structure of scientific revolutions, the recognition of a defect or anomaly within current practice, the search for corrective modification, the growing magnification of problems and the acknowledgement of crisis, the casting about for alternatives, and the pursuit of new leads will often entail a complex and massive reshuffling of all the elements of the field until a solution has been found. In Alexander's case, practically every single element has had to be redefined and restructured into a new constellation of facts, values, theories, and methods. It is not surprising, therefore, that his investigations have touched base with so many lines of thought, both old and new. What is unusual — and perhaps problematic — is that the terrain of his journey covers a tenuous intellectual landscape midway between the often conflicting worlds of both art and science. For Alexander, however — who has origins in both worlds — the apparent conflict is not intrinsic to the subject matter of his work.

To recall Schopenhauer's distinction, the object of science is a description of the universal that contains many particulars; the object of art is the making of particulars that contain a universal. The distinction appears to be mainly between "describing" things and "making" them. The problem is in trying to identify which parts of Alexander's work have to do with science and which parts have to do with art. To him, a more accurate way of looking at it is to say that *all* of it has to do with both — but in different ways:

The relation art has to this quality is usually in creating it. In that sense, my activities have to do with art. On the other hand, the scientific side of it is in trying to identify processes which are likely to create this quality, conditions under which it manifests itself, and what you might call the network of facts surrounding the existence of it. All of that is what one would normally call scientific investigation.

In A PATTERN LANGUAGE, for example, we attempted to define several hundred patterns which, when present in the world, help in the manifestation of this quality. You could say it is science insofar as there are some fairly exhaustive inquiries in different patterns as to whether that is so, why it might be so, and exactly what it is that is likely to do that in given cases. Insofar as it has to do with the creation of buildings which possess a great density of this thing, it is art. It is both art, in itself, and an instrument of art in the sense that the intention is quite clearly that people will be able to make more and more of this thing by working within that language.

So in this case, art is concerned with the making of it and science with the explanation of it — but there is a continuous interplay between these two because obviously to the extent that you understand more about the phenomenon — the kinds of processes which create it, and so forth, which are all scientific questions — the more you are able to make it.

For Alexander, however, it is not a matter of integrating two different activities called art and science. To him, the importance of the phenomenon of the unity of space is that it exists in a realm that is fundamental and basic to *both* — and that what we call art is part of it and what we call science is part of it. They are not two distinct activities but, rather, two differnt ways of looking at the same thing. Instead of integrating these two activities, it is more a question of realizing that there is simply one activity. The current separation and conflict he sees as both an "historical" and cultural imposition, endemic to 20th century western thought:

There are some periods in history — the high period of Sephardic art in Persia, for example — in which the main artists of the day — painters, architects, tile makers, rug weavers, etc. — were completely connected to science. In other words, there was no sense in which there was a distinction between what they were doing and what mathematicians were doing. For example, the Arabic mathematicians who were aware of the discussions going on in Italy about Copernicus retained the idea of a centralized cosmos — even after the discussions had moved into the realm of Newton, Leibnitz, and the infinite universe — on the grounds that those discussions constituted

216

bad art.

I think this is very important to understand and so I want to press the point slightly. In FROM THE CLOSED WORLD TO THE INFINITE UNIVERSE, Alexandre Koyré presented the chronology of extremely disturbing and unsettling philosophical and scientific events that essentially disconnected man from divinity at the same time that it seemed to present what looked like a mathematically adequate picture of the cosmos. Well, the Arabic mathematicians' view of this was that the idea of a cosmos which you could not draw was incomprehensible. In other words, the point about being able to draw it is that not only must it be accurate as a representation of what is "out there," but also, it has to be accurate as a representation of what is "in here" — namely, inside the mind of the person looking at it.

So the Arabic mathematicians who were insisting that this was bad art meant that an image which is fundamentally incomprehensible at the human level must be incorrect because all of science is actually as much a description of what is in us as what is out there — and that a correct description of the universe has to be faithful at both *ends.*

Of course in terms of 19th and early 20th century scientific thought, this was just philistine. But in terms of the beginnings of changes that are now taking place, in physics even, that is no longer so clear. There are now beginning to be more serious attemps to say that, ultimately, there is no difference between physics and psychology. In fact, the congruence between the interior world and the exterior world is a theme that is actually begining to affect 20th century western science, and all I am pointing out is that in the 16th and 17th centuries, when this was first an issue, the Arabic mathematicians refused to go along with the western view on the grounds that it violated this principle of congruence.

They happen to have been the same people who were living in a culture in which art and science were not separable. In other words, the actual business of making a painting of the cosmos was taken as seriously as giving a mathematical description of it — and there was no distinction between the two in terms of what you might call the proper field of investigation.

We are now in a period three hundred years later than this example — and presumably a lot more sophisticated. Alexander's discussion of the subject was not to suggest that what he has been doing is a reversion to an earlier time period but, rather to give an example, in the history of science, when there was actually a complete union between art and science:

217

The fact that, in the conventional sense, there is scientific truth in many of the things I have said or discovered, is really only one side of this coin. The main point, and the one that actually concerns me more, is that there is artistic truth there — namely, that it is actually dealing with the fundamental problem of making something. It happens to have truths in it and around it which are scientific, but basically it is a making problem and always has been the problem of all art. However, when art gets disassociated from truth — and just becomes manipulations, like the New York Abstract Expressionists, for example, or the recent history of Modern Architecture, also in New York — then it is just a nonsensical place for art to be. It isn't really serious art at all.

But it is also true that science has gotten into some pretty absurd subject matter. The situation of science in the mid-20th century is that there have been unbelievable experiments with both unprecedented intellectual as well as technical results, especially in the last one hundred years; but at the same time, there is more and more the feeling that science doesn't have anything to do with what life is all about — to the point that there is a very strong anti-scientific sentiment among intellectuals today, not to mention architects. And this of course comes back to the famous quality without a name. If there is this something — call it life, or call it something that is beautiful, or call it essence, or this "it" that manifests itself when the universe appears to melt, so to speak — if this is not just poetic metaphor, but is actually for real, and possible to do, then you could say two things about it in the context of this discussion.

First, doing it is very difficult and requires tremendous patience and concentration, and that is art — perhaps with a little science thrown in. On the other hand, you could say that a science which is going on its merry way without taking this into account is deficient. If this is indeed true, and there really is such a phenomenon, which can be dealt with, then you have to say that the science which isn't dealing with it is in very bad shape as well. Perhaps art is more obviously in a bad state because it is not considered very respectable and not taken seriously. And perhaps science has a legitimacy which comes from the fact that you can perform technological miracles. But still, the fact is that if it isn't dealing with this matter it is definitely one-sided.

In the very begining of THE TIMELESS WAY OF BUILDING there is a comment about chemistry and physics which says that, within the canon of those fields as we know it, there is no sense in which one system can be more alive or more intense in itself than another. I then say that this is a problem in chemistry and physics. In other words, it is a shortcoming in those fields that they cannot recognize this as they are presently constituted. If indeed, serious recognition of this topic became widely understood among scientists, it would produce drastic changes in that it would remove the one major stumbling block on the escutcheon of modern science.

At the moment, science tends to concern itself with natural phenomena. This "it" — this quality — is of course implicit in natural phenomena; but as a distinction, it only becomes relevant when you get into the man-made realm, because it is only there that the question of its presence or absence becomes so crucial and so clear. So one could ask if science is going to address itself to man-made phenomena. If that became clear, I believe that this topic would very rapidly become central. At the moment, man-made phenomena are not approached with the same kind of seriousness and reverence with which the great scientists approached nature.

What I am getting at here is that when you start to construe the making of a work in painting, or in building, in these very serious terms, the distinction between what you are doing and science completely disappears because you are actually dealing with a real phenomenon — mysterious perhaps, but completely real — and you have to be as exacting and serious about what will do it and what wont do it as any scientist conducting his experiments in chemistry or physics.

If there is a problem today, it is because both art and science are somehow out in the woods with respect to this phenomenon. Art, because it isn't taken seriously enough and intensely enough to pursue its own goals; and science perhaps because it wont admit to the existence of this "it." But within the framework of the whole paradigm that we have been speaking about, the problem does not exist. There is no problem. There is no split between art and science.

As Alexander points out, the product of the unity of art and science is not likely to be a mixture of two distinct disciplines. In other words, what is definitely not being discussed is some kind of redefined art which is somehow "scientific," like computer graphics or crystalographic silkscreening:

The one thing I do want to make quite clear is that the central issue of all art, even as it is understood by today's artists in their struggling, is to make things which have this luminous spirituality in them and which actually take your breath away and lead you into these very, very deep realms. And when you honestly pursue that, and learn how to do it, with full seriousness, it leads you into matters that are completely discussable and straightforward and where both artistic and scientific problems merge and where you do not have to maintain the split between the two.

There is however a slight paradox here. Only by appealing to a phenomenon which is basic to both art and science is there a resolution of the apparent conflict between them. Obviously some paradigmatic reshuffling in both fields needs to occur; but the critical point is that the origin or source of the adjustments has nothing to do specifically with either field. The fact that Alexander himself has origins in both art and science only accounts for his ability to negotiate the terrain of both; it does not fully explain the motive or driving force behind his focused attention on this one phenomenon. In other words, just trying to make seriously beautiful things, or just trying to discover scientific truths, or even a combination of both, is not likely, in the end, to entirely account for and explain this body of work. In the end, it is a much more personal search which both completes the explanation of the uniqueness of Alexander's achievement and brings the argument to its conclusion:

There is an unchanging principle which I have described in THE TIMELESS WAY and which I have felt now for several years and which these recent discoveries in geometry and color have only confirmed. This principle is very simply that to make a thing which lives comes about to the extent that you can succeed in letting go of yourself.

In the end, it has to do with freedom. It is only the word freedom which connects up these somewhat esoteric and spiritual matters in the realm of color and ornament with the possibility of making a building which is like a life lived rather than some abstract, architected, formal object. It also connects up to the questions of the political organization of a neighborhood, the forms of taxation, the way people live when they actually design their own houses for themselves and cooperate to design the larger common land, and so on. Whether you want to talk about letting go of your smaller self while you embrace the large self, or whether you want to talk about genuine human freedom, real freedom of the spirit, freedom from the tyranny of one's own self and of others is the crux of the whole thing. It unifies the two strands, the political strand on one hand and the strand that has to do with the deep artistic problems of "The One" on the other hand. When I think about the little road in Denmark, and the experiences of the families in Mexico, and the activity of building — of actually handling wet concrete — and the questions of color, the breath that blows through all of them is

220

freedom.

What Alexander means by freedom can best be summarized by referring to an essay written by Max Wertheimer — one of the pioneers of gestalt psychology — entitled "The Story of Three Days." In this story, Wertheimer takes the notion of "appropriateness," which is very close to the heart of perceptual gestalt, and he accepts that as a given. He then arrives at the conclusion that freedom is the capacity to live in a state, both internally and externally, which permits one to act appropriately to whatever happens — a conclusion which also happens to be completely congruent with the teachings of zen. In zen, freedom means that, far from having many choices, you only really have one choice because you are free to do the most appropriate thing possible in any situation you encounter. In short, you only have one possibility — which you are free to choose; and consequently, you are free when you can identify the most appropriate response and can do it.

The meaning and impact of Alexander's discovery can perhaps best be understood in the context of that definition. For what he has uncovered is that there is an actual phenomenon which we have the faculty to perceive which can help us to distinguish and choose between more or less appropriate actions. And that is why he says it is a fundamental criterion for looking at anything — a town, a building, or a moment in a person's life. And when he speaks of the possibility of making a building which is like a life lived, rather than some formal object, that is exactly what he means.

Beethoven said that the fourth of the series of late quartets that he wrote presents "a day in the life" of the composer. The last movement of the last quartet is subtitled "The Difficult Resolve." Under the opening phrases he penned in the words: "Must it be? It must be!" All kinds of interpretations have been offered to explain this seemingly mysterious statement. Most of them try to locate a referent for "it." But as Morse Peckham points out in his own interpretation, the "it" of "It must be!" can be anything at all. The ostensible object or referent does not have to be "fate" or "joy" or a "religious ritual"; it can be absolutely anything in the day of a life:

> Further, what the day exhibits is what every day for every human being exhibits: the failure of traditional ways of structuring experience, the randomness, meaninglessness, and pointlessness of

events-in-themselves, and the continuous struggle, the assymetric, non-rhythmic, irregular effort of the perceiving subject to shape order out of life's chaos. Beethoven's epigraph ... is remarkably like the words of Goethe's dying protagonist, "Only he deserves freedom and life who conquers them every day."[1].

The word freedom unfortunately carries a lot of baggage with it, but whether or not every one would express it in quite that way, it is the ultimate concern of every person. When you get right down to it, I think that this is what everyone's yearnings come to — including my own. Because it is obviously true that, as a person, forgetting all of this work, being free in that sense and living unencumbered and undaunted by my own images and fears is much more important to me than anything else.

But take a simple practical matter, like being involved in construction. I can say, intellectually, that in order for buildings to become beautiful and alive, it is necessary for people like myself to be directly involved in the act of construction rather than fiddling around on paper. But that makes it seem as though the basic reason for it is purely in order to make better buildings. And that indeed may be so. But, on the other hand, it also happens to be true that when I'm out on a construction site I actually feel more complete and alive as a person, and I enjoy myself in a way that I never can when I'm sitting around in an office drawing. So it would be equally true to say that I do the construction myself because it makes me feel better. But then the question is, Which one is it? One or the other? What's the real reason? What's the guiding issue?

The whole point is that if you wanted to summarize this body of work, it is that there is no tension between the two. What I can say — and in a way I am uniquely able to say this — is that whenever I do what makes me feel right I will be doing something that is congruent with this body of work; and whenever I do something that is congruent with this body of work, it will make me feel good. In other words, the unique feature of this particular body of thought and experience is that there never is a choice involved because the two are always congruent — and if there ever appears to be an incongruence, it undergoes transformation until it is congruent.

If you take the case of the relationship between architects and contractors, and think about it in a way that doesn't have anything to do with how it feels to actually do the construction, and you just ask which one produces a better building, it is demonstable that unless the person that is actually responsible for making the building is also literally involved in building it, it cannot be quite right. But how remarkable that that fact should be congruent with the incredible, living breathing pleasure that you have while

222

you're out on the construction site mixing concrete, for example — because that was not explicitly a part of the theoretical formulation connecting the master-builder to the building. In other words, there are undercurrents here that connect what is theoretically correct with what feels good. Yet the theory is decided according to the inner necessities of the formulation which, in this case, indicate the need for a master-builder; but then it turns out that that in itself is life-liberating.

There is also the formulation which indicates that families should be designing their own houses because, after looking at countless cases of traditional architecture, that is obviously what was happening. When you think about adaptation as a biological phenomenon, you realize that every spot has to be unique because of its unique locus in space and therefore the people that are to live there have to help shape it — and that's all in the formulation of the theory. But then you actually have families that are doing that — as we did in Mexico — and suddenly they feel incredibly good, liberated, and full of powerful emotions that have no correlation with anything predictable that would emanate from the theory. So there's something pretty amazing going on here.

To me, the fact that this whole theory, which is internally coherent and structured in terms of generative processes, should also happen to create such wonderful feelings at every point of its own implementation, in the end, is perhaps the most remarkable feature about the whole thing.

Remarkable indeed; but not necessarily new. Recall Kuhn's observation about the ideas upon which new paradigms are built being themselves almost always rooted in tradition. The congruence between beauty, truth, and goodness is of course an ancient idea; and just as Copernicus was not the first to suggest the earth's motion, neither is Alexander the first to suggest this remarkable idea. But he has arrived at it by way of an unprecedented linguistic and even mathematical system which distinguishes him from his predecessors. And this, as Kuhn observes, is the crucial ingredient in paradigm shift — the ability to be precise about the consequences of a reality only believed to be existing independently of our knowing it.

Whether or not Alexander's work will actually inaugurate a revolution in architecture comparable to the great scientific revolutions described by Kuhn is a question that cannot be answered either at the present moment or within the confines of this analysis. Regardless of the outcome, however, he has set a standard for inquiry and debate long overdue in the field of architecture. As Kuhn points out, "scientific progress is not different in kind from progress in other fields, but the absence at most times of competing schools that question each other's aims and standards makes the progress of a normal-scientific community far easier to see."[2] For this achievement alone, Alexander has changed the field. And if his work also succeeds in fostering an architecture that is based on human freedom and liberation, it would indeed be — as the subtitle of his first book with Chermayeff suggested — "a new architecture of humanism."

REFERENCE NOTES

1. Morse Peckham, BEYOND THE TRAGIC VISION (New York: George Braziller, 1962), p.66
2. Thomas Kuhn, THE STRUCTURE OF SCIENTIFIC REVOLUTIONS, 2nd ed. (Chicago: University of Chicago Press, 1970), p.162

CONCLUSION

It was Geoffrey Scott who first coined the term "the architecture of humanism" at the turn of the century. For Scott, the capacity to seek congruence between our own feelings and the external world is an ancient, deep-seated, and universal instinct:

> It looks in the world for physical conditions that are related to our own, for movements which are like those we enjoy, for resistances that resemble those that can support us, for a setting where we should be neither lost nor thwarted. It looks, therefore, for certain masses, lines, and spaces, tends to create them, and recognize their fitness when created.[1].

For Scott, this is the "natural" way of perceiving and interpreting what we see. It is the way of the child, primitive peoples, and the ancient Greeks, "whose mythology is one vast monument to this instinct." In his formulation, it is the basis of poetry and the foundation of architecture — but in its absence, architecture appears singularly inauthentic. This is the real problem of modern architecture today: in its effort to meet the exigencies of industrial society, it has lost touch with the foundation of its own authenticity. And yet, this is a uniquely 20th century problem, not necessarily confined to architecture.

Heidegger's phrase "forgetfulness of being" summarizes the sentiment of a great deal of 20th century literature, art, philosophy, and even social science.[2]. There is a general feeling that the certainties once provided by religion have been lost and can never be replaced, and that science, by its dazzling solutions to practical problems, can only make this inner void more painfully obvious. Although these are problems which Medieval man would have found inconceivable, Heidegger is only restating a problem that has been recognized since the Greeks.

The problem of modern architecture is a bit like the problem of the prisoners in Plato's cave who endlessly manipulate the shadows of images cast on a cavern wall. No matter how adept they become in figuring out the order and sequence of appearance, they cannot see what's really casting the shadows. And the increasing tendency of architecture to lapse into an almost geometrical version of this allegory is felt like a wall of forgetfulness going up between the meaning and the existence of things like buildings and towns.

Plato believed that authentic reality could be regained in the world of "Ideas." Before a carpenter can make a chair, he must have an idea — or pattern — of a chair; consequently, this idea must be more important than the actual chair. One can destroy the chair, and it is easy enough to make another; but if the idea were destroyed, no chairs could be made. The "idea" is like the mold in which all real things are cast — what Banham calls the "precious vessel." And somewhere behind the walled facade of reality, according to Plato, there is a timeless world in which these molds are kept.[3]

The problem with modern architecture is that it seems to be unaware of this distinction. Like the prisoners in the cave, it has its back to the wall; or like carpenters who have forgotten the "idea" of a chair, modern buildings take on the appearances of images of a forgotten world. And the architects of these shadows, like the prisoner's in Plato's cave, have devised an elaborate language of cardboard-like signs and symbols to convey the order and meaning of the images they manipulate. These "painted words" — as Tom Wolfe calls their equivalent in modern painting — constitute the inauthenticity of modern architecture.

Such comparisons, however, are only useful in establishing a philosophical reference to Alexander's inquiry. Unfortunately, they may obscure the fundamental difference between his approach to these problems and those of philosophers like Plato and Heidegger. The purely philosophical approach tackles the problem mainly with the mind. Alexander's approach is much more empirical. This is a matter of necessity. As Suzuki puts it in his comparison between zen swordmanship and philosophy, "The question is at the door, over the head, 'sizzling the eyebrows.' If the answer is not forthcoming, all is ruined. The situation here is more critical than the philosopher's."[4] For Alexander, the perception of authentic or inauthentic architecture is a matter of life or death —

and he uses the terms literally.

His sensitivity makes him unusually aware of the negative; yet all his faculties are exerted in a search for the positive — the instinctive, absolute, yea-saying confirmations of authenticity. Like all artists, he has moments when he seems to be in complete accord with the universe and himself, when he feels that the universe and himself are made of the same stuff. The rest of the time is a struggle to regain that insight and that feeling.

If there is an order, a structure in the universe, if he can sometimes perceive that structure and feel himself completely in accord with it, then it must be seeable, touchable, so that it could be regained by some discipline — entered through by some gate. That this discipline should include a mathematical account of that structure is somewhat astonishing and constitutes part of Alexander's uniqueness as an architect.

Yet even as an approach to the problem in purely philosophical terms it is unique in its insistence upon and search for an empirically objective criterion that can actually distinguish cases of good and bad. In other words, Alexander's claims — that for this thing to have any reality at all one must be able to see the degree to which the quality of authenticity is present in any situation — are actually startling, especially in light of the more meta-physical account of the problem in modern philosophy. Consequently, there is no guarantee that Alexander is talking about the same thing as Plato and the others.

The question is difficult to answer insofar as it is often excruciatingly difficult to know for sure just what philosophers are talking about. Although Alexander himself discounts the relevance and even accuracy of such comparisons — with the possible exception of Whitehead — I believe they are useful in understanding the objectivity of his claims beyond published research or personal experience. My purpose here is not to contest that experience — for I believe it to be true; but rather, to try and explain its relationship to a wider body of thought. My own opinion is that Plato is much less abstract than scholarly interpretations often suggest. I think he is very realistic indeed when, in the REPUBLIC, he describes the return of one of the now-liberated prisoners back to the cave:

> And if he were forced to deliver his opinion again, touching the

227

shadows aforesaid, and to enter the lists against those who had always been prisoners...would he not be made a laughingstock, and would it not be said of him, that he had gone up only to come back again with his eyesight destroyed, and that it was not worth while even to attempt the ascent? And if he endeavored to set them free and carry them to the light, would they not go so far as to put him to death, if they could only manage to get him into their power?[5]

This is hardly an abstraction intended to be accessible only to other philosophers. Plato is describing a very real problem, with serious personal implications. But it is also true that he never identifies the criterion for distinguishing the real from the shadows. The same is true for all those philosophers after Plato who tried to tackle the problem. And although the purpose of philosophy is not really to furnish empirical criteria, without something more concrete to go on the relationship of these ideas to architecture seems uninteresting.

But that is precisely the point of distinction between Alexander's ideas and those of his predecessors. The purpose of the comparison therefore is not only to illustrate the scope of the problem and its relationship to a wider body of thought, but also to highlight the unique features of Alexander's solution — namely, its particular claims to objective reality. For without those claims, his theories could easily be dismissed as idiosyncratic and highly personal opinions about the meaning of life. That this is not the case, is in fact what makes his story both interesting and relevant to the search for new paradigms — and particularly to the search for those which might resolve the crisis of modern architecture.

REFERENCE NOTES

1. Geoffrey Scott, THE ARCHITECTURE OF HUMANISM: A STUDY IN THE HISTORY OF TASTE (Gloucester: Peter Smith, 1965), p.174

2. See Colin Wilson, BEYOND THE OUTSIDER (London: Pan Books, 1965), pp.17, 104-109; cf. Martin Heidegger, BEING AND TIME (1927)

3. See Wilson, OP. CIT., p.52

4. D.T. Suzuki, ZEN AND JAPANESE CULTURE (Princeton: Princeton University Press, 1970), p.124

5. Plato, THE REPUBLIC, Book Seven, trans. by H.D.P. Lee (Harmondsworth: Penguin Books, 1964), p.281

ALEXANDER BIBLIOGRAPHY
BOOKS, PAPERS, MONOGRAPHS AND PROJECTS
(Buildings and projects are marked with an asterisk)

"Perception and Modular Coordination," *RIBA Journal,* Vol. 66, No. 12, October, 1959, pp. 425–429.

"A Result in Visual Aesthetics," *British Journal of Psychology,* October, 1960, pp. 357–371.

"The Revolution Finished Twenty Years Ago," in *Architect's Year Book 9,* London, 1960, pp. 181–185.

"Information and an Organized Process of Design," *Proceedings of the BRI,* Washington, Spring, 1961, pp. 115–124.

"The Use of Diagrams in Route Location," (with Marvin Mannheim), Civil Engineering Systems Laboratory Publication 161, MIT, March, 1962. Also in Highway Research Board Reports, 1965.

"The Design of Highway Interchanges" (with Marvin Mannheim), Civil Engineering Systems Laboratory Publication 195, MIT, March, 1962. Also in Highway Research Record No. 83 Highway Research Board, Washington, D.C., 1965.

"Hidecs 2: A Computer Program for the Hierarchical Decomposition of a Set with an Associated Graph," (with Marvin Mannheim), Civil Engineering Systems Laboratory Publication 160, MIT, June, 1962. Also in *Behavioural Science,* Vol. 8, No. 2, April, 1963.

"The Origin of Creative Power in Children," *British Journal of Aesthetics,* Vol. 3, No. 2, July, 1962, pp. 207–226.

"The Determination of Components for an Indian Village," *Proceedings of the Conference on Design Method,* London, September, 1962. Also published by Pergamon Press, 1963, pp. 83–114.

*Village school, Bavra, Gujarat, India, 1962 (with Janet Johnson).

*Master plan for village of Bavra, Gujarat, India, 1962.

Community and Privacy: Toward a new architecture of humanism (with Serge Chermayeff), Doubleday, New York, 1963. Also published in Japanese, Tokyo, 1966; Spanish, Buenos Aires, 1967; and German, Mainz, 1972.

229

Program for Urban housing, Arthur D. Little, San Francisco, 1963.

"Hidecs 3: Four Computer Programs for the Hierarchical Decomposition of Systems Which Have an Associated Linear Graph," Civil Engineering Systems Laboratory Publication Report No. R63–27, MIT, June, 1963.

"Main Structure Concept" (with B. V. Doshi), *Landscape,* Vol 13, No. 2 (Winter), 1963-64, pp. 17–20, reprinted in *Ekistics,* Vol. 17, No. 103 (June 1964) pp 352–354.

*Courtyard house plans, Newhaven, Connecticut (with Serge Chermayeff), 1963–64.

Notes on the Synthesis of Form, Harvard University Press, 1964. Also published in Italian, Milano, 1967; French, Paris, 1970; Spanish, Buenos Aires, 1973; Japanese, Tokyo, 1973.

*Schematic design of Rapid Transit Stations for the Bay Area Rapid Transit System (with Van King and Sara Ishikawa), for Wurster, Bernardi & Emmons, San Francisco, 1964.

"On Changing the Way People See" (with A. W. F. Huggins), *Perceptual and Motor Skills,* 19, July, 1964, pp. 235–253.

"A City is Not a Tree," *Architectural Forum,* April–May, 1965, pp. 58–62. Also in *Design,* February, 1966, pp. 46–55; *Cuadernos Summa-Nueva Vision,* No. 9, September, 1968, pp. 20–30; *Hefti Birtingur* 13, 1967, pp. 50–72; *Architecture Mouvement Continuite* 1, November, 1967, pp. 3–11; *Stichting Werkgemeenschappen Bergeijk,* 2; *Approach,* Spring, 1968, pp. 26–27.

"The Coordination of the Urban Rule System," *Regio Basiliensis Proceedings,* Basel, Switzerland, December, 1965, pp. 1–9. Also published by the Centre for Planning and Development Research, University of California, Berkeley, July. 1966.

"390 Requirements for the Rapid Transit Station," (with Van Maren King and Sara Ishikawa), Library of the College of Environmental Design, Berkeley, California, 1965.

"The Question of Computers in Design," *Landscape,* Vol. 14, No. 3, Spring, 1965, pp. 6–8.

"The Theory and Invention of Form," *Architectural Record*, April, 1965, pp. 177–186.

"The Universe of Form", burnt ms, 1965.

"From a Set of Forces to a Form," in *The Man-Made Object,* Vision and Value Series, Volume 4 (edited by Gyorgy Kepes), George Braziller, New York, 1966, pp. 96–107, reprinted in *Interior Design,* October, 1967, translated into French, 1968.

"Relational Complexes in Architecture" (with Van Maren King and others), *Architectural Record,* September, 1966, pp. 185–190.

"The Pattern of Streets," *Journal of the AIP,* Vol. 32, No. 5, September, 1966, pp. 273–278. Also in *Architectural Design,* November, 1967, pp. 528–531, and *Approach,* Spring, 1968, p. 25; "Reply to Carson and Roosen-Runge," *Journal of the AIP,* November, 1967.

"Twenty-Six Entrance Relations for a Suburban House," Ministry of Public Buildings and Works, Directorate of Research and Development, London, 1966, pp. 17–73, reprinted in *Emerging Methods in Design,* Gary Moore, (ed.), MIT, 1971.

"The Atoms of Environmental Structure" (with Barry Poyner), Ministry of Public Buildings and Works, Directorate of Research and Development, London, 1966, pp. 3016. Also published by the Center for Planning and Development Research, University of California, Berkeley, July, 1966; reprinted in *Emerging Methods in Environmental Design and Planning,* Gary Moore, (ed.), MIT, 1971.

"Systems Generating Systems," Booklet, published by Inland Steel, 1967. Also in *Architecture Canada,* No. 11, Vol. 45, November, 1968, pp. 39–44; *Casabella,* 321, 1967, pp. 4–11; *Approach,* Spring, 1968, pp. 14–19; and *Architectural Design,* December, 1968.

"The City as a Mechanism for Sustaining Human Contact," in *Environment for Man: The Next Fifty Years* (edited by W. Ewald), American Institute of Planners Conference, Indiana University Press, 1967, pp. 60–102. Also published by the Center for Planning and Development Research, University of California, Berkeley, Working Paper No. 50, October, 1966; *Cuadernos Summa-Nueva Vision, No. 9,* September, 1968, pp. 3–19; *Approach,* Spring, 1968, p. 24., and *Transactions of the Bartlett Society,* Volume 4, 93–136.

"The Center for Environmental Structure: Theory, Organization and Activities," Brochure, Center for Environmental Structure, Berkeley, California, 1967.

"Design Innovation" (with others), *Progressive Architecture,* November, 1967, pp. 126–131.

"Proceedings of the Seminar of the Center for Environmental Structure" (with Sara Ishikawa, Murray Silverstein and others), Center for Environmental Structure, Berkeley, California, 1967.

"Subsymmetries" (with Susan Carey), *Perception and Psychophysics,* Vol. 4 (2), February, 1968, pp. 73–77.

"A Sublanguage of 70 Patterns for Multi-Service Centers" (with Sara Ishikawa and Murray Silverstein), report submitted to the Hunts Point Neighborhood Corporation, Hunts Point, Bronx, New York, January, 1968.

"Thick Walls," *Architectural Design,* July, 1968, pp. 324–326.

"The Bead Game Conjecture," *Lotus 5,* 1968, Alfieri, Venezia, pp. 151–154.

"Major Changes in Environmental Form Required by Social and Psychological Demands," Second International Seminar, Japan Center for Area Development Research, September 1968. Also published in *Ekistics,* Vol. 28, No. 165, 1969; *Architectural Design,* March 1970; reprinted in *Cities Fit to Live In,* Walter McQuade (ed.), New York, 1971.

A Pattern Language Which Generates Multi-Service Centers (with Sara Ishikawa and Murray Silverstein), Center for Environmental Structure, Berkeley, California, 1968.

*Design for multi-service center, Hunts Point, Bronx, New York (with Sara Ishikawa and Murray Silverstein), schematics, 1968.

"Cells of Subcultures," occasional paper of the Center for Environmental Structure, Berkeley, California, 1968.

"Mosaic of Subcultures," Center for Environmental Structure, Berkeley, California, 1969.

Tres Aspectos de Matematica y Diseqno, Barcelona, 1969.

Houses Generated by Patterns (with Sanford Hirshen, Sara Ishikawa, Christie Coffin and Shlomo Angel), Center for Environmental Structure, Berkeley, California, 1969; reprinted in *Architect's Yearbook 13,* London, 1971; also in *The Growth of Cities,* David Lewis (ed.), London, 1971.

*Design for a community of 1500 houses for Lima, Peru (with Sanford Hirshen, Sara Ishikawa, Christie Coffin and Shlomo Angel), invited competition entry, United Nations, 1969.

Eighty-panel exhibit for the 1970 Osaka World's Fair, Japanese Pavilion, entitled "A Human City," with Ronald Walkey and others, 1970.

*Program and design for Berkeley City Hall Complex, for the City of Berkeley (with Ronald Walkey and Barbara Schreiner), 1970.

A Human City. (With Ronald Walkey, Murray Silverstein, and others). Kajima Publishing Company, Tokyo, 1970.

"The Environment," *The Japan Architect,* 165, 1970.

*Furniture, design and construction, various experimental pieces, 1970–78.

Interview with Max Jacobson, "A Refutation of Design Methodology," in *Design Methods Newsletter,* 1971, reprinted in *Architectural Design,* December 1971.

Interview with Maria José Ragué Arias, in Maria José Ragué Arias, *California Trip,* Barcelona, 1971, pp. 53–59.

La Estuctura del Medio Ambiente. Barcelona, 1971.

*Construction of fourteen prototype houses, Lima, Peru, 1971.

*Master Plan for the University of Oregon, Eugene, Oregon, 1971–1972.

*Design and construction of Community Mental Health Center, Modesto, California (with Murray Silverstein and Nacht and Lewis, Sacramento), for Stanislaus County, California. Completed and occupied, 1972.

"The Shirt-Sleeve Sessions in Responsive Housebuilding Technologies," Department of Architecture, MIT, Cambridge, Massachusetts, May 3-5, 1972.

"An Attempt to Derive the Nature of a Human Building System from First Principles," in *The Responsive House,* Edward Allen (ed.), MIT, 1974, pp. 22–32.

"Specifications for an Organic and Human Building System" (with Max Jacobson), in *The Responsive House,* Edward Allen (ed.), MIT, 1974, pp. 33-51.

"Can a housewife design a home?" *Christian Science Monitor,* February 18, 1972.

*Master planning process for the town of Märsta, Sweden. Fourteen panels, 27″ × 40″, English and Swedish (with Max Jacobson and Ingrid King), 1972-1973.

"An Early Summary of 'The Timeless Way of Building'," in *Designing for Human Behaviour,* Jon Lang et. al. (eds.), 1974, pp. 52–59.

"The Grass Roots Housing Process," with Halim Abdelhalim and others, Center for Environmental Structure, Berkeley, 1973.

"Economics, Politics and Implementation of the Pattern Language," working paper of the Royal Institute of Technology, Stockholm, 1973.

233

*Master Plan for Tourist Resort, Fuerteventura, Canary Islands, with Ingrid King, Halim Abdelhalim, and Lisa Heschong, 1973.

*Master Plan and preliminary design for Town Square, Walnut Creek, with Ingrid King. 200,000 square feet of commercial space, to be built incrementally, by Miller and Facchini, Walnut Creek, 1974.

*Experimental Building Project: two-storey building built of featherweight concrete, vaults, columns, beams, all built of featherweight concrete, with Walter Wendler, Donald Corner, and others, 1974.

"A Collection of Patterns which Generate; Multi-Service Centers," (with Sara Ishikawa and Murray Silverstein). Summary of book in Declan and Margrit Kennedy, *The Inner City,* London: 1974, pp. 141–180.

Tourist Development Project for Malaga, Spain, on behalf of the Spanish Ministry of Tourism. 1,000,000 square feet, to be built over a ten-year period (with Halim Abdelhalim, Walter Wendler, Ingrid King, Donald Corner, and Howard Davis), 1974.

*User designed apartment building, 27 families, St. Quentin-en-Yvelines, Paris. Schematic design, program, and construction schedule with Ingrid King and Walter Wendler, 1974.

"People Rebuilding Berkeley: The Self-Creating Life of Neighbourhoods" (with Howard Davis and Halim Abdelhalim), report to the Master Plan Revision Committee, City of Berkeley, California, November, 1974.

"The New Apartment House," with Ingrid King and Walter Wendler, Center for Environmental Structure, Berkeley, 1975.

"The Andalusian Project" (with Halim Abdelhalim, Walter Wendler, and others), report to the Ministry of Tourism, Madrid, 1974; also in *Architectural Design,* January, 1975.

"The Growth of Order from Small Acts," unpublished working paper, Center for Environmental Structure, Berkeley, California, 1975.

"A Conjectured Mapping Density Theorem," unpublished working paper, Center for Environmental Structure, Berkeley, California, 1975.

The Oregon Experiment, (with Murray Silverstein, Shlomo Angel, Sara Ishikawa, and Denny Abrams), Oxford University Press, 1975; Spanish and French translations 1980, Japanese and Italian translations 1981.

*Rockridge plaza, shops and apartments, Oakland, California, 1975.

*Experimental block production factory for producing soil-cement interlocking blocks. Design, erection and management, Mexicali, Mexico, 1975–76.

*Tiles, and paintings, multicoloured, various experimental works, 1975–78.

"The architect builder," John Lawrence Memorial lecture, Tulane University, New Orleans, 1976.

*User built housing. Eight low cost experimental houses with community facilities, Mexicali, Mexico, 1976.

"The Construction of Thin Shells," unpublished working paper, Center for Environmental Structure, Berkeley, California, 1976.

A Pattern Language, (with Sara Ishikawa, Murray Silverstein, Max Jacobson, Ingrid Fiksdahl-King, and Shlomo Angel), Oxford University Press, 1977, Spanish translation 1980, Japanese Translation 1981.

*Plans for an $8000 migrant workers house, Department of Migrant Services, State of California, 1977.

"On Value," *Concrete,* Vol. 1, No. 8, December, 1977, pp. 1, 3, 6–7.

"The Architect Builder: Toward changing the Conception of what an Architect is," *San Francisco Bay Architects Review,* September, 1977, p. 4.

The One, unpublished ms. early version of *The Nature of Order,* Berkeley, 1977.

*Experiments in sprayed concrete, University of California, 1977–78.

*Experimental sprayed concrete house, Martinez, Calif., 1978–79.

The Timeless Way of Building, Oxford University Press, 1979.

*Master Plan for Segev H, Israel (with Amos Gitai), Center for Environmental Structure, Berkeley, California, 1979.

"Art and Design for the 21st Century," in *Design is Unsichtbar,* edited Liesbeth Waecheter Bohm, Locker Verlag, Vienna 1980, pp. 101–110.

"The Progress of My Work," *ibid,* pp. 385–394.

"Notes on the Design of the Linz Cafe," *ibid,* pp. 664–667.

"The Timeless Quality of Things," *ibid,* pp. 111–114.

*Paintings (1980):
  White cross on green field
  Blue gateway
  Green yellow and red alcove
  Three colored square
  Magenta and violet arches

*Tiles (1980):
  White diamonds on black ground
  Green spiral
  Yellow arabesque

*The Linz Cafe, building completed in Linz, Austria, 1980.

*Furniture: Chairs, stools and tables, designed for the Linz Cafe, Linz, 1980.

*Design for restaurant on the Hudson River for Robert Schwarts, New York, 1980.

*Design for extension to Tarrytown Conference Center, Tarrytown, N.Y., for Robert Schwarts, 1980.

"Rebirth of the Inner City: The North Omaha Plan," (with Howard Davis), Center for Environmental Structure, Berkeley, California, 1981.

The Linz Cafe, Oxford University Press, 1981; German edition, Vienna, 1981.

"Beyond Humanism," Christopher Alexander interviewed by Howard Davis, Journal of Architectural Education, Vol. 35, No. 1, Fall 1981, pp. 18–24.

*House for Mr. & Mrs. Stuart Card, Palo Alto, Calif., 1981.

*House for Mr. and Mrs. John Lighty, Berryessa, Calif., 1981.

*Plan and layout for Moshav Shorashim, Galilee, Israel, 1981.

Geometry, Second unpublished early MS version of The Nature of Order, 1981.

*Furniture:
  Blue music cabinet for Pamela Patrick, 1981.

"Sketches of a New Architecture," unpublished manuscript, 350 pages, 250 illustrations, 1981.

The Production of Houses (with Howard Davis and others), Oxford University Press, 1982.

"Rules for House Layout," Definition of process for layout of houses in Moshav Shorashim, Center for Environmental Structure, Berkeley, California, 1982.

*The Eishin School — high school and university complex, Tokyo, Japan, 1982.

*House for Mr. and Mrs. Andre Sala, Albany, Calif., (with G. Black) 1982.

*House design for Mr. and Mrs. Kinsey Anderson, Bodega Bay, California, 1982.

*10-storey apartment building design for Mrs. Keiko Inoue, Sapporo, Japan (with Ingrid King), 1982.

*Tiles: thirty-five multi-colored blue diamond tiles, all hand drawn and painted, for Berryessa house, 1982.

*Layout and design of twenty houses, all different, each one laid out in conjunction with the family, Moshav Shorashim, Galilee, Israel, 1982.

A New Theory of Urban Design (with Ingrid King, Hajo Neis, Artemis Aninou), Oxford University Press, in press.

"The One," unpublished manuscript, 1200 pages, to be published by Oxford University Press, as The Nature of Order.

Geometry, Oxford University Press, in preparation.

"Very Early Turkish Rugs," unpublished manuscript, 600 pages, 100 illustrations, 1982.

AN ALEXANDER COLLAGE

The following photographs and drawings, provided by Christopher Alexander, are deliberately not in chronological sequence. They are in random order and intend to convey, as a whole a visual impression of Christopher Alexander and his personality.

Modesto clinic, 1973.

Balustrade of Sala house, Albany, California, 1982.

Modesto clinic, 1973.

Dome in Mexicali, 1976.

Martinez house under construction, 1979.

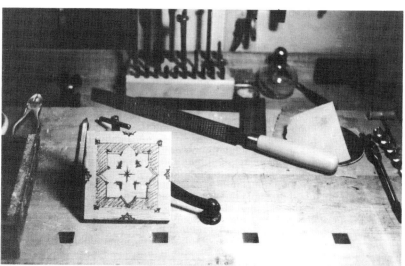

CA's workbench, and sketch for a stamp used for stamping patterns into concrete, 1977.

CA in India, 1962.

Four domed school, Bavra, India, under construction, 1962.

Street facade of Mexicali project, 1976.

Hand painted flowers in the Linz cafe, 1980.

Model for Paris apartment building, 1974.

247

Interior of Linz cafe, 1980.

Interior of Linz cafe, 1980.

Hand made tile, 1977.

Interior vault, Mexicali, 1976.

Tiles for foundation of Berryessa house, 1981.

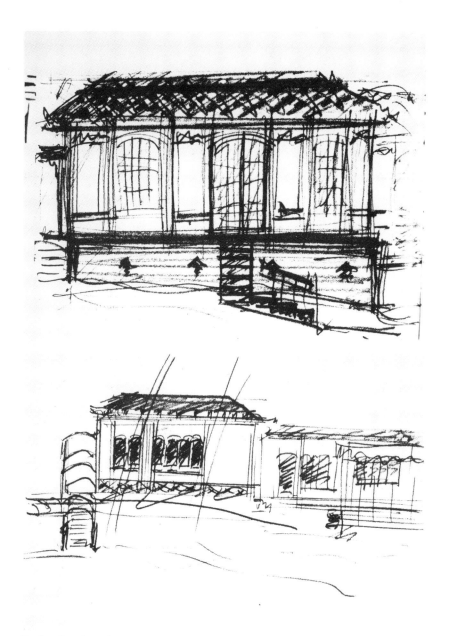

Early sketches for Berryessa house, 1980.

Linz cafe, exterior, 1980.

Bedside table, 1975.

Inauguration of village school, Bavra, India, with Janet Johnson, 1962.

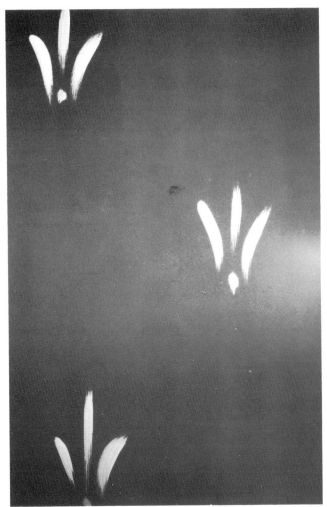

Flowers from Linz cafe, 1980.

Domes in Mexicali, 1976.

Construction experiments, 1977.

Etna street cottage, Berkeley, 1973.

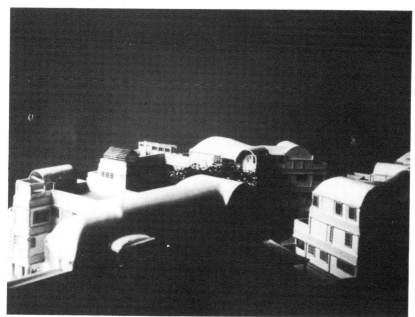

Paris apartment house, model, 1974.

Martinez workshop, sprayed concrete, 1979.

L

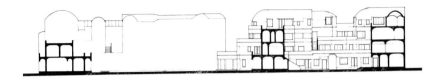

Paris apartment house, sections and elevations, 1974.

Ten storey building, Sapporo, Japan, model, 1982.

CA's block making yard, Mexicali, 1976.

Sketching an interior opening
during construction, 1982.

Buffooning, Florence, 1980.

Families preparing to build their houses, Mexicali, 1976.

Painting, green, cinnabar, pale green and white, 1977.

Alcove in the Linz cafe, 1980.

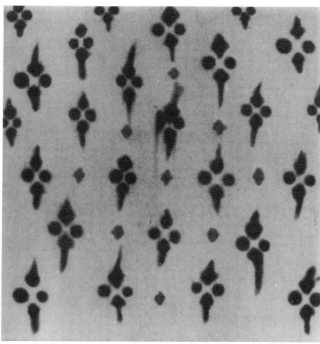

Hand made tile, 1977.

Taking a break, Linz, 1980.

Working in bed, 1981.

Hand made tile, 1978.

Martinez, California, 1980.

One of CA's turkish rugs: 17th century Ladik.

Mexicali, 1976.

Etna street cottage, wood and burlap basket, ready to receive lightweight concrete shell to form vault, 1973.

CA's daughter Lily, 1982.

Block making yard, Mexicali, 1976.

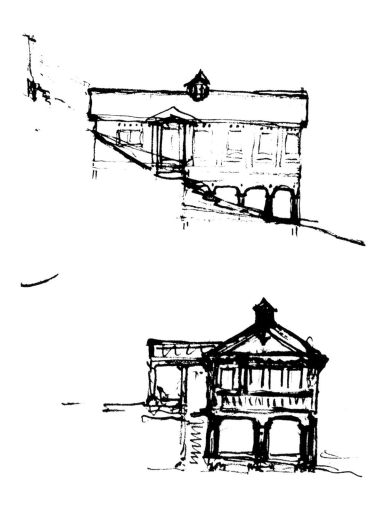

Sketches for La Loma house, Berkeley, 1978.

University of Oregon foundry, built by students under the guidance of the Oregon master plan, mid-seventies.

Pamela and Lily, 1982.

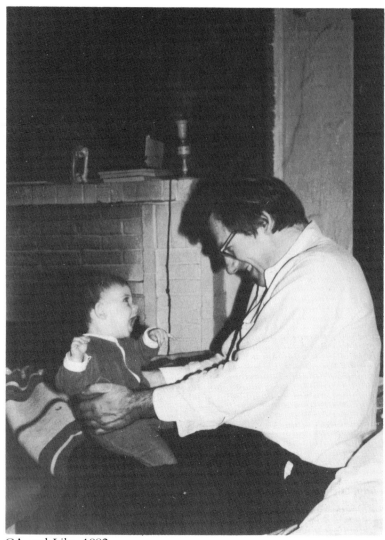

CA and Lily, 1982.

With a favourite kitten, 1979.

Wooden tray, green oil stain, french polished, with hand painted ornaments, 1976.

CA as a PhD student, 1960.

Houses in Mexicali, under construction, 1976.

A proud householder on her front porch, Mexicali, 1976.

Painting on wood panel, blue, yellow, black with touches of minor colors, 1978.

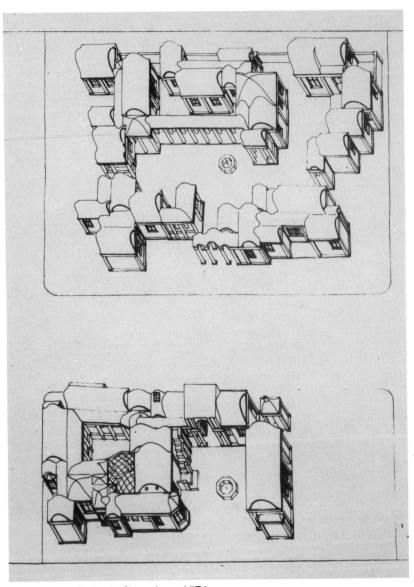

Overview of Mexicali project, 1976.

Mexicali, under construction, 1976.

In Florence, 1980.

Arcade in Mexicali, 1976.   Alcove in Mexico, 1976.

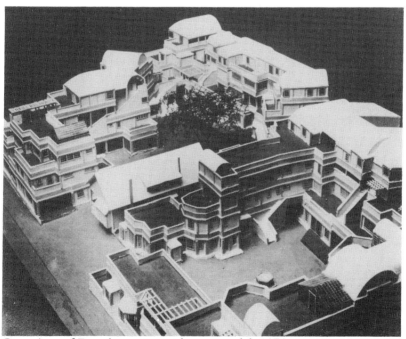

Overview of French apartment house model, 1974.

Clinic, Modesto, California, 1973.

Experimental Count Rumford fireplace, built in concrete, Martinez, California, 1981.

Martinez project, third building under construction, 1982.

Concrete bracket, CA's craftsmanship, Sala house, Albany, California, 1982.

Linz cafe, balcony, 1980.

Laying out houses with the families, Mexicali, 1976.

Vaults under construction, Mexicali, 1976.

A sunny corner of the Linz cafe, 1980.

Mockup for a ceiling ornament, 1977.

CA's favorite prayer rug, a 15th century Turkish rug from Konya.

CA and fellow student at Cambridge, high jinks in the woods, 1955.

Tying reinforcing wires.

Etna street cottage, 1973.

Martinez building site, 1979.

Preparing to shoot concrete, 1979.

Foundations of the Berryessa house, 1981.

Martinez workshop, spayed concrete, 1979.

CA nine years old,
Chichester, 1946.

CA seventeen years old, with a summer job
as a bus conductor, 1953.

Shooting concrete, 1979.

Writing *Notes on the Synthesis of Form*, Cambridge, Mass 1960.

With Lily, on the beach at Santa Cruz, 1982.

Mother and son, Oxford, 1945.

Father and son, 1959.

Zurich, 1979.

Mary Louise Rogers, Sara Ishikawa, CA, Ron Walkey, Christie Coffin, Murray Silverstein, and Denny Abrams, Center for Environmental Structure, 1970.

Interior of Oregon foundry, built by students under the guidance of the
Oregon master plan, mid seventies.

With the people who built the school in India, 1962.

Music cabinet, before painting, 1980.

Getting the right size for a window, Etna street cottage, 1973.

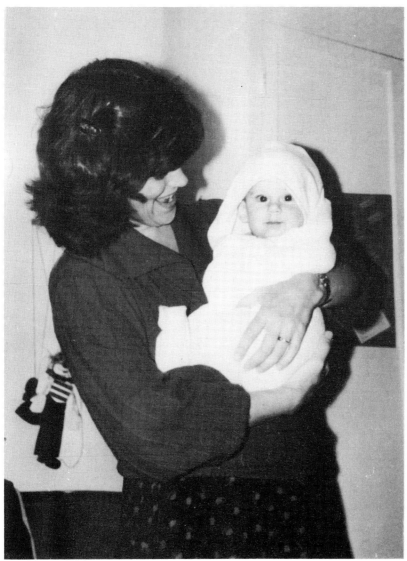

Pamela and Lily, 1981.

Martinez, 1981.

With Lily, and the experimental fireplace, 1982.

Painting on wood, 1968.

A window seat of the Linz cafe.
Painted ornaments near ceiling
are pale green on apricot yellow.

Chris and Ingrid, Berkeley, 1972.

CA's workshop, 1982.

Raising a beam, Berryessa, house, 1982.

Painting, red and silver, 1970.

"Boxhill": Locomotive made from sheet brass, 1950.

Hand made tiles, 1978.

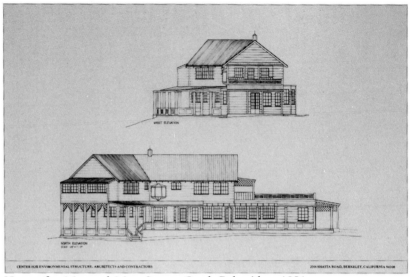

House for Mr. and Mrs. Stuart Card, Palo Alto, 1981.

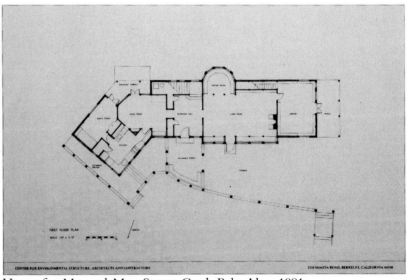

House for Mr. and Mrs. Stuart Card, Palo Alto, 1981.

302

Sapporo apartment building, 1982.

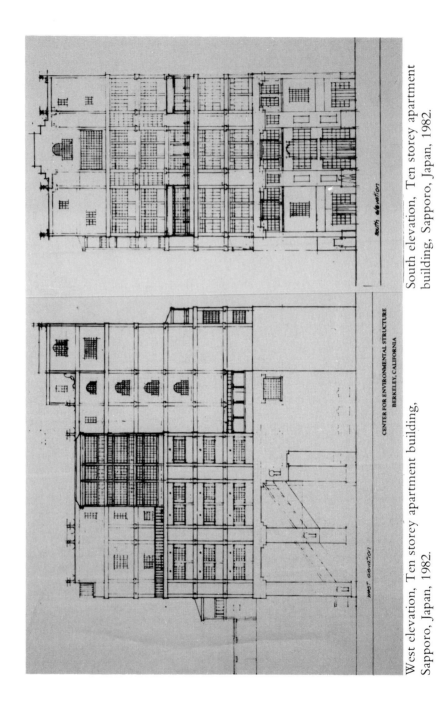

South elevation, Ten storey apartment building, Sapporo, Japan, 1982.

West elevation, Ten storey apartment building, Sapporo, Japan, 1982.

ILLUSTRATION CREDITS

This list gratefully acknowledges the many photographers and institutions whose illustrations were reproduced for this book.

Frontispiece. Jean-Michel Folon; Harry N. Abrams, N.Y., 1978
PLATES
 1. Alinari; Societa Editrice Internazionale, Turin, 1967
 2. Doeser-Fotos, Laren; Verlag Gerd Hatje, Stuttgart, 1958
 3. Jürgen Joedicke; Verlag Gerd Hatje, Stuttgart, 1958
 4. J.M. Richards; Hugh Evelyn, London, 1966
 5. Jürgen Joedicke; Verlag Gerd Hatje, Stuttgart, 1958
 6. Heinz Geretsegger and Max Peintner; Rizzoli, N.Y., 1979
 7. Morley Baer; Walker and Company, N.Y., 1966
 8. Yukio Futagawa; Thames and Hudson, London, 1970
 9. Wim Swaan; Stein and Day, N.Y., 1965
10. Alexandre Georges; Walker and Company, N.Y., 1966
11. Wim Swaan; Stein and Day, N.Y., 1965
12. Leopoldo Torres Balbas; Editorial Plus Ultra, Madrid, 1949
13. Antoine Trincano, Lyon; B. Arthaud, Paris, 1966
14. Municipal Museum, The Hague; J.M. Meulenhoff, Amsterdam, 1956
15. From Theo van Doesburg; with permission of Florian Kupferberg Verlag, Mainz, 1966
16. Matila Ghyka; Sheed and Ward, N.Y., 1962
17. Peter Cook; Reinhold, N.Y., 1967
18. Photograph courtesy, Mies van der Rohe Archive, Museum of Modern Art, N.Y.
19. Christopher Alexander; Harvard University Press, Cambridge, 1964
20. Halvor Vreim M.N.A.L., Oslo; Dreyers Vorlag, Oslo, 1958
21 Christopher Alexander; Harvard University Press, Cambridge, 1964
22. Christopher Alexander; Harvard University Press, Cambridge, 1964
23. Christopher Alexander; Harvard University Press, Cambridge, 1964
24. Christopher Alexander; Architectural Record, 1966
25. Christopher Alexander; Architectural Forum, 1965
26. Christopher Alexander; Architectural Forum, 1965
27. Christopher Alexander; Doubleday and Company, Garden City, N.Y., 1963
28. Christopher Alexander; Center for Environmental Structure, Berkeley, 1968
29. Christopher Alexander; Center for Environmental Structure, Berkeley, 1968
30, Christopher Alexander; Wiley Interscience, N.Y., 1971
31. Christopher Alexander; Wiley Interscience, N.Y., 1971
32. Gertrude Jekyll; Country Life Ltd., London, 1913
33. Photograph courtesy, Mies van der Rohe Archive, Museum of Modern Art, N.Y.
34. S.F. Murasawa; George Braziller, N.Y., 1963
35. D'Arcy Wentworth Thompson; Cambridge University Press, London, 1966
36. J.C. Chenu; Cambridge University Press, London, 1966
37. Brookhaven National Laboratory; Addison-Wesley, Reading, Mass., 1965
38. Gallerie H.J. von Wirth, Dusseldorf; Klinkhardt and Biermann, Munich, 1955
39. Photograph courtesy, Mies van der Rohe Archive, Museum of Modern Art, N.Y.
40. Herbert Wise; Copyright, The Putnam Publishing Group, N.Y., 1978
41. R.S. Magowan; Hamlyn Group Picture Library, Feltham, 1961
42. Veli Roth, Zurich; Werk, January, 1967
43. Ezra Stoller, ESTO, Mamaroneck, N.Y.; Oxford University Press, N.Y., 1976
44. Anonymous
45. Victor Harris; The Overlook Press, Woodstock, N.Y., 1974
46. Christopher Alexander; Oxford University Press, N.Y., 1977
47. Christopher Alexander; Oxford University Press, N.Y., 1977
48. Christopher Alexander; Oxford University Press, N.Y., 1977
49. Zauko Press, Tokyo; George Braziller, N.Y., 1963
50. Henry Reinhard Moeller; Verlag Gerd Hatje, Stuttgart, 1958
51. Marcel Gautherot; Verlag Gerd Hatje, Stuttgart, 1958
52. Christopher Alexander; Oxford University Press, N.Y., 1975
53. Christopher Alexander; Oxford University Press, N.Y., 1975
54. Christopher Alexander; Oxford University Press, N.Y., 1975
55. Christopher Alexander; Oxford University Press, N.Y., 1975
56. Christopher Alexander; Oxford University Press, N.Y., 1975

57. Christopher Alexander; Oxford University Press, N.Y., 1975
58. Christopher Alexander; Oxford University Press, N.Y., 1979
59. Morley Baer; Oxford University Press, N.Y., 1976
60. Ezra Stoller, ESTO, Mamaroneck, N.Y.; Walker and Company, N.Y., 1966
61. Christopher Alexander; Oxford University Press, N.Y., 1979
62. Christopher Alexander; Center for Environmental Structure, Berkeley, 1974
63. Copyright by William A. Garnett; Harper & Row, N.Y., 1969
64. Myron Goldfinger; Lund Humphries, London, 1969
65. Christopher Alexander; Oxford University Press, N.Y., 1977
66. Myron Goldfinger; Lund Humphries, London, 1969
67. Bernard Rudofsky; Anchor Press, N.Y., 1969
68. Wim Swaan; Stein and Day, N.Y., 1966
69. Laurin McCracken; Oxford University Press, N.Y., 1972
70. Jürgen Joedicke; Verlag Gerd Hatje, Stuttgart, 1958
71. Christopher Alexander; Oxford University Press, N.Y., 1979
72. Harry Van Oudenallen, Milwaukee, 1976
73. Christopher Alexander; George Braziller, N.Y., 1966
74. Pier Luigi Nervi; Edizioni di Comunita, Milan, 1957
75. Fotovasari, Rome; Edizioni di Comunita, Milan, 1957
76. Harry Van Oudenallen, Milwaukee, 1976
77. Harry Van Oudenallen, Milwaukee, 1976
78. Wim Swaan; Stein and Day, N.Y., 1965
79. Harry Van Oudenallen, Milwaukee, 1976
80. Harry Van Oudenallen, Milwaukee, 1976
81. Riksantikvariatet, Oslo; Dreyers Forlag, Oslo, 1958
82. Harry Van Oudenallen, Milwaukee, 1976
83. Yukio Futagawa; Grosset & Dunlap, N.Y., 1970
84. Robert Laeuffer, Colmar; B. Arthaud, Paris, 1961
85. Copyright by Luciano Coen and Louise Duncan; Harper & Row, N.Y., 1978
86. Gallerie H.J. von Wirth, Dusseldorf; Klinkhardt & Biermann, Munich, 1955
87. Christopher Alexander; Perceptual and Motor Skills, 1964
88. Christopher Alexander; Perception and Psychophysics, 1968
89. Copyright by Luciano Coen and Louise Duncan; Harper & Row, N.Y., 1978
90. Basilio Pavon Maldonado; Estudios Sobre La Alhambra, Granada, 1975
91. Y. Watanabe; George Braziller, N.Y., 1963
92. Guy Desbartes; Grosset and Dunlap, N.Y., 1966
93. Christopher Alexander; Oxford University Press, N.Y., 1981
Alexander Collage, Christopher Alexander